ISSUES IN

SOCIAL JUSTICE

Citizenship and Transnational Struggles

Tanya Basok
Suzan Ilcan

OXFORD
UNIVERSITY PRESS

Oxford University Press is a department of the University of Oxford.
It furthers the University's objective of excellence in research, scholarship,
and education by publishing worldwide. Oxford is a registered trade mark of
Oxford University Press in the UK and in certain other countries.

Published in Canada by
Oxford University Press
8 Sampson Mews, Suite 204,
Don Mills, Ontario M3C 0H5 Canada

www.oupcanada.com

Library and Archives Canada Cataloguing in Publication

Basok, Tanya, 1958-
Issues in social justice : citizenship and transnational struggles
/ Tanya Basok & Suzan Ilcan.
(Themes in Canadian sociology)
Includes bibliographical references and index.

ISBN 978-0-19-543775-1

1. Social justice. 2. Citizenship. 3. Transnationalism. 4. Social
action—International cooperation. 5. Human rights. I. Ilcan, Suzan,
1960- II. Title. III. Series: Themes in Canadian sociology

HM671.B38 2013 303.3'72 C2012-906299-5

Cover image: Nick White/Taxi/Getty Images

Printed and bound in the United States

Contents

Acknowledgements

We thank Susan McDaniel and Lorne Tepperman, the Series Editors, for initially inviting us to contribute a volume to the series. At Oxford University Press, we thank Lisa Peterson for her continued support of our work and for seeing this book through to completion. We appreciate the fine work of Jennifer McIntyre and express our thanks for her editorial expertise and patience with us during the production process. We acknowledge the generosity of the three anonymous reviewers who provided insightful comments and suggestions, and express our gratefulness for their time and efforts during the process of peer review. This jointly written book would not have been possible without the generous research support provided to us by the Social Science and Humanities Research Council of Canada (SSHRC), the SSHRC Canada Research Chairs program, and the International Development Research Council of Canada (IDRC). In particular, both SSHRC and SSHRC Canada Research Chairs provided invaluable support to Suzan Ilcan's research on social justice, global governance and international relations, and citizenship. Both SSHRC and IDRC provided much-appreciated support to Tanya Basok's research on migration, citizenship, and human rights. This research funding made possible all our archival, field, and policy research for our respective research projects, and ultimately our writing of this book.

In our journey towards the completion of this book, we were assisted by some outstanding graduate students who provided us with valuable assistance and feedback. Jessica Barnett supplied us with a literature review of some key social justice debates, which was an enormous help to us in writing the theoretical chapter of this book. Laura Connoy and Marie Fuki prepared excellent, concise summaries of case studies used in two chapters, and Victoria Simmons was particularly talented at putting together drafts of the tables, some figures, and "boxes" that appear in the text. We would also like to acknowledge the dedicated work of Steven Richter for his assistance in conducting library research and providing us with policy and internet materials throughout our research and writing of this book. A very talented graphic designer, Galina Yeverovich, helped us translate our ideas into visual images.

And last but not least, we would like to thank each other for our collaborative spirit and friendship.

1 Introduction

During the writing of *Issues in Social Justice: Citizenship and Transnational Struggles* in 2011, important social and political events have unravelled. From the social justice perspective that we offer in this book, this year has left an unforgettable mark in social history. In the very first month of the year, we began witnessing mass mobilizations of people discontent with the current economic and political climate. At the end of January a wave of demonstrations seized Egypt. Demonstrators demanded the resignation of President Hosni Mubarak, who had ruled Egypt for 30 years in an authoritarian and repressive fashion. In response to the police crackdown against the protesters, mass rallies continued until the resignation of Mubarak on 11 February. Concurrently, rallies and demonstrations sprang up in Syria, Yemen, Bahrain, and Libya. In Libya, for example, the uprising against the 42-year rule of Moammar Gadhafi was met with extreme violent repression by the armed forces loyal to the president. The civil war that followed lasted several months and, after Gadhafi's death on 20 October, the rebel forces seized power.

These events, coined the "Arab Spring," along with parallel events in Wisconsin, USA, where protesters stormed and occupied the Wisconsin statehouse in defence of collective bargaining in February and March (Davey and Greenhouse 2011), inspired activism in other parts of the world. In Spain, on 15 May demonstrators who called themselves *indignados* (the "indignant") started occupying city squares in Madrid and other Spanish cities. Committed to nonviolent civil disobedience strategies, they denounced the injustice of the political and economic system. They were particularly disturbed by Spain's adoption of austerity measures (such as cuts to public spending) aimed to relieve the country's foreign debt at the time when unemployment had reached 20 percent. They blamed the country's political leaders and global economic institutions for the country's looming social crisis. They engaged in activism to protect the most vulnerable. For example, they blocked evictions of poor families from repossessed homes, stopped the detention of undocumented migrants, and attempted to prevent the closing of public hospitals following the introduction of austerity measures. Critical of Spain's political leadership, the *indignados* called for "real democracy." Under the slogan of "democracia real ya" (real democracy now), the *indignados* organized popular assemblies in city squares. Through these popular assemblies and neighbourhood committees, they tried to rebuild the social fabric threatened by draconian economic policies and to formulate proposals for alternative economic and social development (Ouziel 2011; Hardt and Negri 2011).

This wave of protests quickly spread to other countries. In June, there were mass protests against economic austerity measures in Athens (Chakrabortty 2011). In July, tent encampments against economic injustice sprang up in Tel Aviv, Israel (Sanders 2011). On 17 September 2011, over 2000 people in New York City marched toward Wall Street to denounce the banks, corporations, and governments for their complicity in provoking an economic crisis that had threatened the livelihoods of millions of people in the United States and elsewhere. Since 15 October the Occupy Wall Street movement has been replicated in many North American and other cities worldwide (see Figures 1.1 and 1.2), with protesters occupying financial districts and setting up camps near town halls to protest inadequate political leadership and unfair economic policies (read more on the Occupy movement in Box 2.6). Similar to the *indignados*, people involved in the Occupy movement are not only protesting against economic and political injustice; they are also experimenting with new democratic practices, involving frequent assemblies, participatory decision making and the building of horizontal, non-hierarchical political structures. Hardt and Negri refer to such democratic structures as "multitude form" and expressions of "real democracy" (Hardt and Negri 2004: 2011).

This wave of activism has brought to our attention two important messages. First, protesters have made it clear that social and economic justice requires sustainable policies that revamp the social protection infrastructure. The protesters have repeatedly expressed their frustration with the unequal distribution of economic resources across the globe and within individual countries. Critical of neoliberal policies (the policies that call for cuts in social spending on health care, education, public housing, and nutritious and inexpensive food), protesters call on global and national policy makers to prioritize people over markets. While the "Arab Spring" uprisings were aimed at specific authoritarian rulers, protest participants also expressed frustration at the neoliberal austerity policies these countries had pursued for several decades (see, for example, Joya 2011; Hanieh 2011). Second, around the globe, protesters involved in the aforementioned rallies, demonstrations, occupations, and uprisings have called for democratic decision making.

While these two concerns—economic equality and democratic politics—have been voiced clearly at the events mentioned above, these are not the only social justice issues that are relevant today. Another important political issue that has gained much visibility in the last few years is the struggle of Palestinian people for recognition as an autonomous nation. Their plea for statehood has been recognized and supported by many activists worldwide. There are also numerous struggles that often go unnoticed by the majority of people and the media. Among them are the struggles of women against domestic violence; of gay and lesbian people for legal and social recognition;

of indigenous peoples for self-government; of ethnic and racial minorities for the right to practise their culture and uphold their beliefs; of progressive intellectuals for the right to produce alternative forms of knowledge; and of indigenous and local people for the protection of their knowledge against bio-piracy.

FIGURE 1.1 The Occupy Movement in Canada

Source: Alamy CEMHT4

FIGURE 1.2 The Occupy Movement in the US: Protesters gather in front of the George Washington statue on Wall Street

Source: AP Images #120316151063

Three Faces of Social Justice

These social justice–oriented struggles express three main objectives: (a) access to protections, benefits, and privileges; (b) democratic political participation; and (c) recognition and acceptance of cultural diversity. These three issues are related to what we call "social inclusion" in this book. They represent *what* is relevant in a socially just society, or the content of social justice. This is the first aspect of social justice. The second important issue that needs to be addressed by social justice scholars and activists is that of who gets included in the first place—that is, *who* gets to claim protections, benefits, privileges, political voice, and respect for diversity. In other words, the boundaries of social inclusion constitute the second dimension of social justice. Thirdly, we need to ask a procedural question, that is, who gets to decide and *how* the decisions on the content and boundaries of social justice are made. To use Fraser's terminology, these three aspects of social justice are related to the struggles for redistribution, recognition, and representation (see Chapter 2 for further discussion).

Social Justice as a Multidirectional and Perpetual Process

We see social justice as a *process of change* towards equal distribution, wide recognition, and democratic representation. This process of change is often sparked by popular struggles led by feminists, labour organizations, environmentalists, indigenous peoples, gay and lesbian rights activists, anti-racist activists, disability rights supporters, and others. The goals of this change could include: revised national legislation (e.g., the recognition of same-sex marriage); new international conventions (e.g., the recently adopted International Labour Office Convention Concerning Decent Work for Domestic Workers); improved school curricula (e.g., inclusion of indigenous languages); changed attitudes (e.g., towards women, elderly people, people with disabilities, visible minorities, gays and lesbians, etc.); better social relations (e.g., between workers and employers); supportive social programs (e.g., poverty reduction programs, investment in preventative health); and increased self-confidence and assertiveness for marginalized people. The latter is captured by the frequently used concept of "empowerment."

As discussed by various feminist scholars, "empowerment" refers to the ability to make choices, or exercise agency, in situations where these choices were previously denied (Kabeer 1999). One of the meanings of empowerment is linked to the ability to exercise *power over* people, resources, and institutions. This notion of power and empowerment is expressed through the changing relations that occur with the state. However, in conceptualizing power as fluid, dispersed, relational, and linked to control over discourses and the production of knowledge, some feminists incorporate two additional meanings of empowerment. One meaning of empowerment builds on the notion of *power within*, and it recognizes the importance of individual consciousness and understanding (Parpart, Rai, and Standt 2002: 5). This notion of empowerment is closely related to the notion of conscientization (or consciousness-raising) advanced by the Brazilian radical educator Paulo Freire (Stromquist 2002). The other notion of power relates to collective action or *power with*. It expresses the collective power to organize for the purpose of transforming conditions that marginalize some people (Parpart, Rai, and Standt 2002: 5–8).

As we emphasize in this book, social justice should be seen not as a linear process of change but as a complex process that involves advancement, resistance, derailment, backlash, and reversal. For example, much of the advancement in social protections of disadvantaged groups and workers that was achieved under the welfare state regime has been reversed by the neoliberal agendas of the state and attacks on organized labour, as discussed in Chapter 4. Women and people of colour employed under affirmative action programs have suffered from the backlash of their co-workers who resent special treatment for these disadvantaged groups of individuals. Terrorist attacks in New York, London, and Madrid have triggered strong anti-Muslim sentiments in those countries that had begun to accept cultural diversity. In addition, various security measures unleashed by North American and European states in response to the terrorist attacks have resulted in the violation of various forms of civil rights that immigrants had enjoyed prior to these events. The increased mobility of transnational corporations has led to the removal of certain labour rights and the demise of trade unions. While the January and February 2011 street protests in Cairo had called for democracy, the Supreme Council of Armed Forces that assumed control after president Mubarak's resignation has become even more repressive than the previous form of rule. What we observed through mass communications media in November 2011 is that Cairo's Tahrir Square has once again become the stage for mass rallies against the authoritarian government (see, for example, the Guardian, 22 November 2011). These are just some of the numerous examples of how social justice achievements can be reversed.

Furthermore, even when some groups of people achieve greater protections, there may be some among them who are still disadvantaged. For example, while trade unions have advanced the rights of workers in many ways, female workers within these unions have not always had their specific needs recognized (see, for example, Franzway and Fonow 2011). At the same time, Western feminist organizations have often been criticized for their failure to represent the interests of women in the global south (see, for example, Mohanty 2003). Thus we see social justice as an ongoing (and possibly, never-ending) process that involves struggles for change that aim to attain greater social inclusion.

Finally, it is important to recognize how the language of social justice can be appropriated and used for certain objectives that contradict original intentions. For example, under neoliberal agendas, the concept of empowerment has been used by corporations, international organizations, non-governmental agencies, and national states as a means for increasing productivity through capacity-building (see, for example, Parpart, Rai and Staudt 2002: 5; Ilcan and Lacey 2006). As discussed in Chapter 7, UN organizations often employ this neoliberal notion of empowerment when they design and implement poverty-reduction programs. In this book, we see these initiatives—which remove the responsibility for the provision of social benefits and protections from the state and place the burden on the poor people themselves—as a way of derailing, rather than advancing, social justice aims.

Social Justice as "Contentious Politics": Actors and Players

In order to understand social justice as a process of change we need to identify the actors involved in the process. Most social justice initiatives are propelled by grassroots activists and social movements. Other actors respond to the demands for change by either accepting or rejecting them. These actors include: national states, voluntary organizations, transnational organizations (such as the United Nations [UN]), and transnational corporations, among others.

Social activists struggling to bring about greater social inclusion engage in what McAdam, Tarrow, and Tilly (2001) call "contentious politics," or "episodic, public, collective interaction among makers of claims and their objects" (5). Contentious politics can include rallies, demonstrations, lobbying, and other forms of protest through which claims are advanced. When these activities are sustained over time, we can talk about a social movement. Social movements can be defined as "collective challenges, based on common purposes and social solidarities, in sustained interaction with elites, opponents, and authorities" (Tarrow 1994: 3–4). In Chapter 2 we will discuss how activists in different social movements struggle to bring about greater social inclusion. Social movement networks working in solidarity across international borders are called transnational movements (as discussed in Chapter 7). While much of social movement activism is directed towards the nation-state, other types of authorities, such as corporations or UN organizations and such global organizations as the International Monetary Fund, the World Trade Organization, and the World Bank, can also be targeted (Tilly 2004: 4; also see Chapter 7). Among other things, grassroots organizations and social movements have pressured national states and the UN to introduce legal changes, new UN conventions, and/or support programs for particular vulnerable groups. They have also protested against environmental pollution, displacement, and human rights abuses perpetrated by transnational corporations even though only nation-states can demand that transnational corporations change certain destructive practices. At the same time, and under pressure from grassroots activists, Human Rights voluntary organizations, and some UN organizations and transnational corporations, have adopted the ethic of "corporate social responsibility" which expresses their alleged concern for the environment and investment in such fields as education, job training, and other practices. Many analysts remain sceptical of these initiatives since the ethical orientations and the actual practices related to these orientations do not always coincide (see, for example, Wells 2009; Banerjee 2008).

It should be pointed out that while social movements and other grassroots initiatives can result in greater social inclusion, it is possible that the opposite is the case. First, not all social movements are pursuing the goals of social inclusiveness. And second, some social activism has been met with repression unleashed by certain states' and corporations' private armies.

We should also recognize that, while social activists can influence certain policies and programs initiated by national states or the UN, they can in turn be influenced by these institutions. For example, many UN conventions make it possible for social movements to launch campaigns and demand greater benefits and recognition for particular groups of excluded people. By funding specific initiatives, nation-states can also encourage certain forms of activism.

Voluntary organizations are also important players in the social justice field. Some voluntary organizations grow out of grassroots activism. They attempt to improve the lives of vulnerable and marginalized people who face poverty, discrimination, or other types of social injustices, and their actions can be important in presenting the life circumstances of marginal groups and assisting them in having a voice with which to share their own perspectives and to advance claims for social inclusion. Funding provided by national states, international non-governmental organizations, international organizations (such as the World Bank) or UN agencies has made it possible for voluntary organizations to pursue their objectives even though this funding comes with certain conditions that are imposed unilaterally by the funders. Increasingly, however, voluntary organizations are being faced with funding cutbacks by many nation-states across the globe, and they are being forced to support neo-liberal policies and agendas to varying degrees. These organizations often find themselves less and less involved in advocacy issues and much more involved in fundraising and in performing services that were once the responsibility of national states (see, for example, Trudeau 2008a). In the context of urban activism, Mayer (2007) suggests that "[m]uch of what used to constitute urban activism . . . now has demobilizing effects, where community-based organizations have become too busy training, feeding, and inserting their clients into job programs instead of representing them, lobbying for them" (100). Depending on the specific nation-states and other forms of governance, these and other similar organizations are becoming progressively less involved in the democratization of political relations. Instead, as Jaeger (2007: 260) warns, these organizations can engage in and contribute to forms of liberal processes of self-regulation and self-surveillance.

Figure 1.3 represents the complex interaction between various players involved in the social justice field. It is important to understand that this interaction does not always lead to greater social inclusion. Social justice goals can be derailed and subverted by some of the players and, despite the remarkable

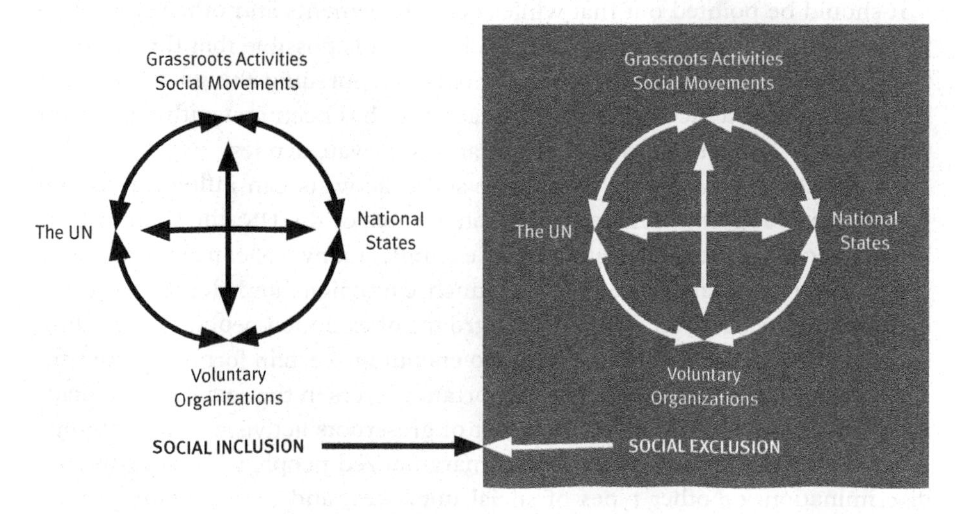

FIGURE 1.3 Social Inclusion–Social Exclusion

Source: T/K

efforts made by other players, result in social exclusion. These two outcomes are presented in Figure 1.3. This figure also reveals the two-way movement between social inclusion and exclusion. It is thus crucial to recognize social justice as a perpetual process of change aimed at correcting practices of exclusion through negotiations and struggles between various players.

Outline of the Book

Focusing on the contributions of key social justice theorists, such as John Rawls, Nancy Fraser, Iris Young, Karl Marx, David Harvey, and others, Chapter 2 explores how social justice has been conceptualized. We relate social justice to social inclusion and examine various aspects of social inclusion addressed by particular political thinkers. These aspects include: (1) equal access to protections, benefits, and privileges; (2) democratic political participation; and (3) acceptance of cultural diversity. In this chapter we also explore how the creation of boundaries of social inclusion (i.e., rules of membership) simultaneously produces the social exclusion of certain groups. In this regard, we define social justice in relation to struggles for social inclusion by those who are excluded in one form or another and by those who support them. We then explore how social justice, defined in relation to social inclusion, can be attained. We thus examine Nancy Fraser's notion of redistribution, recognition, and representation, and the two strategies that she identifies, namely the affirmative and the transformative.

The notion of social justice as a process of change that is directed towards greater social inclusion is captured by the ideals and practices of citizenship. In Chapter 3, we explore how the notion of citizenship has evolved from civil rights (protecting individual freedoms), to political rights (protecting the right to political organization and participation), to social rights (providing access to social protections). We point out that while social rights do not guarantee economic equality, they do improve the lives of economically disadvantaged groups. In this chapter, we also discuss how the allegedly universal principles of citizenship do not adequately protect certain groups of individuals, such as women, cultural minorities, people with disabilities, gay and lesbian people, etc. Thus, we discuss how struggles for equal rights can be combined with the recognition of differences. The notion of differentiated citizenship captures this principle.

Struggles waged by various social movements in the second half of the twentieth century were, in fact, struggles for differentiated citizenship. While certain advancements towards the social inclusion of various groups have been made through these struggles, the ideals and practices of citizenship remain problematic. With its ties to the nation-state, the notion of citizenship sets limits on who is recognized as an individual with the rights to have rights.

Focusing particularly on social citizenship, Chapter 4 discusses the welfare state and its social programs. Starting with an historical overview of the emergence of the welfare state after the Second World War, the chapter explains how the welfare state approach cushioned the hardships of economically disadvantaged people through such programs as social insurance and poor relief and invested in social programs (such as health, education, public housing) that were aimed at improving citizens' wellbeing. The chapter then turns to the erosion of social citizenship on a global scale. As discussed in this chapter, during the late twentieth century, the welfare state approach came under criticism in many countries around the world. Critics viewed the social welfare system as being costly and inefficient, and called for a broad range of reforms to reduce public spending and expand global markets. These reforms and the practices and policies that underpin them have become known as neoliberalism. Although neoliberal policies are diverse in form and in their impact, and have been revised in the last three decades, neoliberal principles are firmly entrenched in global governance today. The decline of social citizenship has been characterized by a broad spectrum of social implications which are illustrated in this chapter.

While welfare states have renounced some of their responsibility for supporting marginalized and disadvantaged groups, non-governmental, non-profit, and community organizations, including voluntary organizations, have assumed a greater responsibility for these groups. National and international work pursued by these organizations is the subject of Chapter 5. This chapter questions whether these initiatives have led to greater social inclusiveness. It identifies limitations faced by these organizations in their efforts to bring about sustainable change for disadvantaged groups. In fact, it argues that voluntary organizations involved in such activities as poverty reduction and health provision are constrained by the demands for efficiency placed upon them by national states and international organizations that fund them. Under neoliberal conditions, the commitment to defending the rights of vulnerable groups has been replaced by the provision of services in the most cost-effective manner. Moreover, some voluntary organizations have turned themselves into the instruments of neoliberal agendas as they attempt to transform vulnerable people into citizens responsible for their own relief.

In recognizing the declining ability of welfare states to address the need for social inclusion of its various citizens, the incapacity of voluntary organizations to fill these gaps, and the social exclusion of various groups of non-citizens, we turn attention to the discussion of allegedly universal human rights principles and practices in Chapter 6. The Universal Declaration of Human Rights and various other human rights treaties establish a set of principles that are meant to apply universally to all human beings merely by virtue of their membership in humankind. Yet, as we illustrate in the chapter, this is scarcely the case. In particular, the rights of workers and economically disadvantaged people are subordinated to the protection of the freedoms of corporate elites. More generally, social and economic rights are protected considerably less than civil and political rights. Human rights treaties are not always sensitive to cultural differences and do not protect women as much as men. Collective rights of Aboriginal peoples clash with the protection of individual rights enshrined in core human rights instruments. Furthermore, just as nation-states exclude non-citizens, human rights protections are too weak to rectify this exclusion. Finally, the recognition of the sovereign power of nation-states severely limits the extent to which human rights principles can be employed to address protection gaps in the practices of national citizenship. Nevertheless, we do not suggest that human rights principles expressed through international treaties are irrelevant. Social activists around the globe have in fact used human rights language to persuade national states to advance the rights of certain disadvantaged groups.

Social activism is the topic of Chapter 7. We are particularly interested in *transnational* forms of activism given that many social problems related to social exclusion are shaped by practices and policies that have a global reach (e.g., transnational corporate investments, financial markets, and global governing institutions such as the IMF, World Bank, and the World Trade Organization), and that are identified as requiring transnational approaches for their resolution. As such, we examine those forms of struggles and activism that transcend national borders and include such actors as inter-governmental and international organizations, and activist networks. We distinguish between activism "from above" and activism "from below." Transnational forms of activism from above refer to advocacy efforts by international organizations that use the language of rights, protection, or humanitarianism to bring about change for disadvantaged or vulnerable groups. In this chapter we focus on three such organizations: Oxfam International, the International Organization for Migration (IOM), and the United Nations High Commissioner for Refugees (UNHCR). Examining these organizations through a critical lens, we point out that while they are committed to social justice ideals, in practice these organizations often engage in excessive control measures. Furthermore, their support for neoliberal governing agendas undermines the very principles they claim to uphold. Transnational forms of activism from below refers to the advocacy efforts of diverse transnational activist networks (TANs) that consist of local and national organizations working in collaboration with their counterparts in other parts of the world. We recognize that while some TANs are critical of neoliberalism, others support neoliberal objectives. We inquire about what makes TANs successful in attaining their goals. We then turn our attention to the Global Justice Movement, which has been gaining strength since the 1990s and is critical of neoliberal perspectives and agendas. We question how and to what extent any meaningful change can be attained through these initiatives.

Finally, in the Conclusion, Chapter 8, we ask how social justice can be attained. We expand on the ideas of Global Social Justice that have been advanced by some scholars, and place particular attention on notions of cosmopolitanism and global (or cosmopolitan) citizenship. We then ask what role global justice networks can play in the process of change towards a more inclusive global society. We view the World Social Forum as a model for creating democratic spaces that allow a wide spectrum of grassroots participants to articulate their concerns and offer new visions for social justice. Although the World Social Forum has been critiqued by some analysts for leaving out some groups of people and for its failure to advance practical and viable solutions, we see this forum as an imperative step towards attaining social justice. Finally, we explore proposals that call for these global justice networks to "reclaim" national states and the United Nations.

2 Exploring Social Justice

Learning Objectives

- Explore the links between morality and social justice
- Conceptualize social justice in relation to social inclusion
- Critically assess three aspects of social inclusion, namely: (1) equal access to benefits, privileges and protection; (2) political participation; and (3) acceptance of cultural diversity
- Understand how the boundaries of social inclusion can simultaneously result in social exclusions
- Understand how the notion of citizenship captures all three aspects of social inclusion and defines the boundaries of social inclusion
- Discuss and assess Nancy Fraser's three main approaches to bringing about social justice, namely, redistribution, recognition, and reframing
- Examine affirmative and transformative strategies for bringing about social justice

Introduction

This chapter offers an approach to social justice that links it to processes of change that are often impelled by various writers, researchers, and social activists who challenge some forms of social exclusion and strive towards establishing a socially inclusive society. From our vantage point, the concept of social justice involves relationships at every level of society. We begin our discussion by focusing on the meaning of social inclusion and putting stress on three dimensions associated with the term: equal access; democratic political participation; and cultural diversity. The chapter then turns to the importance of understanding not only *what* rights, privileges, and benefits are provided to people but also *who* is included in these provisions. In this regard, it highlights and discusses the creation of boundaries of social inclusion and how these boundaries can lead to the exclusion of certain groups and their struggles for social justice. It poses the question of *how* social justice, defined in relation to social inclusion, can be attained. In answering this question, the chapter calls attention to those social struggles over citizenship rights that have reversed many policies and practices that excluded people from social benefits, denied them respect and equal treatment, and imposed constraints on their freedom to act. It outlines Nancy Fraser's three approaches to social justice—redistribution, recognition, and representation—and distinguishes between two strategies for redressing injustice: affirmative and transformative. In our discussion of these three approaches and two strategies, we raise some questions about their implications and level of adequacy. In this chapter, as well as in other chapters of this book, we acknowledge that the current meta-frames of justice that identify who is the subject and object of justice no longer neatly fit with many people's contemporary social life and relations. The increasing mobility of capital, communication, ideas, and people necessitates, amongst other things, much rethinking and renewal of such meta-framing of justice.

Morality and Social Justice: A Problematic Link

Many philosophers understand social justice in relation to notions of morality (Rawls 2003a, Sen 2003a, and Nussbaum 1992). Morality refers to a culturally specific set of beliefs or principles that distinguishes rights from wrongs, and there are many examples to draw upon in this regard. The period immediately following 1945, for example, served as a dividing line for emerging human rights and social justice demands. Although the Nuremberg Trials were not the first occasion in social history when the victors passed moral judgements on the vanquished, the extent of the Nazis' crimes against humanity appears to have justified both the moral and legal penalties (Sklair 2011: 14). Most current social justice struggles can be linked to certain moral principles. For example, the eradication of child labour initiatives is based on the moral principle that children should enjoy their childhood and that child labour outside the household deprives them of their dignity and of the ability to fully engage in educational opportunities (ILO 2012).

Not all moral principles, however, are as clear as the ones mentioned above. There is as much disagreement over what constitutes morality in many social and political contexts across the globe as there is concerning what constitutes social justice. For example, differences in moral attitudes towards sex work have resulted in conflicting approaches towards the legalization of this profession as well as approaches to immigrant women smuggled over international borders to work in the sex trade. On the one hand, those who view the sex trade through the "violence against women" lens and emphasize the violence and danger involved in this occupation, advance the position that calls for the eradication of sex trade. On the other hand, those taking the "harm-reduction" position call for the normalization of commercial sex in an effort to make this employment less risky and more socially acceptable (Agustín 2005; Macklin 2003). With respect to immigrant women in the sex trade, most states and international organizations (such as the International Organizations for Migration, discussed in Chapter 7) have adopted an anti-trafficking approach (Dauvergne 2008; Berman 2010). This approach calls for increased border surveillance and the criminalization of migrant smugglers. In contrast, from a human rights perspective, women's rights activists and scholars recognize that migration for sex work is propelled by the need to secure a living for migrants themselves and their households. In this regard, the way to address exploitative, demeaning, and dangerous working conditions that immigrant women face in the sex trade would be to legalize their status and widen opportunities for legal labour migration (Agustín 2005; Macklin 2003; Chapkis 2003).

To address these and other disagreements, the approach put forward in this book is that social justice is to be understood as involving processes of change that are often propelled by various writers, researchers, and social activists who challenge some forms of social exclusion and strive towards establishing a socially inclusive society. As we will see, social justice involves relationships at every level of society, including those relationships we have with significant others, families, schools, prisons, government departments, and international organizations, including relationships with those in institutions that aim to advocate for or enforce rights. In order to understand social justice, we first need to understand what is meant by the term social inclusion. In the following sections we will define three aspects of social inclusion: (1) equal access to protections, benefits, and privileges; (2) democratic political participation; and (3) broad acceptance of cultural diversity.

Social Inclusion

Equal Access to Protections, Benefits, and Privileges

Social inclusion relates to protections (e.g., by law) and access to such public goods as education, health care, police protection, and positions in public offices (Waltzer 1996: 242). This aspect of social inclusion is based on two principles frequently associated with social justice: freedom and equality.

Freedom

For philosophers and political theorists, freedom (or liberty) is seen as fundamental to social justice. Theorists vary in how liberty is conceptualized, with two main views being: a) liberty as freedom from constraint, and b) liberty as the substantive (i.e., socially and materially supported) opportunity to realize a chosen life. Taking up the first position, John Rawls argues that social justice demands "an equal right to the most extensive liberty compatible with a like liberty for all" (2003a: 21). In other words, people should be free to do as they like up to the point where their doing so interferes with another person's ability to exercise the same level of freedom. Here liberty is conceptualized as freedom *from* things like violence, coercion, and constraint. This type of freedom is called negative rights. Freedom as negative rights, or rights to be free from things, is a classic component of liberal politics. An example of freedom as negative rights is the right mentioned in Article 2 of the UN Convention on the Rights of the Child, which states "Parties shall take all appropriate measures to ensure that the child is protected against all forms of discrimination or punishment on the basis of the status, activities, expressed opinions, or beliefs of the child's parents, legal guardians, or family members" (The Convention on the Rights of the Child 2001: 177). Neoliberal conceptions of social justice as freedom from constraint include shared support for welfare state reform, market liberalization, the centrality of private finance, and deregulated economies (see Chapters 4 and 5; see also Griffin 2011: 138) upheld by national and international organizations, private firms, and government bodies. However, as we argue in this book, these initiatives bring about impoverishment, wider income disparities, particular forms of violence, and new forms of exclusion.

Scholars espousing the second position, liberty as the substantive opportunity to realize a chosen life, argue the inadequacy of these liberal rights. For example, Sen states "that a theory of justice . . . must be deeply and directly concerned with the *actual freedoms* enjoyed by different persons—persons with possibly divergent objectives—to lead different lives that they can have reason to value" (2003b: 350). In other words, liberty should be conceptualized as freedom *to* do and possess things a person values, like sexual pleasure, education, a safe environment, or decent jobs. These are called positive rights. An important aspect of the positive rights approach to liberty is the role of choice (Anderson 2004: 173: Burchardt 2008: 224). At times, in order to enable groups of people to exercise their freedom, there is the need to remove certain barriers. For example, disability rights activists have argued that the freedom from discrimination, guaranteed to persons with disabilities by the Universal Declaration of Human Rights (negative freedom), did not guarantee to them the right to participation in electoral politics or other social benefits to which they are legally entitled, and in which they often can't participate unless certain accommodations are put in place. The UN Convention on the Rights of Persons with Disabilities, adopted in 2006, recognizes the need to create opportunities to realize freedom in its assertion that the right to be equal before the law means that persons with disabilities must have access to "the support they may require in exercising their legal capacity" (Mégret 2008: 503).

Equality

What constitutes equality and how it can be achieved has been debated by many political theorists, including John Rawls, who has made a significant contribution to this field (see Box 2.1). For Rawls, social justice is related to the equality of opportunities. This idea is expressed through the concept of fair competition. Fair competition, as an element of moral relations, presupposes that people will be competing with each other for resources. This kind of competition is one way of distributing resources. For this competition to be fair, everyone must have an opportunity to compete (Rawls 2003a: 21–2). From this perspective, all people must receive education so that they are enabled to compete for jobs (Rawls 2003b: 63). And within these processes,

BOX 2.1 ❋ JOHN RAWLS

John Rawls (1921–2002) was an influential political philosopher. Born and raised in Baltimore, Maryland, he spent most of his academic career on the Ivy League circuit of universities in the United States. A graduate of Princeton and Oxford (UK), he taught at Cornell University and MIT before settling in at Harvard. Rawls' most significant contribution is his theory of "justice as fairness," which lays out a basic framework for the legitimate use of political power in a liberal society in which citizens are free, have equal rights, and engage cooperatively in an egalitarian economic system. Justice as fairness, he argues, reconciles the "freedom–equality" dilemma of liberal societies by going beyond the dominant political philosophy of utilitarianism and proposing an alternative version of social contract theory based on equality and reciprocal advantage. This alternate contract, he contends, must be guided by two basic principles of justice: (1) the equal right of all individuals to a maximum level of basic liberties compatible with like liberties for others; and (2) social or political inequalities in society are to exist only in positions that are equally open to all, and only if those inequalities benefit the least-advantaged members of society. Rawls first outlined these ideas in his book *A Theory of Justice* (1971) and subsequently spent the rest of his academic career revisiting and revising them. In doing so, he extended his thoughts on justice to the international arena in his work *The Law of Peoples* (1999), which examined liberal foreign policy and the creation of a peaceful international order. Late in life, Rawls also expressed an increasing scepticism as to the capitalist welfare system's capacity as a model upon which to build an equal and just society, advocating instead either a highly educated, democratic society with mass property ownership or market socialism. (Sources: Stanford Encyclopedia of Philosophy http://plato.stanford.edu/entries/rawls/; Rogers 2002).

there should be no discrimination or what has often been called arbitrary distinctions (Miller 2004; Piachaud 2008: 44; Rawls 2003a: 21).

In this understanding of equality, people acquire resources as a result of their performance of something valued by society (Miller 2004: 188) or something that contributes "to the common good" (Rawls 2003a: 22). Other criteria (e.g., race) are not to be considered when distributing benefits or to allow unequal benefit based on equal performance (Miller 2004: 195–6). Thus, this notion of equality presupposes that some performances are judged to be more valued or socially important, and are therefore to be compensated *more* than other performances (Miller 2004: 196; Rawls 2003a: 24). It is a notion that links to a "justice as desert" approach because it makes provisions for certain people—those who deserve it—to receive higher benefits than other people.

John Rawls importantly limits these inequalities and suggests that in order to be just they must work to the benefit of a person representative of the least fortunate class of people (2003b: 60). For example, in Rawls' view, it would be acceptable to allow entrepreneurs to take an unequal share of the profits produced by their businesses if, and only if, these benefits provide an (otherwise lacking) incentive for the entrepreneurs to perform the (otherwise unperformed) function of providing jobs and tax revenue that benefit unskilled labourers (2003b: 60).

Nonetheless for philosophers like Sen and Nussbaum, equality of opportunity and liberty as freedom from constraint are inadequate bases for social justice. They draw attention to the empirically documented existence of widespread human differences in the ability to turn primary goods (e.g., money) or opportunities into freedom to live the life of one's choosing (Sen 2003b: 353-54: Young 2008: 81–2). These differences arise from a variety of sources, such as the body (e.g., disability, disease, etc.), physical environment (e.g., extreme cold, extreme heat, etc.), and society (e.g., discrimination, coercion, etc.). It is therefore crucial to shift attention from the just distribution of primary goods to the just distribution of capabilities. Capabilities are like basic skills or conditions that could be deployed in various ways. For Sen, capabilities enable us "to achieve various alternative combinations of functionings, or doings and beings" (Sen 2003b: 352). Some researchers argue that, as humans, we are all entitled to certain basic capabilities, such as the capability to move about or meet our nutritional requirements (Sen 2003a: 346; Nussbaum 1992: 216–22).

The capabilities approach has been used in certain policy interventions, such the one undertaken by the British Equality and Human Rights Commission, which, in October 2007, applied the capabilities approach to monitor and address inequality in Britain. In order to make capabilities an enforceable standard for social justice, the Commission first used human rights norms drawn from United Nations agreements, along with research conducted on British residents, to create a list of domains of capabilities necessary to live a "good life" of one's choosing. These domains consisted of being alive; living in physical security; being healthy; being knowledgeable; being able to understand and reason; having the skills to participate in society; enjoying a comfortable standard of living, with independence and security; engaging in productive and valued activities; enjoying individual, family, and social life; participating in decision making, having a voice and influence; being and expressing yourself, and having self-respect; and knowing you will be protected and treated fairly by the law. Next, the Commission developed a model that identified influences on capability development that could be affected by governmental action. The top level of this model illustrates that entitlements (e.g., healthcare, social support, etc.) are differentially converted into capabilities. The entitlements received, and the personal and social factors affecting the conversion of those entitlements into capabilities, are impacted by the bottom-level factors of social context (e.g., labour market, family, etc.), resources (e.g., income, healthcare, etc.), and characteristics (e.g., gender, age, etc.). This model acknowledges that these bottom-level factors influence each other. Therefore, to design appropriate policy interventions, changes had to be introduced at either the top or the bottom level, or both (Burchardt 2008).

Democratic Political Participation

Social inclusion is closely linked to democratic political participation. Generally speaking, democratic governance means that people are able to give their opinion and have it influence decisions about what happens in the political community (Burchardt 2008: 217; Lister 2008: 118; Walzer 1996: 242). Michael Walzer (1996: 257–59) points out that without the ongoing right to participation in governance, people are highly vulnerable to oppression. Some scholars view governance and participation in governance as occurring within state apparatuses only. These scholars call for formal voting rights. Others view governance as occurring through a variety of state, non-state (e.g., churches), and quasi-state (e.g., schools) institutions (Anderson 2004: 174; Young 2008: 95–8). They call for more direct and intensive forms of participation. Participation, then, can have various levels and locations.

Cultural Diversity

Respect for and wide acceptance of diverse cultural beliefs and expressions is the third aspect of social inclusion (Anderson 2004: 155; Fraser 1997: 14; Lister 2008: 111; Young 2008: 80; Burchardt 2008: 217; Piachaud 2008: 36). The failure to recognize and respect diversity, as realized through actions such as racial slurs, gender discrimination, or legal prohibition of certain cultural practices, can be seen as the failure to treat someone in a socially just manner. Examples of disrespectful treatment of certain cultural groups are widespread. For example, Kurds residing in Turkey are often prohibited from using their language and practicing dimensions of their culture (Rubin 2003: 315–16). Similarly, throughout much of the twentieth century, Aboriginal children in Canada were forbidden to speak their languages in residential schools (Royal Commission of Aboriginal Peoples 1996). The prohibition from engaging in certain cultural practices is another example of the denial of respect for cultural diversity. For example, West Coast native groups were banned from practicing Potlatch, a cultural and spiritual practice that Aboriginal chiefs used to announce marriages, name children, pass titles and privileges from elders to young men, and to mourn deaths. Potlatch ceremonies involved honouring a clan's history and giving away or even destroying valuable gifts, such as blankets, food, canoes, wooden carvings, slaves, and copper. The practice was banned in Canada from 1884 until 1951 because the Canadian government considered them to be "un-Christian" and destructive of property (The Canadian Encyclopedia). Thus, efforts to advance social justice would require recognition and respect for diverse cultural expressions. Box 2.2 discusses how in Paraguay, the official policy that denigrated the Guaraní heritage has been replaced by the policies that instated the Guaraní language as one of the two official languages at schools in that country.

Boundaries of Social Inclusion

It is crucial to ask not only *what* rights, privileges, and benefits are provided to people but also *who* is included in the first place. That is, we need to

Box 2.2 ❊ The Guaraní People

For several centuries, the Guaraní people and culture have been associated with backwardness and lack of civilization. Despite the predominance of Guaraní as the major language of Paraguay, Spanish remained the sole language in the education system for a century, from 1870 to 1970. Nevertheless, the overwhelming majority of children entering the education system have spoken little or no Spanish. In 1953, UNESCO produced its landmark statement that the recommended medium for teaching literacy to a child is his or her first language. Yet its first external review of the Paraguayan education system carried out four years later made no mention of Guaraní or the issue of bilingual education.

In the 1980s, the Ministry of Education began a pilot project in bilingual education that was originally conceived as a means of using Guaraní solely as an oral language to teach Spanish. All subject matter and instructional materials were in Spanish, and Guaraní was used only as the language of instruction. Critics charged that because Guaraní was not taught as a written language, the program was simply "Hispanicized." In response to such criticism, the pilot project gradually evolved into teaching rural children to read and write in their mother tongue during the first three years of primary education, with Spanish introduced gradually as a second language. As a major component of the democratization process, a wide-ranging education reform program was introduced in the early 1990s in which bilingual education figured prominently. The reform's mandate derived from the democratic constitution of 1992, which stated "Primary education will be carried out in the mother tongue of the child" (Article 77). Within months of its promulgation, Law 28 of 10 September 1992 made the teaching of Spanish and Guaraní compulsory at all levels of the public education system. (Source: Nickson 2009).

understand how the **boundaries of social inclusion** are drawn. The opposite side of inclusion is exclusion. In order to understand issues of social justice we need to pay attention to who is excluded and the mechanisms of exclusion, as well as struggles of the excluded to become included. As discussed in Chapter 3, most nation-states exclude non-citizens (e.g., undocumented migrants and some asylum seekers) from benefits that social membership provides. We will also see how some of these non-citizens challenge mechanisms and principles of their exclusion.

The scales of social inclusion are also important. When discussing social inclusion, some scholars privilege inclusion in a nation-state. Other scholars, on the other hand, assert that justice and injustice are produced in both the state *and* in civil society (Anderson 2004: 173; Young 1996: 455). Civil society is a term used to refer to all those institutions, spaces, and relationships that are not formally part of the state or official government bodies in which people connect voluntarily to advance common interests. These common interests are broad and include the involvement of civil society participants in violence-against-women campaigns, anti-poverty initiatives, anti-war plans, citizenship rights movements, and other kinds of social justice initiatives. As an umbrella concept, civil society can include, for example, churches, families, advocacy groups, grassroots organizations, and even for-profit associations. The connections among civil society participants are diverse and complex, and include face-to-face encounters, private-public partnership arrangements, and network relations that span from local to national and international arenas. Relationships in this sphere are not, however, fully determined by laws. Even if these relations are codified in law and are just, that does not necessarily mean that the relations people experience on a day-to-day basis will be just. For example, comprehensive anti-discrimination laws do not prevent visible minority groups from being followed in stores, women from being sexually harassed at work, or Muslims from being harassed at national borders. Civil society is also an important site for producing, directly or indirectly, relations of justice and injustice because it involves many influential institutions, including churches, non-profit organizations, and schools, that can be diverse and even contradictory in their orientations and objectives for change. For Young, therefore, social justice implies full participation in major institutions "with authority over [a group's] actions" (1996: 455–65). Additionally, some scholars prefer to go beyond the nation-state and reframe social inclusion in global terms. In pointing out that people's lives are shaped by processes that extend beyond national territorial borders, Fraser (2005) suggests that "globalization is changing the way we argue about justice" (69). Many theorists of global justice (e.g., Pogge 2008; Cronin and De Greiff 2002; Cabrera 2010) imagine and defend an approach to social justice that transcends national borders in their call for institutions that would offer protections to all human beings.

Politics of Social Justice

The notion of citizenship, with its emphasis on rules of membership, reflect the boundaries of inclusion and exclusion. The concept of citizenship also addresses the three aspects of social inclusion, namely, equal access to privileges, benefits, and protection; political participation; and respect for cultural diversity. As discussed in Chapter 3, many past and current citizenship struggles focus on discourses and practices of exclusion from a given polity. While inclusion can be valued as a symbolic signifier of belonging, in most cases it is not inclusion in a community per se that is the target of social justice change and activism. With inclusion come rights and privileges, respect for diverse cultural expressions, and political participation. These three aspects, of social inclusion, combined with its boundary-setting mechanisms, also correspond to Nancy Fraser's vision of social justice (see Box 2.3). Fraser analytically distinguishes three main approaches to bringing about social justice. The first approach, redistribution, is about socio-economic injustices (e.g., economic marginalization, exploitation) and underscores the politics of equality. The second approach, recognition, views injustices as cultural (e.g., such as those

BOX 2.3 ❋ NANCY FRASER

Nancy Fraser (1947–) is an internationally acclaimed social, political, and feminist theorist who is best known for her contributions to social justice theory. In her book *Justice Interruptus: Critical Reflections on the "Postsocialist" Condition* (1996), Fraser brings together post-structuralist and critical-theoretical approaches to the question of justice. She highlights an increasing separation and polarization of what she calls the "redistribution" and "recognition" paradigms of justice theory and politics. Fraser argues that neither the class-based politics of economic equality (redistribution), nor the identity-based politics of cultural difference (recognition) are capable of sufficiently addressing (in)justice. Instead, she proposes a "bivalent conception of justice [that] encompasses both distribution and recognition *without reducing either one of them to the other.*" Since their original publication, these theoretical propositions have been the focus of intense academic and political debate. Nancy Fraser has contributed regularly to such discussions, through important publications such as *Redistribution or Recognition? A Political-Philosophical Exchange*, which she co-authored with Axel Honneth in 2003. Today, Nancy Fraser continues to inspire debate around the world through her research and teaching at the New School for Social Research in New York. (Source: Victoria Peace Network and Institute for Citizenship and Globalization 2005).

entrenched in patterns of representation) and embraces the politics of difference. The third approach of social justice—political—focuses on representation. Fraser outlines two aspects of representation. The first aspect pertains to procedures that "structure public processes of contestation" (Fraser 2005: 75). More specifically, this aspect of representation focuses on the way those included in the political community "air their claims and adjudicate their disputes" (75). This aspect corresponds to political participation and includes aspects of freedom as defined above. Nancy Fraser calls this aspect "ordinary political" representation. While redistribution, recognition, and the first aspect of representation refer to the content of social justice, the second aspect of representation defines the frame insofar as it defines who can press claims for redistribution and/or recognition. The second aspect refers to rules of inclusion in and exclusion from the community of those entitled to make justice claims on one another. In other words, it is the boundary-setting aspect of social inclusion that is at stake here.

How can social justice, defined in relation to social inclusion, be attained? Social struggles over citizenship rights have reversed many policies and practices that excluded people from social benefits, denied them respect and equal treatment, and imposed constraints on their freedom to act. In today's increasingly globalized world, these struggles require support and inspiration from transnational actors and networks (as discussed in Chapter 7).

In outlining three approaches to social justice—redistribution, recognition, and representation—Fraser distinguishes between two strategies for redressing injustice: affirmative and transformative. For her, affirmative strategies "aim to correct inequitable outcomes of social arrangements without disturbing the underlying social structures that generate them," while transformative strategies "aim to correct unjust outcomes precisely by restructuring the underlying generative framework" (2003: 74). In the section that follows we discuss these three approaches and two strategies and raise some questions about their implications and level of adequacy (see Figure 2.1).

Redistribution: The Politics of Equality

The redistribution approach aims at alleviating social inequalities by distributing various entitlements, such as welfare and social assistance. An affirmative approach to **maldistribution** is compatible with the market economy. It calls for policies that compensate for the inequalities that market economies create. These compensatory practices, in the form of social security provisions, housing subsidies, and similar measures, are represented by what has been called the welfare state (discussed in Chapter 4). Part of the welfare state approach involves the establishment of a **social minimum**, or an amount of material resources below which most persons or citizens are not allowed to fall. In contemporary societies, this most often takes the form of a monthly

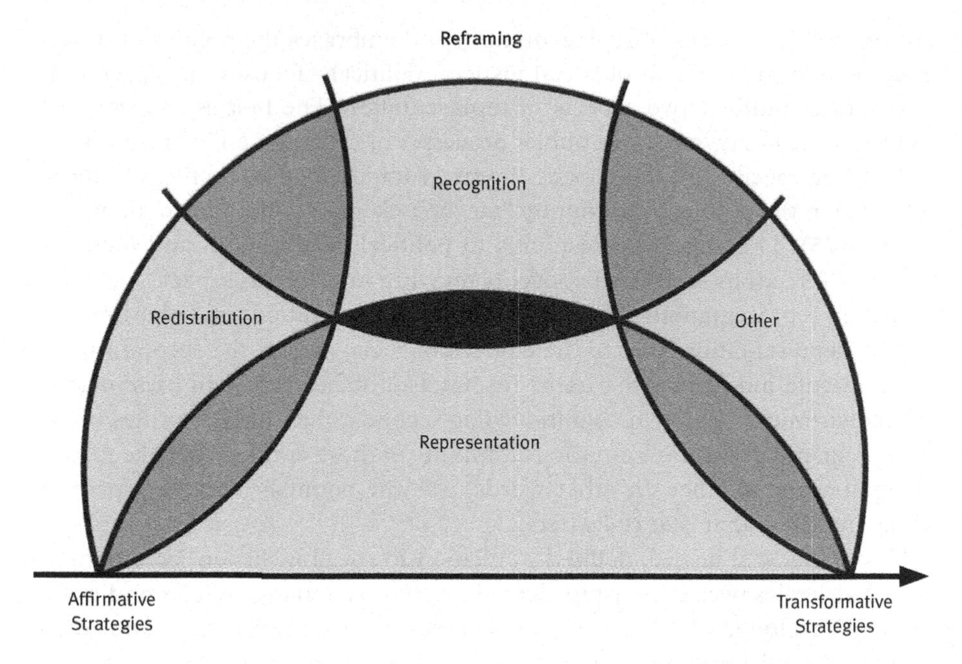

FIGURE 2.1 Reframing

Source: T/K

cheque distributed to adult citizens who do not earn an annual salary large enough to meet their own and/or their children's basic needs. Nevertheless, Rawls asserts that if rational actors who did not know their place in life were deciding on the principles by which to judge between competing claims about how things should be done, they would insure themselves against destitution by establishing a social minimum (2003b: 64). John Rawls argues that "the minimum should be set at the level which, taking wages into account, maximizes the expectations of the lowest income class" (2003b: 67). By expectations Rawls means a reasonable guess about the quality of life it will be possible to enjoy. He guards against the concern that this minimum would be so high as to equalize standings between people by asserting that the "relevant expectation of the least advantaged is their long-term expectation extending over all generations" (2003b: 67). Thus, the expectations of a particular, living individual are not those that establish the minimum, but the expectations of a theoretical, somewhere-in-time member of a particular class of people. In this regard, Rawls is not interested in the particulars of an individual, but rather in the general state of affairs represented by their aggregation. Under the welfare state, the establishment and distribution of the social minimum is the responsibility of government (see Chapter 4; Kymlicka 2008; Lister 2008: 118; Rawls 2003b: 64).

While supporting the welfare state approach in general, some researchers critique certain aspects of it. For example, some call for restructuring the overall distribution of pay and the rewards attached to different kinds of work (see, for example, Lister 2008: 115). Such a restructuring might address the immensity of the gap between the earnings of the top and bottom ten percent of the population. It might also address, for example, the high rewards attached to acting or playing sports in relation to the low rewards attached to teaching or social service work. The principle of desert, which emphasizes that people should receive benefits commeasurably with the value of their contribution to society (as discussed above), could be used in economic restructuring. It could provide a "non-discriminatory" way of re-evaluating benefits based on performances valued by society.

One specific performance often identified as requiring a revaluation of benefits is care work. Care work can include a wide variety of tasks necessary for the bodily and emotional health of other people, such as cleaning, bathing, cooking, feeding, providing emotional support, advocating for "rights," and facilitating another's ability to get around. It can be argued that they do not receive fair value for their labour because they are not recognized by others for their productive contributions, particularly when they perform unpaid work such as "stay-at-home" parenting or caring for elderly parents or family with disabilities (Anderson 2004: 169, 174). Broader social changes are needed for the value of this work to be recognized. It is important to acknowledge that care workers do perform tasks that are necessary for the continuation of life, the production of a "human" quality of life, the reproduction of the work force, and the ability of others to engage in other types of work. Social justice thus requires action to effect such revaluation in political and cultural economies. This approach would have particular implications for women, since women continue to provide the majority of both paid and unpaid care work (Young 2008: 89). It is possible to take this argument further and suggest that the devaluation of the work of care-givers is due to the devaluation of attributes and positions associated with particular assigned notions of femininity or the assignment of devalued attributes and positions to women. This observation points to the importance of revaluation not only for the women who perform care work "full-time" but for all women.

In raising other questions about the welfare state, Fraser critiques it on the grounds that it is "aimed at correcting inequitable outcomes of social arrangements without disturbing the underlying framework that generates them" (1997: 23). For Fraser, the underlying framework that generates economic injustice is capitalism, her analysis of which is rooted in Karl Marx's (see Box 2.4) critique of capitalism. As discussed in Marx's *Das Kapital* and other writings, capitalism is defined by the following characteristics: private ownership of the means of production (such as factories, land, water); commodification (or market orientation) of production aimed at capital accumulation; and antagonism between the proletariat (or the working class) and the bourgeoisie (the owners of the means of production). Under capitalism, according to Marx, the legal framework governing commerce, industrial production, and social and private rights guarantees support for the goals of capital accumulation. He believed that while the capitalist class accumulates more and more

BOX 2.4 ⁂ KARL MARX: "FROM EACH ACCORDING TO HIS ABILITY, TO EACH ACCORDING TO HIS NEED"

Karl Marx (1818–83) was born in Trier, Germany to a Jewish middle-class family. He completed his PhD in philosophy at University of Berlin in 1841. Considered "too radical," Marx never formally worked in the academic world. Instead, he turned to journalism for a brief period of time before being forced into exile as a result of his writings. In 1843, Marx fled to Paris, where he met Friedrich Engels and established what would be a lifelong friendship of academic and political collaboration and even financial support. Later, following his expulsion from France in 1845 and the failure of the revolutionary movements of 1848, Marx moved to London, England, where he remained for the rest of his life. It was in England that he wrote some of his most important contributions to economic and political thought, including *A Critique of Political Economy* (1859) and *Das Kapital* Volume 1 (1867).

Drawing heavily from the works of Hegel, and from the traditions of French socialism and British political economy, Marx developed a critical perspective on the effects of capitalist society on overall human welfare. He argued that capitalism organizes production in a manner that alienates the human being from his/her "natural" impulse toward creative production for the satisfaction of his/her own individual needs. Individuals, he contended, are alienated from this natural impulse because, with the creation of private property, many are no longer able to access the means (land, technology, etc.) to produce for themselves. Instead, he explained, individuals must sell their production time and energy (labour) to a person who does own such means (capitalists). As Marx pointed out, however, once goods have been produced in this manner, they are sold at a value that is greater than the value accorded to workers for their labour, thereby creating a "surplus value" that is then appropriated by capitalists to enhance their own personal lifestyle and power and/or to reinvest in the development and expansion of future production.

The exploitation of the labour of one social class (workers) by another social class (capitalists), Marx argued, was "unnatural" and ultimately detrimental to overall human welfare. He believed that this fundamental contradiction would eventually lead to the demise of the capitalist system and usher in an alternative system.

For Marx, human welfare would reach its highest potential through a communist organization of society. In one of his lesser-known works, entitled *Critique of the Gotha Program* (1875), Marx defines a communist society as one that is guided by the following principle: "From each according to his ability, to each according to his need," meaning that every individual would contribute to society according to their ability and receive according to their need. This powerful idea has been a source of inspiration and heated debate for more than a century now. (Sources: Ritzer 2008; Stanford Encyclopedia of Philosophy 2011).

wealth, the wages of the working class do not rise beyond subsistence level and this results in an increase in workers' exploitation. Parallel to the rise in workers' exploitation is the expansion of the "reserve army" of the unemployed who are squeezed out of production by the growing mechanization of production (Giddens 1971: 46–64; Harvey 1999). More recently, Marxist scholars have applied Marx's political economy approach to explain racial and gender inequalities, as well as other forms of exclusion. While several aspects of Marx's analysis of capitalism have been questioned by both contemporary Marxist and non-Marxist scholars, many critical analysts recognize that contemporary capitalism continues to be driven by "accumulation by dispossession," to use the famous phrase coined by David Harvey, an important Marxist theorist of social justice (see Box 2.5). Under neoliberalism (discussed in Chapter 4) the drive to accumulate leads to the privatization of public assets, the deregulation of the economy, and the development of taxation and fiscal policies that support corporations while further impoverishing the poor and the workers (Harvey 2003). It is these practices that the recently emerged "Occupy Wall Street" movement opposes as socially unjust (see Box 2.6). A number of social theorists argue that it is imperative to find alternatives to unbridled capitalism (e.g., Wright 2010).

Nancy Fraser follows Marx and other radical critiques of capitalism when she argues that remedies that only correct outcomes (which will be continually regenerated by the undisturbed underlying frameworks) are insufficient. In order to prevent economic and related cultural injustice from being perpetually recreated, Fraser calls for "transformative" strategies. In addition to providing social welfare programs, these strategies would call for public or collective ownership, a non-market public sector, and basic socioeconomic priorities in the distribution of resources. As such, transformative strategies would also undermine class differentiation and reduce social inequality (Fraser 1997: 24–6).

BOX 2.5 ❊ DAVID HARVEY

David Harvey (1935–) is one of the world's most influential social theorists today. Born and raised in the United Kingdom, he received his PhD in Geography from the University of Cambridge in 1961. Years later, he moved to the United States to continue his academic work at Johns Hopkins University. Currently, he holds the position of Distinguished Professor of Anthropology at City University of New York. While David Harvey's academic work has undergone several changes over the years, he is best known for his neo-Marxian approach and critical spatial analysis of subjects such as uneven development, urbanization, the environment, and neoliberal globalization. He is an outspoken critic of contemporary global capitalism and, thus, an intellectual ally of the global justice movement. He has published many powerful books which have inspired political and social debate around the world. Some of his most recognized works include *The Condition of Postmodernity* (1989); *Spaces of Hope* (2000); *The New Imperialism* (2003); *A Brief History of Neoliberalism* (2005); and, most recently, *The Enigma of Capital* (2010). (Sources: Kreisler 2004; Ritzer 2008; davidharvey.org).

BOX 2.6 ❊ THE OCCUPY WALL STREET MOVEMENT OCCUPIES THE GLOBE

On 17 September 2011, over 2,000 people in New York City marched toward Wall Street to denounce the role played by the banks, corporations, and governments in creating and perpetuating the economic crisis which, since 2008, has threatened the livelihoods of millions of people in the United States and around the world. Inspired by the popular democratic uprisings that took place in Egypt and Tunisia earlier in the year, trade unionists, students, environmentalists, and community groups in New York united that day chanting "We are the ninety-nine percent" in an expression of outrage over a global financial system that is governed by and for the benefit of the richest one percent of the world's population. Following the march, some 150 people set up camp in Zuccotti Park, renaming it Liberty Square and occupying it in continuous protest. Nearly one month later, on 15 October, the Occupy Wall Street movement went global, with protesters occupying financial districts in over 80 countries around the globe. In Canada, peaceful sit-ins and occupation camps were set up in over a dozen cities as thousands of Canadians joined the world in demanding a global system based on greater democracy, economic equality, and social justice. Sources: Occupy Wall Street Home page. 2011. "Occupy Wall Street Marks One Month." Last modified and accessed on 17 October 2011. http://occupywallst.org. CBC News. 2011. "Occupy Canada protests persist as work week begins." Published and accessed online on 17 October.http://www.cbc.ca/news/canada/edmonton/story/2011/10/17/occupy-canada-wrap.html).

Recognition: The Politics of Difference

A wide variety of social struggles have come under the label of recognition. These social struggles have ranged from civil rights and women's movements, to environmental, lesbian and gay rights, disability rights, peace, postcolonial, and indigenous peoples' movements, and to racialized movements. The claims made by those participating in these struggles are often known as struggles for recognition (see Isin et al. 2008: 5; Juteau 2008). A leading researcher whose work is well known in the field of recognition and the politics of difference is Iris Young (see Box 2.7). She advances a notion of social justice as a recognition of differences. She argues that in order to support difference while maintaining inclusion, we need a "dual system of rights: a general system of rights which are the same for all, and a more specific system of group-conscious policies and rights" (1996: 456). Young points to the dual rights of Native American or Indigenous peoples in the US as an example of such a system (1996: 461–2). In this system, people have US citizenship with all the general rights entailed, as well as tribal citizenship with all the tribe-specific rights entailed. Young also gives examples of necessary group-specific policies, including childbearing and work-leave security, pay for labour (such as unpaid care work, discussed above) and sports funding, bilingual-bicultural maintenance programs (1996: 457–61), and institutional

BOX 2.7 ❊ IRIS YOUNG

Iris Marion Young (1949–2006) has been described as a radical democrat, a feminist, a socialist, a social justice activist, and one of the most important political philosophers of the late twentieth century. Born and raised in New York, she began her academic career as an undergraduate student at Queens College in New York; she later went on to Pennsylvania State University, where she completed her PhD in Philosophy in 1974. Young strongly believed that political theory can and should contribute to practical questions of social and political reform. Her research covered a wide range of themes, including global justice, women and gender; human and labour rights; race; and democracy. Nevertheless, it was her book *Justice and the Politics of Difference* (1990) that gained her much acclaim. In it, she critically examined the basic concepts underlying the dominant theories of justice at the time. She argued for a new conception of justice and for the affirmation—instead of suppression—of social group differences. At the time of her death in 2006, she was a Professor of Political Science at the University of Chicago and a popular figure in academic and activist circles around the world. (Sources: Scheuerman 2006; University of Chicago News Office 2006).

accommodation for the "needs of menstruating, pregnant, and breastfeeding women" (2008: 87). This idea is reflected in the notion of "differentiated citizenship" as discussed in Chapter 3.

Young calls for the direct inclusion of social or positional groups in public decision making (1996: 464). Social groups are defined by shared affinities and ways of life, while positional groups are defined by their structural positioning. By "structural positioning," Young refers to practices that affect "opportunities for self-development and access to resources, to make decisions about both the conditions of their own action and that of others, or to be treated with respect or deference" (2008: 80). The purpose of directly including these groups in public decision making is to "equal the playing field," given that people from one or a few privileged groups typically monopolize positions of political power and make decisions based on their own values and interests about the conduct and content of different people's lives. In this regard, Young also argues that this type of participation in decision making should apply not only to government bodies but also to "any institution with authority over [a group's] actions" (1996: 464). This extension reflects the concern, discussed previously, that civil society can be a potentially crucial site of social inclusion and for addressing issues of equality or inequality.

Concerned mainly with ethno-cultural differences, Kymlicka repudiates policies that either exclude or assimilate (i.e., require people to change so they seem "the same" as the majority) (2008: 56–7). He is a strong advocate of multiculturalism or the incorporation of various ethno-cultural groups in one polity or political community. He argues that this kind of incorporation of ethno-cultural groups can both "reduce historic inequalities between groups" and strengthen "practices of democratic citizenship" (2008: 61). Such incorporation can happen because while the effects of unjust state policies, such as "the adoption of official language laws" (Kymlicka 2008: 55), are taken into account in order to reduce inequalities between groups, at the same time all groups are subject to the accommodation of human rights norms (Kymlicka 2008: 60). Human rights norms, discussed in Chapter 6, are argued to be universal and not particular to any one social group. Multiculturalism is thus an attempt to maintain certain universals while accommodating a range of differences instead of involving the imposition of dominant majorities onto others.

Will Kymlicka reviews common attempts to institutionalize (i.e., pattern and stabilize) multiculturalism. These attempts include "the explanation/celebration of multiculturalism in the school curriculum; the inclusion of ethnic representation/sensitivity in the mandate of public media; exemption from dress codes [and] Sunday-closing legislation; allowing dual citizenship; the funding of ethnic group organizations or activities; the funding of bilingual education or mother-tongue instruction; and affirmative action for disadvantaged immigrant groups" (Kymlicka 2008: 69–70). These actions are intended to notice, value, and support differences among citizens while incorporating these different citizens as equals in one political community. Nancy Fraser, on the other hand, argues against "mainstream multiculturalism," viewing it as a strategy for recognition that fails to disrupt the "underlying generative framework" (1997: 26). These strategies are "affirmative." In other words, the actions of multiculturalism continually regenerate distinctions between groups and *presume* a dominant group or a normal group that is accommodating a subordinated or abnormal group. For example, exemption from Sunday-closing legislation presumes a dominant Christian group that is accommodating subordinated non-Christian groups, which in turn can underscore hierarchal thinking. While repudiating official policies of multiculturalism, Fraser calls for "transformative" approaches or the deconstruction of social identities (Fraser 1997: 26–32).

Nancy Fraser is not alone in endorsing the deconstruction of social identities as a strategy for making the world a better place. Postmodern and queer theoretical traditions, among others, have situated identity deconstruction as a key, effective strategy for "resistance," though scholars in these traditions may not connect these goals with the concept of social justice per se. There are many variations on what such deconstruction means. One line of thought calls for the recognition of our bodies, selves, and identities as being always in a state of *becoming* (Braidotti 2003; Grosz 2005). In other words, we are always changing in the most fundamental sense and never solidify into something bounded, unified, or fixed. This understanding of the self as becoming is different from developmental stage models. The idea that we are infants, then toddlers, then kids, then teens, then adults, and so on is a fairly common developmental model. These and other similar developmental models often presume a boundedness (i.e., there is a clear set of things that are "inside" being a teenager and other things that are clearly "outside"), unity (i.e., there is one self that is, rather than multiple concurrent selves), and fixedness (i.e., for this moment the body, the self, and identity are "congealed" or fixed in place). In this understanding we *are* one thing, then we undergo a change and become something else—here "self" is a noun. This is different from being in a state of *becoming*, with the self understood as a verb. As Grosz claims, "[t]here never was the self-identity and stasis necessary for a fixed identity, a given boundary and clear-cut states, that is, for objects as they are conceptually understood" except those that are cut out for us by our bodily and perceptual needs (2005,12).

Another way of thinking about deconstruction is articulated by Judith Butler. Butler argues, following Michel Foucault, that social identities are a mechanism of social regulation. This means that they shape our behaviour in particular, predictable ways that facilitate the reproduction of the current social order (1999: 173–6). For example, we do certain things because that is what "men" do and "manly" actions are concerned with those of "women" who do other certain things because that is what "women" do. This way of thinking, however, both limits our possibilities for everyday life and reproduces relations of domination. In contrast to scholars like Young who argue for cultural revaluation of different identities, Butler argues that no project of revaluation will fundamentally disrupt socio-cultural domination (1999: 170–4). Revaluation does not disrupt the "underlying generative framework." As long as there are traditionally conceived social identities, there will always be a hierarchal social order based on those identities.

For Butler, the deconstruction of social identities requires practices that reveal the constructed nature of identities most people take as natural. One way to do this is through the combination of practices or performances that seem to belong to different identities (e.g., man/woman) in a way that makes them seem like they might belong together (e.g., man-woman). Such practices call into question the boundaries that demarcate things as belonging to one identity or another and thus the existence of these identities (1999: 179). Butler uses drag as an example of such a combination (1999: 156–57). In drag, things clearly identified with one gender (e.g., waxed legs and lipstick or a bulge and necktie) are displayed along with things that visibly identify with the "other" gender (e.g., chest hair or breasts). According to Butler, identity politics colludes in a system of domination (or injustice) through identity. This is an important point since any pressure to become "woman" or "man" does not come from "sex" but from knowledge and power relations that work together to establish a set of ideas for thinking about the world in these and other kinds of ways (Butler 2004: 215). The conclusion we draw from this discussion is that while diverse identities and cultural lifestyles matter to many people (although not all and not to the same degree) and should be fully recognized, these identities and life preferences are fluid (i.e., constantly changing) and hybrid (often combining several seemingly opposite dimensions). For the goals of social justice to be attained, these identities should be fully recognized as socially relevant (at least for some) and non-hierarchical.

Beyond Redistribution and Recognition

Struggles around redistribution and recognition have had and continue to have varying degrees of success. There have been improvements in some people's lives as a consequence of the demands that have been waged for better healthcare services, social housing, affirmative action programs, and fair wages, although many governments since the 1980s, including the Canadian government, have been abandoning the concept of social security and reducing social program spending (Basok and Ilcan 2003; Brodie 2008b: 39; Ilcan 2009; see also Chapter 4). Pursuing the route of redistribution or recognition, or both, to resolve wide-ranging social justice issues can, however, be inadequate and pose other questions and dilemmas. By this we mean that it is not sufficient to presume that some social struggles are simply about economic redistribution and others are merely about cultural recognition, such as requiring cultural change, cultural readjustment, or cultural accommodation (Isin et al. 2008: 6).

With respect to the recognition approach, there are some differentiated groups, such as racialized ones, that do question the existence of a category that "naturalizes and fixes their identity" (Juteau 2008: 74). To classify social struggles as either redistribution or recognition misses the complexity of these struggles. As Isin et al. point out, "When people mobilize for legalizing same-sex marriage, rally for social housing, protest welfare rate cuts, debate employment insurance, advocate for the decriminalization of marijuana, wear attire such as turbans or headscarves in public spaces, seek affirmative action programs, or demand better health care access and services, they do not imagine themselves as struggling for the maintenance or expansion of social cultural or sexual citizenship rights. Instead they invest in whatever issues seem most related and closest to their social lives, and dedicate their time and energy accordingly. ... To classify such struggles as redistribution (economism) or recognition (culturalism) misses the complexity" (2008: 6). The struggle for same-sex marriage clearly illustrates how the struggle for recognition is combined with the struggle for redistribution (see Box 2.8).

At the same time, some social justice struggles do not centre on either redistribution or recognition. For example, some struggles focus on the construction of diverse counter-hegemonic social visions (see, for example, Basok 2009; Carroll 2007) or alternative forms and practices of knowledge that aim to foster political and cultural relations that are equitable and socially inclusive in orientation. The Transnational Institute, for example, established in 1974, is a transnational network of scholar-activists whose mission is "to provide intellectual support to movements struggling for a more democratic, equitable and environmentally sustainable world" (www.tni.org; also see Carroll 2007). In the Canadian context, the Canadian Centre for Policy Alternatives, established in 1980, is a research centre concerned with social, economic, and environmental justice. Its mandate is to challenge conventional wisdoms and offer critical analyses on such issues as privatization of health care, educational reforms, Aboriginal people's issues, trade, growing income gaps, and others. As stated on their website, "The CCPA debunks myths—like the myth that an aging population will cripple public health care, or that meeting our climate change obligations is a job-killer" (www.policyalternatives.ca). Thus it is critical to bear in mind that struggles for social justice are about more than simply redistribution and recognition as we discuss in later chapters.

Box 2.8 ❊ The Battle over Same-Sex Marriage in Canada: A Struggle for Redistribution and Recognition

The issue of same-sex marriage moved into the spotlight in Canada during the 1990s, as activists and individuals alike seized the opportunity to pursue legal and public policy changes using Section 15 of the Canadian Charter of Rights and Freedoms (Smith 2008). Section 15's open-ended guarantee of equality rights and non-discrimination offered same-sex couples the opportunity to legally challenge the non-recognition of their relationships and their consequent exclusion from many legal rights, benefits, powers, and obligations which were linked to conjugal partnerships in Canada and reserved solely for "spouses," interpreted to mean heterosexuals (Hurley 2010). Thus, following the Charter's introduction, a series of legal battles ensued: In *Canada (AG) v. Mossop* (1993) a federal public servant claimed the right to bereavement leave after the death of his same-sex partner's father; in *Egan and Nesbit v. Canada* (1995) a same-sex couple struggled for spousal benefits under the federal Old Age Security Act; and in *M. v. H.* (1999), a woman sought post-separation support from her former same-sex partner. The Court's decision to grant support in this latter case was by far the most significant of the three since it affirmed the Court's position that same-sex and opposite-sex couples were to receive equal legal treatment (Matthews 2005: 847–8).

Although same-sex couples managed to defeat many of their legal barriers to redistributive justice, they continued to struggle for *recognition* by challenging their exclusion from the institution of marriage. In 2001, for example, the Metropolitan Community Church of Toronto (MCCT) and members of its congregation decided to use the ancient practices of the church (the proclamation of banns) and freedom of religion to challenge marriage laws by marrying two same-sex couples. When one of the couples—Kevin Bourassa and Joe Varnell—was asked why they wanted to marry, given that they already had access to most spousal benefits, they explained that marriage represented a necessary first step towards their attainment of social equality; it validated their relationship as equally valuable and legitimate—on par with their heterosexual counterparts (Nicol and Smith 2008: 681). They saw "changes in official [marriage] law not as ends in themselves but as part of a broader set of social and attitudinal changes in their families, personal relationships and their children" (Nicol and Smith 2008: 684). It was not just a struggle for *redistribution* (equal rights and benefits), but also one for *recognition*. In 2005, the federal government legally recognized same-sex marriage in Canada with the approval of the *Civil Marriage Act.* (Sources: Hurley 2010; Nicol and Smith 2008; Matthews 2005; Smith 2008).

Representation: The Politics of Political Participation and Reframing

As discussed above, Fraser's notion of representation refers to: (a) mechanisms through which political decisions are made and justice claims are adjudicated; and (b) boundary-setting mechanisms that define who is and who is not a subject of justice. Therefore, the politics of representation embraces either one or both of these aspects. With respect to political decision making rules, certain questions need to be addressed. Can representative democracy, prevalent in most liberal democratic societies, assure justice for all? Are the interests of women, visible minorities, and Aboriginal people assured in the political system that under-represents them? Who sets the agenda and procedure rules in the negotiations for self-government between the Canadian federal government and Aboriginal peoples? Do male-dominated trade unions properly represent women's interests and the interests of workers in non-union jobs (e.g., domestic work)? Do civil society organizations participating in UN forums get a chance to voice their concerns and put forward their proposals for change? These and other questions have been raised and activists have called for more democratic representation.

As mentioned earlier, the second aspect of Fraser's notion of representation refers to boundary-setting mechanisms that define who is—and who is not—the subject and object of social justice claims. Currently, the dominant boundary-setting model centres on the sovereign power of a nation-state to define who has the right to claim rights. However, through processes of globalization (or cosmopolitanization, as some call it), this model has lost much of its relevance (if it ever was relevant). As Beck and Sznaider (2006: 9) emphasize, "Cosmopolitanization thus points to the irreversible fact that people, from Moscow to Paris, from Rio to Tokyo, have long since been living in really existing relations of interdependence; they are as much responsible for the intensification of these relations through their production and consumption as are the resulting global risks that impinge on their everyday lives." Nancy Fraser (2005) directs attention to the new sense of vulnerability that has been fostered by such forces as transnational corporations, international currency speculators, transnational financial investors, supranational and international organizations, global mass media, and cybertechnology. She asserts, "Faced with global warming, the spread of AIDS, international terrorism and superpower unilateralism, many believe that their chances for living good lives depend at least as much on processes that trespass the borders of territorial states as on those contained within them" (2005: 71).

Within this context, it is vital to make these transnational forces responsible for the harm they may cause. As discussed in Chapter 7, some social activists have advanced justice claims against transnational corporations and such transnational actors as the World Bank, the International Monetary Fund, and the World Trade Organization for destroying the environment, displacing and/

or impoverishing people, and instigating ethnic and regional wars. For Fraser (2005), these and similar claims destabilize the current framing of social justice based on national territorial states. She sees them as part of the politics of reframing. In addition, the increasing mobility of people across state boundaries has also challenged this nation-based framing of social justice. Non-citizens (such as migrants without authorization to live and work in a country, refugee claimants, and asylum seekers) are often denied access to basic rights such as housing, healthcare, and education. They are excluded from the wider benefits of the welfare state and, in Sweden for example, they are "at risk of frequent moves, exclusion from education and health care, sometimes resulting in unnecessary death" (van dan Anker 2011: 123). Nation-states do not recognize the right of these people to have rights and therefore the struggles faced by non-citizens as well as similarly positioned groups cannot be resolved through struggles for redistribution or recognition. Justice for these people would require re-framing, as many migrant rights activists (including the No Borders movement and other organizations discussed in Chapters 3 and 7) have demanded. Luis Cabrera (2010) calls for the creation of global institutions that would offer protection to all individuals regardless of their place of birth by treating them as "global citizens" and "making them the actual addresses of justification" (259).

Conclusion

In this book we view social justice as involving processes of change that are fuelled by social struggles over redistribution, recognition, representation, and other issues that do not fall neatly into these aforementioned categories. We recognize that the concrete struggles led by social activists often include more than one goal. We also acknowledge that the current meta-frames of justice—that is, who is the subject and object of justice in the first place—no longer fit with many people's current social life relations as these meta-frames require a reframing and revisioning of social justice. Figure 2.1 summarizes this vision. As we will see in the chapters that follow, contemporary social relations are mediated through a range of everyday practices that are increasingly characterized by the mobility of capital, communication, ideas, and people, and that raise questions about issues related to social justice.

Questions for Critical Thought

1. What are the key links between social inclusion and exclusion? How and to what extent might certain initiatives and forms of activism bring about a socially inclusive society?

2. Discuss how Nancy Fraser's notion of representation defines who is and who is not a subject of justice. In the context of political decision making, discuss the extent to which the interests of women, visible minorities, or Aboriginal peoples are assured in the political system that under-represents them.
3. In light of this chapter's discussion of the debates around social justice and processes of change, how do you understand the concept of social justice? What vision or visions of social justice do you have that can assist in bringing about a more socially just world? In this regard, how do your views on social justice differ from or parallel those discussed in this chapter?

Annotated Additional Readings

Loretta Capeheart and Dragon Milovanovic. 2007. *Social Justice: Theories, Issues, and Movements*. New Brunswick, New Jersey, London: Rutgers University Press. This book focuses on some of the common views of criminal justice that often accept a politically established definition of crime which, the authors argue, is too limited in scope. The authors examine a wide range of contemporary issues, from globalization to the environment, that engage ideas of social justice. In their analyses, they question the limits of the law in order to advance a fairer system that operates within and at different scales.

Matthew Clayton and Andrew Williams. Eds. 2004. *Social Justice*. Wiley-Blackwell Publishers. This edited book brings together debates and discussions on social justice in the fields of philosophy, law, politics, and economics. It begins with classic discussions by Locke and Hume, then turns to contemporary theories of social justice that stress the work of Rawls, Nozick, Dworkin, and some of their critics. It concludes with readings on issues such as family, world poverty, and cultural rights that challenge common conceptions of justice.

David Miller. 2001. *Principles of Social Justice*. Harvard University Press. This book presents divergent views about what is required to bring about justice. Drawing upon different principles that are used in different social contexts, the author presents principles of need, desert, and equality that are put together to form an integrated theory.

Related Websites

CAW/TCA Canada Social Justice Fund
www.caw.ca/en/services-departments-social-justice-fund.htm

Centre for Studies in Social Justice
www.uwindsor.ca/socialjustice/

Centre for the Study of Social Justice
http://cssj.utk.edu/critical.php

Ministry of Social Justice and Empowerment, Government of India
http://socialjustice.nic.in/

Social Justice Studies
http://web.uvic.ca/socialjustice/

Social Justice Tribunals Ontario
www.sjto.gov.on.ca/english/default.html

3 Citizenship: Challenging Exclusions

Learning Objectives

- Explore the concept of citizenship and its relation to social justice
- Understand the link between nation-states, citizenship, and social justice
- Assess T.H. Marshall's contribution to the understanding of citizenship
- Identify limitations in the liberal notion of universal citizenship
- Understand the notions of "differentiated citizenship" and "differentiated universalism"
- Question the relationship between diversity and equality
- Recognize how citizenship institutions and practices are shaped through social struggles
- Explain and question the link between the Westphalian system of nation-states and the exclusion of non-citizens

Introduction

In Chapter 1, we explored why social justice is important and how it can be understood. Now we need to ask: how is social justice to be applied? Can social justice principles be applied universally, to all human beings worldwide? While the universal application of social justice principles has been contemplated (see Chapter 6 for more discussion), in today's world, it is the **nation-state** that, to the large extent, defines the boundaries of social justice. This political system is rooted in the political developments of the seventeenth century. In 1648, major European countries signed the Peace of Westphalia accord and agreed to respect the principle of territorial integrity. Since then a **Westphalian system** has been in place. Under the Westphalian system, the application of social justice principles is intimately tied with the notions of nation-state citizenship.

What is citizenship? **T.H. Marshall**, a British sociologist who has inspired much scholarly thinking on citizenship (see Box 3.1), defined it in the following manner: "Citizenship is a status bestowed on those who are full members of a community. All those who possess the status are equal with respect to the rights and duties with which the status is endowed" (Marshall 1965 [1950]: 92). Even though it appears straightforward, this definition has actually created much controversy and numerous aspects of it have been debated. What is a community? What does it mean to be full members of this community? What rights are provided to all citizens? These questions correspond to the issue of boundaries of social inclusion (as discussed in Chapter 2). Does equality

BOX 3.1 ❊ T.H. MARSHALL ON CITIZENSHIP AND INEQUALITY

Thomas Humphrey Marshall (1893–1981), more widely known as T.H. Marshall, was a British sociologist who made significant contributions to citizenship theory. His most renowned work, entitled *Citizenship and Social Class*, is based on a lecture he presented in Cambridge, England in 1949. In it, he responds to a question which was central to the political debates of the Cold War period, that is, whether or not it was possible to achieve equality of citizenship given the socially stratifying nature of capitalism. Marshall saw great promise for equality in the expansion of social citizenship rights under the welfare state during the twentieth century. This expansion, he said, embodied the final stage in the evolution of citizenship rights in Great Britain, which began with the extension of civil and political rights during the eighteenth and nineteenth centuries. Marshall argued that social citizenship rights—such as access to education, healthcare, and unemployment benefits—had a much greater effect in abating social disparities since they enabled individuals to overcome previous barriers (access to economic resources, for example) to the full exercise of their citizenship. Upon re-examination of this question, Marshall recognized that, while the preservation of economic inequalities had been made more difficult by the expansion of social citizenship, citizenship and social class inequality could still be considered compatible. His examination of education as a social citizenship right provides an illustration. The drive to universalize the opportunity to receive education has been accompanied by an ever closer relationship between education and occupation. As children move through the education system, they are evaluated and "categorized" according to their performance, which ultimately determines their occupation later in life. Thus, " ... through education in its relations with occupational structure, citizenship operates as an instrument of social stratification," and "the status acquired by education is carried out into this world bearing the stamp of legitimacy, because it has been conferred by an institution designed to give the citizen his just rights." (Sources: Marshall 1965 [1950]: 121; Turner 1993).

under the law always guarantee equality in practice? How is the right to be different to be reconciled with the right to be equal? What kinds of duties should the state have in order to guarantee rights to all citizens? What duties are expected from citizens? These questions correspond to the *content* of social inclusion, as discussed in Chapter 2. What is the role of political participation, social activism, and other forms of political acts in shaping citizenship? These questions address the *politics* of social inclusion, as discussed in Chapter 2. We will address these questions in this chapter.

We will begin by discussing the notions of modern citizenship rooted in the French Revolution. Three ideas—social justice, citizenship, and nation-state—became intimately intertwined at the time of the French Revolution and the upheavals and political processes that followed. We will then consider T.H. Marshall's contribution to understanding citizenship in relation to three basic rights—civil, political, and social. While acknowledging Marshall's contribution to our understanding of citizenship, we will nevertheless question its **Eurocentric bias.** In other words, does Marshall's perspective privilege the principles, ideas, and views of the world that emerge from Europe and apply them to other contexts? We will also question whether Marshall's analysis captures the experiences of such groups as women, people with disabilities, gay and lesbian people, ethnic minorities, and other excluded groups. To recognize differences among various groups of individuals, we will turn our discussion to the notions of "cultural citizenship" or "differentiated citizenship."

The notion of "differentiated citizenship" poses a dilemma for many activists and theorists: does respect for difference undermine equality? We will address this debate and argue that it is possible to reconcile the two. One concept that has been proposed to underscore both difference and equality is that of "differentiated universalism." We will explore what this means. It is important to point out that citizenship is never set in stone. The definition of the rights to be guaranteed to citizens, duties required from them, who is to be considered a citizen, and many other aspects related to citizenship have changed over time. These changes can be attributed to struggles between those who feel excluded from the privileges of citizenship and those who wish to limit the scope of citizenship to the select few and/or govern others in a particular way. We will discuss how citizenship is linked to social struggles for equity.

We will then turn our discussion specifically to those who have been denied formal (legal) citizenship in nation-states—immigrants and refugees. We will examine not only past attempts to keep some people out, but also current trends, particularly the securitization of borders and increased policing of citizens perceived to pose a threat to national well-being. We will then explore how, despite such tough measures, millions of migrants defy these restrictions and settle in nation-states without authorization. We will discuss whether migrants who are denied formal citizenship have de facto rights in nation-states. Finally, we will examine how unauthorized migrants have asserted their right to be recognized, heard, and granted certain rights by engaging in "**acts of citizenship**" and the politics of representation (see Chapter 2).

Modern Citizenship, Social Justice, and Nation-States

The French Revolution (see Box 3.2) established the links among citizenship, social justice (in the form of equality, solidarity, and freedom), and membership

Box 3.2 ❋ The French Revolution and Modern Notions of Citizenship

The French Revolution is often thought of as the starting point for modern notions of citizenship involving individual nation-state membership and a shared set of rights and obligations to the state. Prior to the French Revolution, France's *ancien régime* was organized around a monarchy that governed civic life in a manner that privileged some groups over others according to their sex, social class, occupation, religious affiliation, place of residence, and so on. The French Revolution changed this by establishing a new regime based on the recognition and guaranteed preservation of the natural and legal rights of man, including the right to liberty, security, property, and, above all, the right to equality. The Declaration of the Rights of Man and of the Citizen, drawn up by the new regime's National Assembly in August of 1789, outlined these guiding principles, providing rational criteria and a legal reference for resolving disputes within society. Today, this document is considered to be a major precursor of the establishment of international human rights instruments. (Sources: Brubaker 1989; Declaration of the Rights of Man and Citizen from the Constitution of Year I www.columbia.edu/~iw6/docs/dec1793.html; Waldinger, Dawson, and Woloch 1993).

in a nation. Even prior to the Revolution, the concept of citizenship had lost its traditional connection to the city and bourgeoisie and expanded to include the political community and the nation. The Revolution rendered the notion of citizenship even broader by emphasizing the role of citizens in the political life of a state (Waldinger, Dawson, and Woloch 1993).

The French Revolution and the upheavals of 1848 laid the foundations of the modern understanding of citizenship. This modern notion of citizenship merged two previous traditions of citizenship. The first one was rooted in the Greek city-state and referred to the reciprocal relationship between those who ruled and those who were ruled. This model emphasized political participation. The second tradition was rooted in the Roman Empire and conceived of citizenship in relation to the legal status, with specific rights and responsibilities. In the nation-state these two traditions merged (Cohen 1999). Thus, the modern notion of citizenship emphasizes the right of citizens to participate in the political life of a nation, as well as the right to be treated equally and have the freedom to pursue one's objectives, as long as they do not harm other citizens.

The model of political membership, as articulated in the French Revolution, was founded on a distinction between nationals and foreigners. This model is based on a division between territorially based national states. Writing on the

French Revolution, Hannah Arendt (see Box 3.3) underlined that, in 1789, the "nation had conquered the state." Thus, for Arendt, the democratic idea of government "by the people, for the people" was then linked to ethnically defined and presumably culturally homogenous nations (cited in Krause 2008, 337). According to Arendt, the French Revolution laid the foundation for the principle that only members of a nation could be citizens and thus enjoy the full protection of legal institutions, and that the laws of a country could not protect people of a different nationality (Krause 2008: 337). Later in this chapter we discuss how this particular understanding of citizenship limits the rights of migrants.

Once the foundations of citizenship were laid, each nation-state embarked on a nation-building process. In the course of these processes, certain categories of persons were prevented from achieving full citizenship. Some nation-states excluded the working class and the poor from the privileges of citizenship. In other nation-states, exclusion from social membership

BOX 3.3 ❖ HANNAH ARENDT'S CONTRIBUTION TO CITIZENSHIP STUDIES

Hannah Arendt (1906–75) is one of the twentieth century's most important political philosophers. In 1941, at the height of the Second World War, this German-born Jewish intellectual fled to the United States, where she subsequently wrote a series of influential books, including *The Origins of Totalitarianism* (1951) and *The Human Condition* (1958). Her work highlighted the tensions between the inclusive abstract principles of human rights and the exclusionary practices of state sovereignty which, when translated into practice—citizenship rights, for example—can produce extreme forms of exclusion and "rightslessness" that threaten people's most basic human rights, especially in contexts of war and imperialist conquest. She was particularly concerned with the way in which state conflicts could render citizens stateless and, therefore, without recourse for claiming either citizenship or human rights, including the right to life.

One of Arendt's most important contributions to citizenship theory resides in the notion that the "first" and most basic of all rights is the "**right to have rights**," that is, the right to belong to some sort of an organized community and to be judged according to one's actions and opinions. Her work illustrated that the "right to have rights" was actually contingent on an individual's membership in a community of political actors (i.e., recognized belonging to a nation-state) rather than their membership in a human community. (Sources: Benhabib 2002; Balibar 2007; Krause 2008; Stanford Encyclopedia of Philosophy online: http://plato.stanford.edu/entries/arendt/).

was based on race and ethnic differences. Everywhere women were denied the rights of full citizenship by preventing their access to the public sphere (Kivisto and Faist 2007: 7). Over the centuries, these different groups of people have claimed and gained citizenship through struggles, as we will discuss later.

The modern notion of citizenship raises two general questions: What kinds of rights (and responsibilities) does citizenship entail and who is to be included? With respect to the first question, T.H. Marshall discusses the evolution of three rights linked to citizenship in the Western world: civil, political, and social. We will discuss Marshall's contribution to citizenship studies in the next section.

From Civil to Political to Social Citizenship

In tracing the historical development of citizenship in Britain, Marshall refers to three elements: civil, political, and social. The civil element, which he associates with the institutions of the judicial system, "is composed of the rights necessary for individual freedom—liberty of person, freedom of speech, thought and faith, the right to own property and to conclude valid contracts, and the right to justice" (Marshall 1965 [1950]: 78). The political element, connected to the institutions of the parliamentary system, refers to "the right to participate in the exercise of political power, as a member of a body invested with political authority or as an elector of the members of such a body" (78). Finally, the social element is "the whole range from the right to a modicum of economic welfare and security to share to the full in the social heritage and to live the life of a civilized being according to the standards of the prevailing society" (78). This last element is connected to education and the social services system. T.H. Marshall believed that these different rights have evolved at different times: fundamental civil rights experienced significant expansion during the eighteenth century, political rights developed during the nineteenth century, and social rights during the twentieth century (81). He also believed that although social citizenship did not eliminate economic inequality, it reduced it (see Box 3.1 for a more detailed discussion of this issue). Figure 3.1 represents Marshall's model of the evolution from civil to political to social rights.

While Marshall's ideas have become very influential among scholars of citizenship, many recognize limitations in Marshall's analysis. Naila Kabeer, for example, has observed that this notion of citizenship is Eurocentric and therefore not entirely applicable to non-Western societies. According to Kabeer, the legacy of colonialism can be found in the *parallel traditions of citizenship* present in the Global South, particularly in Africa. On the one hand, there is the idea of individual memberships based on a social contract of rights and obligations in relation to the nation-state. On the other hand,

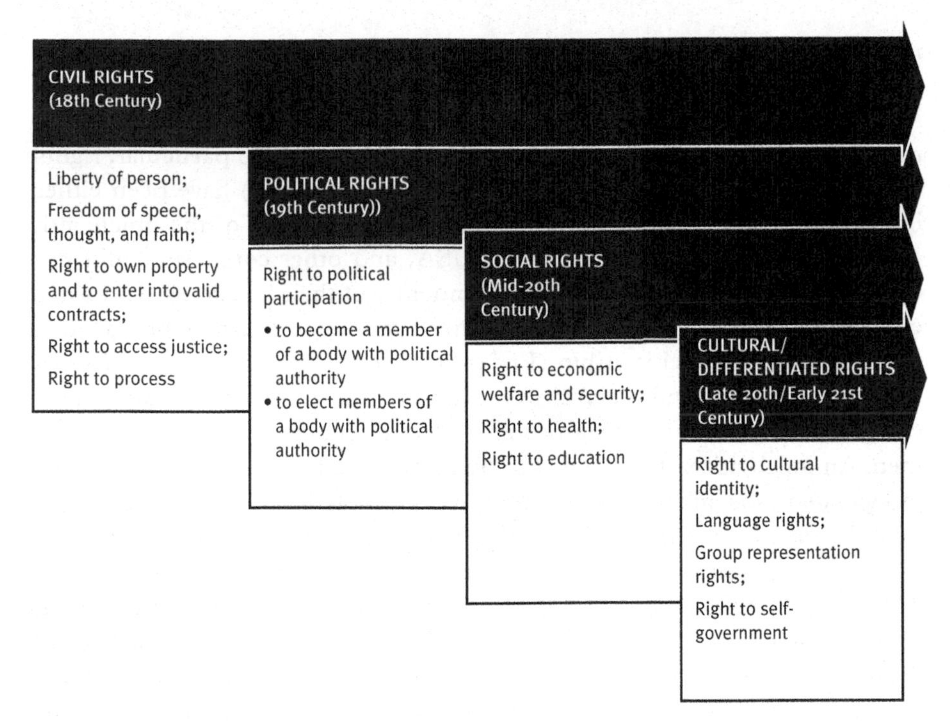

FIGURE 3.1 The Evolution of Citizenship Rights in Advanced Industrial Societies

Source: T/K

simultaneous with this idea of citizenship, group memberships based on diverse social cleavages—place of birth, lineage, religion, caste, sex, etc.—also play a role in citizenship rights and obligations in *practice*. For Kabeer, the co-existence of multiple forms of citizenship can bolster hierarchy, exclusion, and conflict between different groups but can also bring about equality, universality, and dignity for the citizens (2002: 15). For Yuval-Davis (2007), even in Western societies people's lives are shaped by rights and obligations in multiple political communities, such as local, ethnic, religious, national, regional, transnational, and international. She advances the notion of a "**multi-layered citizen**" to illustrate that people can be citizens of more than one political community.

Differentiated Citizenship

T.H. Marshall's analysis of the liberal model of citizenship underscores a set of rights enjoyed universally, that is, by all members of a nation-state, regardless of gender, class, ethnicity, race, or other status. Yet, as feminist and other scholars and activists have pointed out, this notion of universalism masks inequalities experienced by such "second-class" citizens, as women, racialized minorities, gay and lesbians, women with disabilities, and others (see Basok, Ilcan, and Noonan 2008). For example, Walby (1994 and 1997) illustrates that women's rights have developed at a different pace than men's—with women's rights lagging behind male rights. In particular, rights applied exclusively to women (e.g., the right to abortion) have been either ignored or received delayed attention. As late as the end of the nineteenth century, married women in the UK, USA, and other countries could not own property or make contracts independently of their husbands. And since citizenship at that time was conceptualized in terms of civil rights, women were excluded from citizenship (Lister 2003: 69). The exclusion of women from civil, political, and social citizenship has been justified by an essentialist categorization of women's nature and abilities by comparison to those of men. An ideal citizen has been socially constructed as a rational, impartial, independent, disembodied individual. Yet, as Table 3.1 demonstrates, these qualities have been attributed to males. Females, on the other hand, are seen as embodied, rooted in nature, emotional, irrational, dependent, and passive. These characterizations have served as justifications for excluding women from the practices of citizenship (Lister 2003: 71). Thus, women have been portrayed predominantly as reproducers and carers in the domestic sphere. Yet, their domestic work is devalued because it is "natural" and repetitious and thus inferior to the public work performed by males. At the same time, women's identification with their emotionality and sexuality have been viewed as a threat to political order from which they have been excluded (Lister 2003: 71–2). The same essentialist binary characterizations have been employed to exclude from citizenship Black and elderly people, people with disabilities, and gays and lesbians (Lister 2003: 74). Jo-Ann Dillabough and Arnot (2000) call this discursive framing of citizenship "fraternal pact." In addition, they discuss how the portrayal of women as the guardians of cultural morality and catalysts of national identity further marginalizes women by assigning them the responsibility to reproduce and cultivate national citizens.

Table 3.1 Essentialist Categorization of Male and Female Qualities

Public Male Citizen	Private Female Non-Citizen
Abstract, disembodied, mind	Particular, embodies, rooted in nature
Rational, able to apply dispassionate reason and standards of justice	Emotional, irrational, subject to desire and passion; unable to apply standards of justice
Impartial, concerned with public interest	Partial, preoccupied with private domestic concerns
Independent, active, heroic and strong	Dependent, passive, weak
Upholding the realm of freedom, of the human	Maintaining the realm of necessity, of the natural and repetitious

Furthermore, while some people have formal (legal) citizenship in a nation-state, they are denied substantive (*de facto*) citizenship rights. For example, the universality discourse often equates genuine citizenship with a capacity for productivity and thus "if one cannot be productive, one is not worthy of full citizenship" (Devlin and Pothier 2006: 17). As a result, persons with disabilities are relegated to a status of "second-class" citizens. Please see Box 3.4 and Figures 3.2 and 3.3 for a discussion and illustration of the impact this treatment has on persons with disabilities.

Turning to a different example, Box 3.5 illustrates how, prior to 2005, the denial of the right to marriage disadvantaged gay and lesbian partners in Canada. With respect to women, feminists have pointed out that since women are expected to carry the burden of domestic duties and child care, their ability to participate in public affairs is limited (Lister 2997: 133). To make it possible for women to participate in politics, feminists such as Ruth Lister (1997), Lovenduski (2005), and Phillips (1998) call for the removal of social barriers that prevent women from engaging in public life. Furthermore, women's right

BOX 3.4 ❈ THE EXCLUSION OF PEOPLE WITH DISABILITIES

Although Section 15 of the Canadian Charter of Rights and Freedoms (1982) guarantees equal protections and benefits for all persons before the law, disabled populations in Canada continue to face barriers that prevent them from participating fully in society. Many of these barriers stem from norms that privilege able-bodiedness and link an individual's personhood (claim to rights) to his/her capacity for productivity. Able-bodied norms are presented as "natural" or "normal," resulting in exclusions that might not be readily noticeable. For example, urban planning that presumes that all persons have 20/20 vision (with or without glasses) and are able to drive a car can unintentionally exclude or marginalize those persons whose eyesight or physical capabilities fall outside of this norm, since it makes it more difficult for them move about and meet their daily needs. Similarly, the relationship between personhood and productivity in liberal societies disadvantages those individuals whose capabilities are distinct from the imagined norm. Currently, more than half of working-age adults with disabilities in Canada are unemployed or excluded from the labour market. Consequently, they are also more than twice as likely to live in poverty as the rest of the Canadian population. Among the disabled, women, children, elderly persons, and Aboriginal groups experience the highest risk and most acute forms of this poverty. (Sources: Council of Canadians with Disabilities 2007 and 2008; Federal Task Force on Disability Issues 1996; Devlin and Pothier 2006).

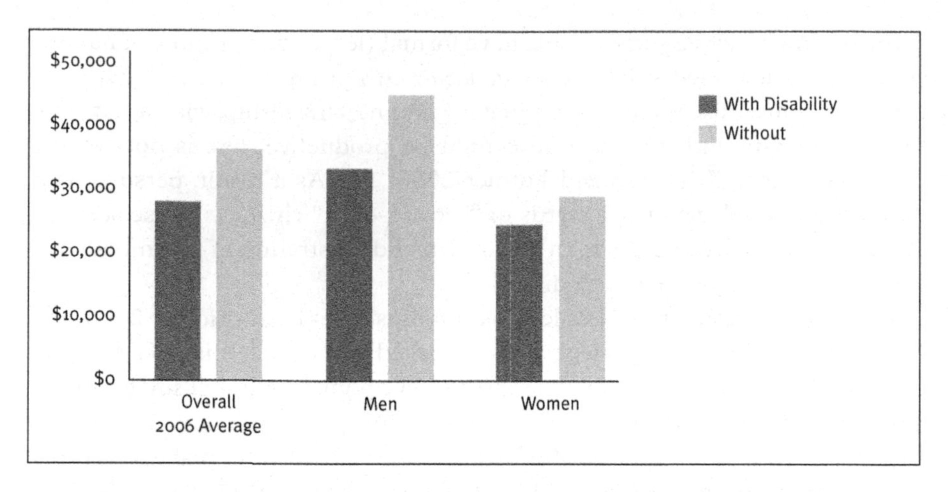

FIGURE 3.2 Canadians' Total 2006 Income according to Ability and Sex Status

Source: Adapted from Statistics Canada (2008) "Total income for adults 15 years of age or older, by disability status and sex, Canada, 2001 and 2006"; accessed online 24 June 2011 at www.statcan.gc.ca/pub/89-628-x/2008011/tbl/5201079-eng.htm

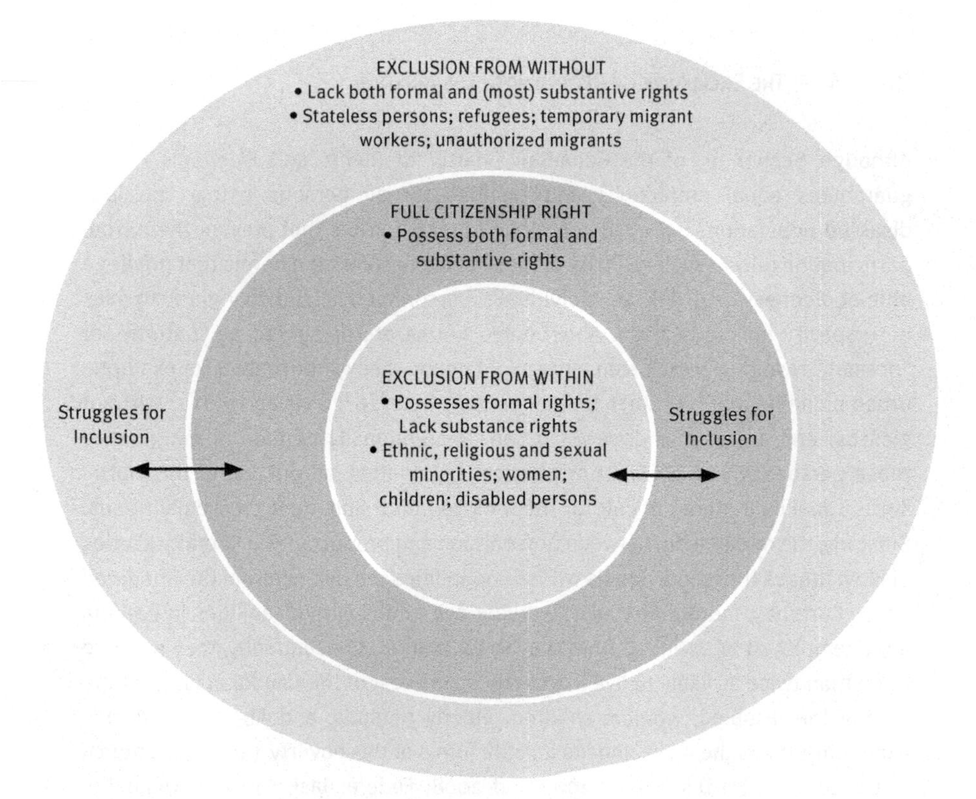

FIGURE 3.3 Citizenship Rights: Exclusions from Within and Without

Source:

BOX 3.5 ❋ DENYING LESBIANS AND GAYS THE RIGHT TO MARRY IN CANADA

In July 2005, the Canadian government approved the *Civil Marriage Act*, a national legal framework that recognizes marriage between two persons regardless of their sex. Prior to 2005, many provinces in Canada had advanced significantly toward ensuring equal rights for same-sex partnerships. Nevertheless, most federal legislation still used the terms "marriage" and "spouse" to allocate rights, benefits, and powers to conjugal partners in Canada. Because the definitions of these terms were based on conjugal partnerships between two adults of the *opposite* sex, same-sex partners were excluded from qualifying for a wide range of federal spousal rights and benefits available to heterosexuals. In the workplace, for example, homosexuals were unable to access spousal employment and health benefits for their same-sex partners. Likewise, pension and old age security plans did not allow same-sex partners to claim survivor's benefits, nor did immigration policy give same-sex couples the right to sponsor a partner for permanent residency. (Sources: Glass and Kubasek 2008; Hurley 2010).

to access welfare benefits and pensions is curtailed by the requirement to engage in uninterrupted full-time employment. The requirement to perform care duties and unpaid work in the so-called private sphere of home and family often prevents women from participating in wage labour (Walby 1994; Nash 2000). Thus, to address the citizenship rights of women, the division between the so-called public and private spheres needs to be deconstructed. In addition, many feminist scholars (e.g., Lister 1997) recognize that gendered patterns of exclusion interact with other divisions such as class, race, disability, sexuality, and age in ways that can be either multiplicative or contradictory. The notion of "intersectionality" captures the interaction of these various forms of exclusions (Yuval-Davis 2007). Understanding that universal liberal citizenship cannot guarantee equality to these people, it can be argued that working towards social justice would be better served if differences among various groups of people were recognized and addressed accordingly.

In Chapter 2, we discussed how social justice includes not only equality but the recognition of differences. In the discussion of citizenship, this ideal is expressed through the notion of differentiated citizenship (Lister 2003). To draw attention to the exclusionary experiences of different groups and the need to redress these inequalities, researchers have introduced such concepts as "multicultural citizenship" (Kymlicka 2008); "cultural citizenship" (Lister 2003), "dis-citizenship" (Devlin and Pothier 2006), "queer citizenship" (Johnston 2008), and others.

Arguing in favour of "multicultural citizenship," Kymlicka (2008) points out that in most countries a range of nation-building policies have encouraged the preferred national identity while suppressing alternative identities, despite the alleged commitment to "cultural neutrality" (54). He suggests that cultural minorities have been treated as second-class citizens and recommends a model that would entail special measures that recognize their cultural specificities. These measures would include language rights, group representation rights, and a form of self-government for some national minorities (Kymlicka 2008: 54). Will Kymlicka's call for multiculturalism is not meant to undermine the values of liberal equality. He believes that multiculturalism can both reduce historic inequalities between groups and strengthen practices of "democratic citizenship" based on the recognition of universal rights (61). Nevertheless, not everyone believes that equality and the recognition of difference can co-exist. As Squires (2007) observes, the notion of "differentiated citizenship" places "the complex inter-relation between equality and diversity at the centre of current citizenship debates" (533). Let us examine this debate.

Equality versus Difference?

The tension between equality and difference was discussed in Chapter 1 in our examination of Nancy Fraser's understanding of social justice. It is also characteristic of much writing on differentiated citizenship. Okin (1999) has expressed concern regarding the demands that minority cultures be protected through special group rights or privileges. She has pointed out that sensitivity to ethnic or religious difference has allowed for the oppression of women. She questioned whether feminism and multiculturalism are always reconcilable. For her, it was important to decide whether to prioritize cultural group rights or women's equality (See an excerpt from Okin's work in Box 3.6).

Okin opened a controversy to which many writers have responded. Okin has been critiqued for being patronizing and disrespectful of other cultures and for generalizing about other cultures and religions. Critics have pointed out that, rather than being a source of oppression, for many women their culture and religious beliefs provide dignity and protection (Fairweather 2000). Box 3.7 illustrates how Muslim women in Canada negotiate their commitment to cultural diversity while demanding equality for women. To reconcile equality and difference, Lister introduces a concept of "**differentiated universalism**" (1997 and 2003) to refer to "a universalism which stands in creative tension to diversity and difference and which challenges the divisions and exclusionary inequalities which can stem from diversity" (Lister 1997: 39). For her, universalism is understood "not as false impartiality but as 'universality of moral commitment' to the equal worth and participation of all" (Lister 1997: 39). In fact, for Lister, the achievement of equality is contingent on attention to difference (Lister 2003: 91). To attain

BOX 3.6 ❊ SUSAN MOLLER OKIN'S VIEW ON DIVERSITY AND EQUALITY

"During the 1980s, the French government quietly permitted immigrant men to bring multiple wives into the country to the point where an estimated 200,000 families in Paris are now polygamous. Any suspicion that official concern over headscarves was motivated by an impulse toward gender equality is belied by the easy adoption of a permissive policy on polygamy despite the burdens this practice imposes on women and the warnings issued by women from the relevant cultures. On this issue, no politically effective opposition galvanized. But once reporters finally got around to interviewing the wives, they discovered what the government could have learned years earlier: that the women affected by polygamy regarded it as an inescapable and barely tolerable institution in their African countries of origin and an unbearable imposition in the French context. Overcrowded apartments and the lack of each wife's private space leads to immense hostility, resentment, even violence both among the wives and against each other's children... The French accommodation of polygamy illustrates a deep and growing tension between feminism and multiculturalist concerns to protect cultural diversity. I think we—especially those of us who consider ourselves politically progressive and opposed to all forms of oppression—have been too quick to assume that feminism and multiculturalism are both good things which are easily reconciled. I shall argue instead that there is considerable likelihood of tension between them—more precisely, between feminism and a multiculturalist commitment to group rights for minority cultures." (Excerpt from Okin 1999, pp. 9–10)

"differentiated universalism," it is important to overcome binary thinking that gives rise to exclusions (as discussed above). A "gender-inclusive" model of citizenship, in particular, requires that we subvert some established dichotomies that equate women with the "ethic of care" and dependence, and men with the "ethic of justice" and independence (Lister 2003: 116). Lister calls for the value to be placed upon care (whether provided by men or women) and "the recognition of care as a political ideal and practice that transcends the public–private divide" (Lister 2003: 199). Thus she calls for public policy that would improve women's position in the labour market (to promote women's economic independence), combined with the policies that would make it possible for men and women to take time for care (i.e., parental and carers' leave and affordable care services). At the same time, she advocates establishing mechanisms to make formal political systems (dominated by men) more accessible to informal political groupings or grassroots initiatives where women frequently find fertile grounds for political participation (Lister 2003: 200–02).

BOX 3.7 ❋ CAN RESPECT FOR CULTURAL DIVERSITY COEXIST WITH GENDER EQUALITY?

Can adherence to multiculturalism be combined with commitment to gender equality? Let's examine the reaction of Muslim women's organizations to the proposed instauration of Islamic tribunals in Ontario, Canada. In 2004, the Islamic Institute of Civil Justice announced that it intended to conduct arbitrations according to Islamic Shari'a-based law. This proposal was in line with the Arbitration Act of Ontario, set up in 1991 to resolve most civil matters—including family conflicts—privately, without recourse to the Canadian judicial system. Supporters of this proposal justified it by evoking respect for cultural diversity. Yet many women's organizations, such as the Canadian Council of Muslim Women, the National Organization of Immigrant and Visible Minority Women of Canada, and the internationally based Women Living Under Muslim Law, expressed strong opposition to the Islamic tribunals. The Canadian Council of Muslim Women pointed out that the Islamic tribunals contradicted Article 28 of Canada's Charter of Rights and Freedoms that guarantees equality to women. They argued that this right should supersede when women are treated unequally as a consequence of cultural or religious practices. Yet this opposition to Islamic tribunals should not be read as a rejection of multiculturalism. In its written submission, the Council of Muslim Women wrote: "CCMW is a strong believer in Canada's multiculturalism policy, for it celebrates our differences and allows groups such as ours to be proud of our multiple identities" (quoted in Juteau 2008: 90). At the same time, CCMW cautions that the celebration of difference could be a tool of gender oppression. Therefore, CCMW expresses a firm position that cultural practices that disadvantage women should not be tolerated. The national campaign to criminalize female circumcision has also politicized Muslim women in Canada. Muslim immigrant women in Canada who participated in these campaigns asserted their claims for equality without undermining the value of diversity. As Macklin observes, "claiming their entitlement as legal citizens of Canada to participate in governance, they demanded equal citizenship as Canadian women" (Macklin 2009: 276). At the same time, these women refused to renounce their cultural citizenship. (Sources: Juteau 2008; Macklin 2009).

Analyzing cultural citizenship, Danielle Juteau (2008) proposes a distinction between two types of multiculturalism: Multiculturalism 1 and Multiculturalism 2. For Juteau, Multiculturalism 1 refers to the recognition and respect of cultural differences shared by a collectivity (86). Multiculturalism 2, on the other hand, stresses the link between power and differentiation and calls for equality in cultural, economic, and political spheres (87). We can call Multiculturalism 1 "multiculturalism without equality" and Multiculturalism 2 "multiculturalism with equality."

Social Struggles for Citizenship

T.H. Marshall has also been critiqued for neglecting the role of social struggles in shaping citizenship. Yet, throughout the world, changes in civil, political, social, cultural, and other forms of citizenship owe much to social activism. Engin Isin and Patricia Wood emphasize the importance of social struggles in the notions of citizenship when they say, "We conceive of citizenship broadly—not only as a set of legal membership in a state, but also as the practices through which individuals and groups formulate and claim new rights or struggle to expand or maintain existing rights" (Isin and Wood: 1999, 4). In fact, it was as a result of its struggles in various industrializing countries throughout the nineteenth and early twentieth century that the working class gained political, civil, and social rights from which working men had been previously excluded (Castles 1985; Kivisto and Faist 2007). For instance, by 1912 the Australian state had introduced such reforms as: factory and shop legislation; old age and invalid pensions; workers' compensation; conciliation and arbitration (which instituted a living wage principle); a maternity allowance; votes for women; immigration restriction; compulsory education; and child welfare allowances for foster parents. For Garton and McCallum (1996), these reforms can be attributed to workers' mobilizations. Measured both by the degree of unionization and the electoral strength of left-wing and labour parties, working-class power was rather impressive in Australia at that time. Although significantly weaker than the Australian working class, Canada's workers also engaged in struggles for an ideal living wage. Consequently, social reforms introduced by the Canadian state in the twentieth century can be linked to the struggles waged by Canadian workers, particularly during World War II, although as Garton and McCallum (1996) argue, political, constitutional, and administrative processes have played a role in the emergence of what Marshall calls "social citizenship."

Yet, working for their inclusion, working men were prepared to leave out women and racial minorities (Kivisto and Faist 2007: 21; Garton and McCallum 1996). And consequently, women and racial minorities waged their own struggles for social inclusion throughout the twentieth century. Race- and gender-based social movements gained strength in the 1960s and 1970s, particularly in the United States. The US civil rights movement inspired other struggles, including the student, peace, women's, and the gay and lesbian liberation movements. Activists struggling for diverse causes often borrowed the ideology, tactics, and strategies from the civil rights movement. Reflecting on social activism in the United States in the twentieth century, Buechler (2000) writes, "The protests of the 1930s were rooted in class structures of power and undertaken by workers and unemployed people, whereas the protests of the 1960s emerged from racial structures of power that sparked resistance by African Americans that in turn became a prototype for social activism across the political spectrum" (131). Similar developments were unfolding in Canada at the same time (see, for instance, Adamson, Briskin, and McPhail 1988 for the discussion of the women's movement; Smith 2008 for the discussion of the gay and lesbian liberation movement; and Ladner 2008 for the discussion of the Aboriginal rights movement in Canada). Although not with the same intensity as in the 1960s and 1970s, these activists have continued since then to demand new rights or fight to protect their achievements from eroding under the assault by neoliberal practices and policies (discussed in Chapter 3).

These social movements have used the language of citizenship to claim or defend rights (Lister 2003: 5–6). For example, appealing to the Canadian Charter of Rights and Freedoms Section 15 (on equality and freedom from discrimination), the lesbian and gay rights activists have fought successfully to legalize same-sex marriage in Canada (Smith 2008). Canadian disability rights activists have first fought to have the term "mental or physical disability" included in Section 15 (which prohibits discrimination on a number of grounds including race, ethnic origin gender, age, and religion). After winning this victory, the disability rights activists fought successfully to challenge various discriminatory practices. Consequently, people with mental disabilities won the right to vote; people with physical disabilities gained the right to physical access to polling stations; and deaf people attained the right to medical consultations in sign language. Furthermore, the Ontario Disabilities Act called for a removal of all physical and social barriers to private and public organizations in the province (Chivers 2008; Devlin and Pothier 2006). The countries of the Global South have also witnessed the rise of activism aimed at achieving social inclusion for various disenfranchised and marginalized groups of people. Box 3.8 provides an illustration of how, in the 1980s and 1990s, Brazilian social movements called for greater political participation for the country's poor and other excluded groups.

Reflecting on the origin, composition, organizational nature, and overall goals of post-1960s social activism, some social movement theorists have argued that these expressions of activism are significantly different from the earlier, class-based, struggles. The so-called "new social movements" were claimed to be more complex in their composition. Rather than being rooted in the class structure, these movements seem to comprise activists from different racial, ethnic, gender-based, sexual orientation–based, and other social groups. "New social movement" theorists (particularly, Melucci 1989 and 1996) draw attention to the centrality of the social construction of collective identities in social struggles. In addition, they point out that for the so-called "new social movements" everyday life, with its personal and intimate aspects (such as sexual orientation, marriage, ageing, etc.) has become the battlefield of political activism. Furthermore, it has been argued that, rather than seeking political power and material resources, the "new social movements" seek

Box 3.8 ❄ Challenging Citizenship in Brazil

In the 1980s and 1990s, social movements in Brazil challenged the conception of citizenship prevalent in that country. Composed of popular movements, excluded sectors, trade unions, left parties and, later, women, blacks, ethnic minorities, homosexuals, and urban and rural workers, among others, these movements underlined the cultural dimension of citizenship and redefined it in a manner that moved beyond the acquisition of legal rights to ". . . require the constitution of active social subjects who would define what they consider to be their rights and struggle for their recognition" (Dagnino 2005, 150). The movements sought to broaden conceptions of politics in relation to its participants, institutions, processes, agenda, and scope. They succeeded in opening up a political space for civil society's direct participation in state decision-making processes through mechanisms such as municipal participatory budgets or federal management councils for public policy. At the same time, these movements called for a radical transformation of cultural practices that reproduced inequality and exclusion throughout society. In Brazil, to be poor meant not only economic or material deprivation, but also "submission to cultural rules that convey a complete lack of recognition of poor people as subjects-bearers of rights." Poverty is seen as a "sign of inferiority, a way of being in which individuals are unable to exercise their rights" (*ibid*, 153). Thus, these Brazilian social movements called for a new notion of citizenship that challenged these cultural expressions. (Source: Dagnino 2005).

autonomy from the intrusive invasion by postmodern technologies (e.g., media, surveillance technologies) and grassroots democracy. And thus, as it has been pointed out, these movements employ cultural and symbolic forms of activism in addition to (or in place of) conventional political forms of contestation (see Scott 1990; Buechler 2000: 45–51 for a critical assessment of the "new social movement" theory). While many of the aspects of the "new social movement" theory have been questioned, this scholarship has made important contributions. In particular, it has drawn attention to the complexity of current social struggles as they relate to issues of equality and difference and seek to bring about material changes (redistribution), cultural changes (recognition), or other types of changes, as discussed in Chapter 1.

Mirza and Reay (2000) view Black supplementary schools (run predominantly by Black female teachers) in London, England, as an example of a new social movement that questions fixed notions of citizenship. These schools, critical of the mainstream education system, embody a radical Black agency aimed at creating collective consciousness and educational achievements in the context of an alternative urban community building.

Mirza and Reay observe that the Black women's community action creates a "third space" that is neither public nor private but rather radical "counter-public" (70). They further argue that the marginal and excluded people find a voice—radical and subversive—in this third space. "In the 'third space,'" they conclude, "Black women educators' acts of belonging and sustenance of community demonstrate new and inclusive forms of 'real citizenship' that deserve to be recognized" (70). Thus, as can be seen from this illustration, social movements not only question exclusion from presumably universal citizenship, but they also question the very notions of mainstream citizenship built on binaries between the public and private spheres of political participation and between individual self-achievement and self-improvement on the one hand and collective community reciprocity on the other.

Exclusions from Without

In addition to "exclusion from within" (discussed above), some people have been "excluded from without," to use Lister's (1997) terminology. Figure 3.4 represents both types of exclusion.

Immigration policies are mechanisms of exclusion from national membership. Historically, various groups of people have been excluded from

FIGURE 3.4 A US Border Patrol surveillance tower at the international border between the United States and Mexico

Source: Alamy CEDB3R

Canada. For example, starting in 1885 Canada put in place a series of head taxes to prevent Chinese immigrants from coming to this country. At the turn of the twentieth century, the Bill of Direct Passage was introduced to cut off immigration from India. In 1919, Canada introduced a new immigration act to exclude individuals who had been classified as "enemy aliens," which, at the time, included Germans among others. In addition, provisions were introduced to deny access to Doukhobors, Mennonites, and Hutterites on the basis that their "peculiar customs, habits, modes of life and methods of holding property," made them unlikely to become "readily assimilated ... Canadian citizens" (Simmons 2010: 56). Jews were also denied entry to Canada between the 1920s and 1945, largely because anti-Semitism was widespread in Canada (Abella and Troper 1982). When an unidentified immigration agent was asked how many Jews would be allowed in Canada after the war, he replied "None is too many" (Abella and Troper 1982). In addition, exclusionary immigration policies were based on class and gender, as well as physical and mental fitness. For example, legislation enacted in 1879 prevented the arrival of British paupers and destitute immigrants. Similarly, the 1910 Immigration Act prohibited the entry of "prostitutes and women and girls coming to Canada for any immoral purpose." The 1910 Immigration Act also prohibited the entry of the "mentally defective," "the diseased," and "physically defective" people. Finally, communists and communist sympathizers were banned from coming to Canada during the Cold War years (Satzewich and Liodakis 2007: 44–5).

The current immigration policy has removed some of these obstacles, but class, race, gender, and other forms of distinction continue to influence admission guidelines. The preferred immigrant is now defined in class terms that privilege candidates who have the economic means to become self-sufficient and capable of supporting their families and bearing the costs of their integration into Canadian society (Abu-Laban and Gabriel 2002: 65; Abu-Laban 2009). The $975 Right of Landing fee, introduced in 1995, reflected this neoliberal preference for self-sufficient individuals who had the means to cover the costs of their settlement. Even though this fee was cut in half in 2006, the fact that it is still collected is an indication of Canada's continued interest in attracting better-off immigrants. In addition to class, gender also influences who gets admitted to Canada and under what immigration category. For example, most women are admitted in the family class and not as economic class immigrants (Abu-Laban 2009: 158–9). As family class immigrants, they are not eligible for various settlement programs, such as language and vocational training (Zaman 2006). In addition, most people with disabilities are found inadmissible (Hanes 2010; Devlin and Pothier 2006).

Since the 1980s, most immigrant-receiving countries have introduced measures to make it more difficult for some people (particularly, poor and racialized individuals) to cross their borders (Dauvergne 2008; McNevin 2011). For example, various tactics have been deployed by the US government to prevent Mexican migrants from crossing the border. Since the 1970s, there has been a marked intensification of border policing. Significant increases in the Immigration and Naturalization Service's (INS) budget made it possible for this agency to employ considerably more border patrol staff and upgrade the border architecture to include aerial surveillance, a more sophisticated electronic ground sensor system, and a variety of vision-enhancing devices, such as night vision goggles, vehicle-mounted infrared telescopes capable of remote imaging, low-light TV cameras, and infrared scopes (Inda 2006).

Around the globe, nation-states have also shut their doors to people fleeing violence and in search of a safe haven (Dauvergne 2008; McNevin 2011). In 1986, Canada received a Fridtjof Nansen Medal from the United Nations for its compassionate refugee policy. Yet, its current treatment of asylum-seekers tells a different story. Not only has it become more difficult for asylum-seekers to be granted refugee status, but the Canadian government has introduced measures to prevent people from even landing on Canadian shores (see Box 3.9).

Following the attacks on the World Trade Center and the Pentagon on 11 September 2001, and the United States' subsequent declaration of a "War on Terror," securitization intensified significantly in North America and Europe. Anti-terrorism legislation was swiftly introduced in Canada and the US, and borders were reinforced via stricter entrance requirements, militarization (especially at the US southern border), and the ratification of bilateral agreements, such as the 2003 Joint Statement of Cooperation on Border Security and Regional Migration Issues. Initiatives such as Canada's 2007 Passenger Protect Program and the US's no-fly lists also placed restrictions on the mobility of individuals who were designated a "threat" to aviation and public security (see, for example, O'Connor and de Lint 2009; Rygiel 2010).

In both countries, the post–9/11 securitization agenda has eroded the rights of citizens, especially those immigrants, refugees, and citizens with real or imagined Muslim or Arab origins. For example, since the passage of the Anti-Terrorist Act (ATA) and the Immigration and Refugee Protection Act (IRPA) in Canada, harassment, intimidation, physical and verbal attacks, arrests, deportations, and racial profiling became "justifiable" realities for many (Dobrowolsky 2008). In the name of national security, the Canadian state issued at least five IRPA "security certificates" allowing for the indefinite detention or deportation—without charge and under secret evidence—of Arab or Muslim permanent residents and foreign nationals (CBC News Canada, 14 December 2009). The rights of certain Canadians who held dual citizenship also became increasingly curtailed, as demonstrated in the case of Maher Arar, a dual Canadian–Syrian citizen whose detention by American

BOX 3.9 ❊ CANADA'S RESPONSE TO ASYLUM-SEEKERS

In August 2010, a boat carrying 492 Tamil migrants from Sri Lanka arrived on the shores of British Columbia. Those on board claimed to be seeking asylum from persecution as a result of a protracted civil war in their country between the Sinhalese and Tamil populations. The Canadian government, however, suspected that many of the Tamil migrants had in fact paid smugglers between $30,000 and $50,000 to secure their passage to Canada. Furthermore, both the Sri Lankan and the Canadian governments raised concerns about possible connections between this particular group of migrants and the Tamil Tigers, a group that fought for Tamil independence in Sri Lanka and that the Canadian government classified as terrorists in 2006.

In response to these events, and in an effort to prevent similar happenings in the future, the Canadian government proposed a series of reforms aimed at persons who seek to profit from human smuggling as well as "queue-jumping" immigrants who claim asylum. These reforms would give the minister of public safety the power to classify migrants as "irregular" arrivals if and when Canadian officials suspect the involvement of smugglers, criminals, or terrorist groups in arranging their travel. Migrants of all ages—including children—determined to be "irregular" arrivals would then be subject to up to one year of detention while their asylum claim is being evaluated. Similarly, they would be barred from applying for permanent residence status, receiving certain health benefits, and from sponsoring family members for five years. They could also have their asylum revoked at any time should the Canadian authorities decide that it is no longer necessary. Immigrant and refugee advocates criticized this proposal, stating that it denied asylum-seekers their most basic rights and that it would establish two "classes" of refugees. The Canadian Council for Refugees questioned the Canadian government's claims to be targeting smugglers and made appeals to the public, saying that people fleeing for their lives must be welcomed not punished. By detaining asylum-seekers for longer and denying them family reunification and freedom of movement, the Council said, the Canadian government would likely be violating the Canadian Charter of Rights and Freedoms as well as its human rights obligations. (Source: Greenaway and Quan 2010).

authorities and deportation to Syria resulted in months of interrogation and torture in 2002 (Dobrowolsky 2008: 471; Stasiulis 2006). Similarly, in the United States, "preventative" national security measures were cited for the approximately 5000 Arab or Muslim foreign nationals who were arrested and subject to lengthy detentions without due legal process in the years following the September 11 attacks (De Genova 2008). US citizens such as José Padilla and Yasser Esam Hamdi were imprisoned indefinitely without any formal presentation of charges relating to terrorism or otherwise, and legal challenges to such detentions were subsequently suppressed by legislative initiatives such as the United States' Military Commissions Act, which, in 2006, granted the Presidency exceptional powers to designate individuals as enemies (De Genova 2008).

The ever-increasing securitization of borders has made it more dangerous for people to cross them as well. A study by Andrijasevic (2003) reveals that borders can take the form of a material barrier (wire or wall) through the operation of technological devices. These devices include the use of coastal radar stations by Italian and Spanish police forces to intercept the arrival of boats, of infrared cameras and x-ray scanners on the English coast, and of carbon dioxide detectors by German border police to discover people hidden inside cargo. Such border policing, along with visa regimes, and detention and deportation policies, has resulted in many deaths of mobile peoples, such as migrants, displaced and undocumented peoples, insurgents, refugees, and asylum seekers. Nonetheless, millions who are denied authorization to enter a country defy these restrictions (Cabrera 2010). Countries that receive unauthorized migrants often depict them as a threat to the well-being of the nation because these migrants are presumed to be "law-breakers" who steal jobs from national workers and drain the social welfare system (Inda 2006). They are coined "illegal" by policy makers to emphasize their violation of the country's immigration laws (De Genova 2004). Nevertheless, Cabrera recognizes that most people who choose to cross international borders illicitly are desperately poor and need to find work outside their country in order to save their families from possible death. To him, "(t)he violation of affluent state-entry laws is a potentially defensible means of addressing those gaps according to the global community's prevailing, or perhaps emerging, sense of justice" (2010, 146). He therefore sees unauthorized migrants not as criminals but as "conscientious evaders" or people "who deliberately but covertly violate a law on principled grounds" (136).

Millions of people live, work, and consume in societies that deny them formal citizenship yet enjoy the privilege of consuming their labour. Without formal citizenship, are they able to enjoy any citizenship rights and privileges? In 1994, Soysal published a groundbreaking book in which she argued that rights that used to be granted solely to nationals are now extended to the foreign population and that we are witnessing a transition from national to post-national citizenship (1994). More recently, Benhabib has argued that today we are moving away from the conceptualization of citizenship as a national membership and more towards citizenship of residency with civil, social, and, in some cases, political participation rights being extended to non-citizens (2007). In fact, in many countries non-citizen migrants enjoy access to emergency healthcare and their children are allowed to attend schools. For example, in some states, such as Tennessee, unauthorized migrants have been granted the right to receive driver's licenses (Ansley 2010). Similarly, various US states, such as California, Illinois, New York, Utah, Washington, Oklahoma, and Texas have passed state-wide legislation to enable children of unauthorized migrants to receive in-state tuition in colleges and universities (Varsanyi 2006).

However, the recognition that some rights have been extended to unauthorized migrants should not blind us to the fact that as non-citizens they experience major forms of exclusion (Bosniak 2006). Unauthorized migrants are among several categories of people who are found in precarious conditions that deny them, in one form or another, citizenship rights in Canada and elsewhere. Other migrants in precarious conditions include: refugee claimants, migrants brought in under family sponsorship, and temporary migrants. Precarious status is marked by the absence of any of the following elements normally associated with permanent residency and citizenship in Canada: (1) work authorization; (2) the right to remain permanently in the country; (3) independence (from a sponsoring spouse or employer); (4) access to social services, such as health and education (Goldring, Berinstein and Bernhard 2009: 240–41). Temporary workers in Canada consist of different categories. Among them are seasonal agricultural workers, live-in caregivers, construction workers, and workers admitted under the Temporary Foreign Worker Program. Entitlements and restrictions vary from one program to another. Box 3.10 provides an illustration of the restricted citizenship rights among Mexican seasonal agricultural workers in Canada.

It can be argued that under the Westphalian system of sovereignty (discussed above), nation-states are morally justified in distinguishing citizens from non-citizens. In fact, some assert that in order to guarantee social benefits to their own nationals, nation-states must deny them to others. Yet, many migrant rights activists disagree with this position. At times these activists invoke universal principles of human rights (to be discussed in Chapter 7) to argue that, as human beings, migrants are entitled to the same protections as citizens. At other times, they use more pragmatic arguments, such as migrants' contributions to national economies. Using a variety of discourses, migrant rights activists have demanded regularization for unauthorized migrants, temporary workers' rights to permanent settlement, more humane treatment of asylum seekers, and an extension of social benefits and protections for various migrants found in precarious conditions (Basok 2009; Cook 2010; Elias 2008).

Despite their extreme vulnerability, migrants themselves have challenged their exclusion and demanded to be treated like citizens (see Box 3.11). Engin Isin and Greg Nielsen refer to such forms of political mobilization as "acts of citizenship." For Isin and Nielsen, "acts of citizenship" are those

Box 3.10 ❊ Mexican Seasonal Agricultural Workers in Canada

Since 1974, Mexican migrants have been coming to work in Canadian fields and greenhouses under the Seasonal Agricultural Workers Program. Today, some 10,000 Mexicans participate in this program, which allows them to work in Canada for up to eight months each year. Under the terms of the bilateral agreement between the governments of Canada and Mexico, these workers are entitled to many of the same benefits to which Canadian citizens and permanent residents have access. For example, in a number of provinces, workers are covered by provincial Employment Standards Acts and Health and Safety Acts. With a few exceptions, they also benefit from coverage under the provincial health plans. When injured at work, they are entitled to receive workers' compensation payments. But there is one fundamental difference between these workers and Canadian citizens and permanent residents. Whereas Canadian workers can move from one job to another, seasonal agricultural workers are authorized to work for a specific employer. Even if their working conditions are unbearable, they are not allowed to seek another job. If the employer terminates their contract, Mexican migrant workers are required to return to Mexico (unless the Mexican consulate reassigns them to another employer). Furthermore, their participation in this program in the consequent years is contingent on a positive evaluation from a current employer. This lack of mobility and dependence on their employers makes seasonal agricultural workers extremely vulnerable. For example, even though under the Ontario Employment Standards Act workers are entitled to a day of rest after having worked six consecutive days, this right is denied to them during the peak harvest season. When injured, instead of taking time off work and collecting workers' compensation, workers often return to work, putting up with severe pain. They do it out of fear of disapproval by their employers. When the employer demands work, the workers comply even when sick or exhausted. Some workers report working up to sixteen hours per day during the peak harvest season. Yet, they do not dare refuse work. For fear of deportation and consequently being banned from the program, Mexican migrants put up with abusive and dangerous working conditions. Despite legal regulations, workers are often asked to spray dangerous pesticides without the benefit of protective clothing. Some are asked to work without masks while others spray pesticides. Thus, while Mexican migrant workers do theoretically enjoy some citizenship rights, their vulnerability makes it difficult for them to enjoy these rights in practice. (Sources: Basok 2002 and 2004; Preibisch 2007; McLaughlin and Hennebry 2010).

BOX 3.11 ❊ ACTS OF CITIZENSHIP AMONG UNAUTHORIZED MIGRANTS

In the spring of 2006, migrants (some legal residents and some unauthorized) in the US organized an unprecedented series of massive protests to be held in major cities across the country. These protests culminated in a National Day of Action on 1 May 2006. Hundreds of thousands of people—citizens and non-citizens—participated in public demonstrations in many cities. By conservative estimates, the numbers reached 600,000 in Los Angeles; 400,000 in Chicago; 50,000 in San Francisco and San Jose; 15,000 in Houston; and 30,000 across Florida, not to mention other cities. Although not as massive as in the US, in Canada "non-status" migrants (or unauthorized migrants, as they are called by activists in Canada) have also challenged their exclusion and formed political action committees. Their demands include: an end to deportations; an end to the detention of migrants, immigrants, and asylum-seekers; the abolition of "security certificates" (discussed earlier in this chapter); and, most of all, the introduction of a program to regularize the status of *all* non-status migrants in Canada. They have staged rallies and organized marches, the most impressive of which was the 200-kilometre march from Montreal to Ottawa that took place during 16–25 June 2005. (Sources: Nyers 2008; De Genova 2010).

acts that occur "when, regardless of status and substance, subjects constitute themselves as citizens or, better still, as those to whom the right to have rights is due" (2008).

Conclusion

This chapter emphasizes the concept of citizenship as a negotiated relationship between those who feel socially excluded and others who wish to consolidate their privilege and shape citizens to comply with their visions of a market-based society. We have traced the notions of modern citizenship and demonstrated how the universal inclusion of liberal democratic states has resulted in the *de facto* exclusions of some groups of people, like the poor, women, gays and lesbians, racialized minorities, and persons with disabilities. We have explored how the struggles for recognition by these groups have brought about the expansion of their rights. While some theorists fear that the focus on cultural diversity on the part of some of these excluded groups of people may undermine their commitment to equality, others contend that the two goals are not necessarily contradictory. Furthermore, in the context of securitization, the exclusion of refugees and migrants from national territories has intensified. Nevertheless, many non-citizens and "second-class" citizens continue to assert their rights and/or engage in "acts of citizenship."

Key Terms

Eurocentric bias a tendency to interpret the world in terms of western and especially European or Anglo-American values and experiences

nation-state a form of political organization in which a group of people who share the same history, traditions, or language live in a particular area under one government

Westphalian system a political system of international relations that recognizes the principles of sovereignty of independent nation-states

Questions for Critical Thought

1. Explain how and in what ways the concept and practices of citizenship relate to notions of social justice. How does the linking of citizenship and social justice help us to understand issues of inclusion and exclusion?
2. What are the major limitations of T.H. Marshall's understanding of citizenship?
3. Does the recognition of diversity as expressed through the notion of "differentiated citizenship" undermine equality? If so, in what ways?
4. How and in what ways is citizenship shaped through social struggles? What particular kinds of social struggles can you identity in this regard?
5. What has been the impact of neoliberal and securitization orientations on the institutions and practices of citizenship?
6. Do you view migrant non-citizens as enjoying any (or all) of the privileges of citizenship? If so, what privileges of citizenship would you include?

Annotated Additional Readings

C. Crouch, K. Eder, and D.Tambini (eds). 2001. *Citizenship, Markets, and the State.* Oxford: Oxford University Press. This edited volume addresses current debates on citizenship and assesses the impact of the marketization of social life on the institutions and practices of citizenship under neoliberalism.

Naila Kabeer (ed.) 2005. *Inclusive citizenship: Meanings & Expressions. Claiming Citizenship: Rights, Participation and Accountability.* New York: Zed Books. This edited volume focuses on the understanding of what it means to be a citizen in relation to various meanings of identity, including national identity; political and electoral participation; and rights.

P. Kivisto and T. Faist. 2007. *Citizenship: Discourse, Theory, and Transnational Prospects*. Malden, MA: Blackwell Publishing. This book provides a thorough overview of the current literature on citizenship by focusing on the importance and the changing nature of citizenship. In particular, it examines changing patterns of inclusion and exclusion, such as the erosion, withdrawal, and expansion of the boundaries of citizenship.

Ruth Lister. 2003. *Citizenship: Feminist Perspectives*. Basingstoke: Macmillan. This widely cited book explores issues and concepts of citizenship from a feminist perspective. It focuses on the inclusion and exclusion of women from public life, and the need to redefine political participation to include the private sphere. The author recognizes differences among women and notes that different women have different relationships towards the nation-state. The book advances the notion of "differential universalism" as an attempt to reconcile the recognition of differences and the need to maintain equality.

Evangelia Tastsoglou and Alexandra Dobrowolsky (eds). 2006. *Women, Migration and Citizenship: Making Local, National, and Transnational Connections*. Hampshire, England: Ashgate Publishing Ltd. This edited volume addresses the gendered implications of migration and the changing regimes of citizenship. Theoretically inspired, the volume contributes to current debates on the interrelationship among gender, migration, and citizenship. It focuses on specific examples drawn from research on immigrant and refugee women.

4 The Welfare State and the Decline of Social Citizenship Under Neoliberalism

Learning Objectives

- Explore the meanings of the welfare state
- Understand the link between the notion of "the social" and the social welfare approach
- Identify different sources of criticism of the social welfare approach and the reasons behind these criticisms
- Examine factors that have contributed to the decline of the welfare state
- Assess how neoliberal agendas have contributed to the decline of social citizenship

Introduction

This chapter focuses on the welfare state. It provides a brief historical discussion of the emergence of the welfare state after the Second World War, particularly its role in the protection and promotion of the social and economic wellbeing of its citizens. In this discussion, the focus is on the social welfare approach, an approach that involved liberal social governments seeking to cushion the hardship of the worst-off people, their fears of unemployment, and the harms produced by an uncertain future by establishing mass education, public housing, public policing, social insurance, national poor relief, national taxation systems, and so forth. Here, the social, as a single space that encompassed a nation, included entitlements and social rights for citizens from the social welfare state. However, during the late twentieth and early twenty-first centuries, many countries around the world experienced challenges to social welfare-state schemes. These challenges, which ranged from issues of efficiency and the free market to the development of entrepreneurialism, contributed to burgeoning support for neoliberal agendas and practices. In light of neoliberal demands for economic, political, and social changes, this chapter demonstrates the move away from the social dimension of liberal social government—from various rights, entitlements, and obligations of the welfare state, to a focus on the decline of social citizenship and its implications.

The Welfare State

As part of a system of relief given to the poor in England and Wales, the early poor laws, such as the British Poor Law of 1834, remained in existence until the emergence of the modern welfare state after the Second World War. The early poor laws distinguished between those categories of poor people who were regarded as deserving of assistance, including the aged, the sick, and children, on the one hand, and other people who were viewed as undeserving, such as unemployed people and idle paupers who were considered capable of work (Oorschot 2006: 23). Present-day welfare states, with their protection schemes and services, go beyond the early poor laws in terms of coverage and generosity, yet the distinction between the "deserving" and "undeserving" poor is still maintained to a certain extent. Contemporary welfare states often treat dissimilar groups of needy people differently. For some groups, social protection is more easily accessible, more generous, longer lasting, or less subject to reciprocal obligations, than for other groups. For example, it is usually the case that elderly people and people with disabilities can rely more strongly on less stigmatizing benefits than, for example, unemployed people; in many countries national benefit schemes offer stronger assistance to widows than divorced women; mostly, core workers can rely on more generous and comprehensive social insurance schemes than peripheral workers (Oorschot 2006: 23).

We understand the **welfare state** as a form of government in which the state plays a critical role in the protection and promotion of the social and economic wellbeing of its citizens. It emerged from the ruins of World War I and the ruins of the Great Depression as one solution to the economic and political turbulence of the early decades of the twentieth century. In many parts of the world, welfare states are not the same in kind. They vary from one another in key areas, including: decommodification (provision of social protections from market mechanisms); approaches to employment; relations among the state, market, and family; and the manner in which social policy affects class divisions (see, for example, Esping-Andersen 1990, 1999). As a consequence of their variation, welfare states produce a diversity of social welfare initiatives, including, for example, insurance schemes, minimum wages, health and education facilities, state-subsidized housing, family allowances, and old age security.

Not only are there different kinds of welfare states, there are also different views of the welfare state. For example, Offe (1982) views the welfare state under advanced liberal democracies as a "peace formula" that aims to limit the struggles between capital and labour, struggles that characterized the pre-welfare state period. The two key dimensions of this formula involved, first, the "the explicit obligation of the state apparatus to provide assistance and support (either in money or in kind) to those citizens who suffer from specific needs and risks which are characteristic of the market society" and, second, the recognition of the labour unions' role in collective bargaining and public policy (Offe 1982: 7). The adoption of the peace formula has taken diverse forms and reached different levels of development in the Western hemisphere.

In Western Europe and North America, for example, welfare states emerged quickly in the post-war period of the 1950s and 1960s.

While the concept of the welfare state may cover various forms of economic and social organization, it is largely based on ideas of equality of opportunity, equitable distribution of wealth, and public responsibility. It recognizes that marginal and vulnerable groups can find themselves in need of social assistance for their own well-being. In this context, how do we understand "the social" and how did the social welfare approach get assembled?

The Social Welfare Approach

An emphasis on the social and on the social welfare approach emerged in the twentieth century partly because of changes in one type of social government, namely the liberal state governments of the industrial economies. These governments conceived of their task in terms of the division between state and society and between the public sector and private sector. In doing so, they created what can be called a social domain, an order of collective being and collective responsibilities and obligations that a particular set of authorities presumed and which gave rise to forms of knowledge and disciplines, such as welfare economics and social statistics (Dean 2007: 88–9). Liberal social governments sought to cushion the hardship of the worst-off people, fears of unemployment, and the "potential harms delivered by an *uncertain* future" (O'Malley 2004: 55). To these ends, they established mass education, public housing, public policing, social insurance, national poor relief, national taxation systems, and so forth. These liberal social programs assembled the social domain and created what some writers call "identification projects" (Rose 1996). Such programs would require state-centred networks of personnel and resources to maintain collective security, social protection, social solidarity, and social citizenship (Brodie 2007; Isin 2000). This form of social welfare government would, ideally, shape and administer the affairs of all sectors of "national society." Here, the notion of national society is viewed as a cohesive domain with a national culture, national population, national territory, and national government.

As a single space that encompassed a nation, "the social" included entitlements and social rights for citizens from the social welfare state as emphasized by sociologist T.H. Marshall (1983 [1950]) (see also Chapter 3). This social welfare approach shifted harm and risk from individual citizens, groups, and firms to society (O'Malley 2004; Urry 2000). It grounded notions of social citizenship in the universalistic aims of state-provided social security and social welfare. It fostered an image of civil society that was consistent with Fordist production, which centred on the adult "male bread-winner" and the notion of a "family wage." It presumed a gendered division of responsibilities in that women would be responsible for social reproduction, both daily and generationally. It also presumed that women would gain access to subsistence through the male wage (see Armstrong and Armstrong 2002; Fudge and Vosko 2001; Vosko 2006). As Walters points out, social security supposed and encouraged "bonds of solidarity and income redistribution" between earning and non-earning sectors, and fostered "lines of mutuality linking men and women, rich and poor, young and old, employed and unemployed" (2000: 129–30). Thus the social welfare model presumed that citizens would understand themselves to be members of a single, integrated national society. While its social policies and programs did, as Donzelot (1988: 397) contends, "compensate for the effects of poverty and reduce the effects of oppression," these social security policies and programs also produced and regulated citizens and national populations. This regulation was achieved through, for example, obligations of caring for and rearing children and techniques of security, punishment, internment, and disqualification (see Brodie 2008b: 32). Many actors were involved in implementing the social welfare approach, and this included the state and its agencies, directly or indirectly, via specific social responsibilities and obligations rather than individual ones (see, for example, Brodie 1996; Dean 2007; Lemke 2002; Peck, Theodore, and Brenner 2009).

Neoliberal Developments

During the late twentieth and early twenty-first centuries, in almost all advanced industrial countries, including Australia, Britain, Canada, France, Germany, Sweden, and the United States, and in some "developing" countries, such as Chile, India, and Mexico, confidence in liberal social government, particularly its social welfare–state schemes, would come under challenge and be recast in new directions. Various interest groups no longer thought that it worked efficiently or smoothly and could handle rapid change. Some groups worried that liberal social government would interfere with the growth and movement of free-market solutions, hinder entrepreneurialism, drain public resources (see, for example, Buǒra and Keyder 2006; Amin 2005; Lakoff 2005), and render certain peoples too dependent on government. For one, the political Right criticized liberal social government and its social welfare approach for creating disincentives to invest (due to tax and regulatory burdens) as well as disincentives to work (due to collective bargaining power and a capitalist work ethic) which ultimately proved to be detrimental to economic growth, inflation, and governability. For example, when President Johnson declared a "War on Poverty" in 1964 (see Figure 4.1), he set the stage for renewed conservative attacks on the welfare state. In contrast, the political left criticized liberal social government and its social welfare approach for being ineffective, repressive, and a source of false politico-ideological consciousness among the working class, that is, a band-aid solution that stabilizes rather than transforms capitalist society (Offe 1982). For people on the moderate left, the solution was not the dissolution of the welfare state but rather its transformation. In the United States, for example, when poor Black women mobilized in the late 1960s to claim the citizenship rights exercised by many White women, they encountered a federal judiciary already sensitized to problems of class and racial disparity in the exercise of citizenship. According to Mayer (2008: 161), these women brought court cases against welfare agents who had denied them access to resources to raise their children and were rewarded in a series of decisions preventing states from imposing eligibility criteria beyond those set by Congress (King vs. Smith 1968).

With the economic downturn of the 1970s, the declining profitability of mass production industries, and the crises of Keynesian welfarism, critiques of liberal social government gained prominence in public debate. Various governing agents, political elites, and actors saw a political opportunity to promote neoliberal agendas and practices during the 1970s and by the 1990s they were pushed forward by an ever-growing range of international participants including states, corporations, and international financial organizations, such as the World Bank and the International Monetary Fund. With links to

The Issue: Poverty

President Johnson's "unconditional war on poverty" is a small beginning toward what could become the most ambitious social venture undertaken in the United States since World War II.

The antipoverty bill passed by Congress is, of course, no promise of achieving a goal that has eluded man through all the ages. It is too limited in means, too timid in ideas, even as a jumping-off point. Yet, the contrasting attitudes Mr. Johnson and Senator Goldwater have exhibited toward this program provide one of the reasons for our belief that the country's interests will benefit from a Johnson victory.

The President has shown an awareness that the onsurge of new technology will in coming years make it realistic, for the first time, to envision the elimination of basic economic distress in the United States. Paradoxically, this same technology closes to large numbers of people direct participation in its fruits through the mass displacement of men by machines in farms, factories and other fields. Poverty has become so ingrained in some areas that one generation succeeds another on the relief rolls.

The antipoverty program is based on the proposition that an America enjoying its greatest prosperity has an obligation to restore hope to prosperity has an obligation to restore hope to the distressed and disinherited. This is a matter not solely of compassion but also of recognition that the nation's economic health is menaced when one-fifth of its citizens live in families with an annual income of $3,000 or less. The program's accent is not on handouts, but on work training and work experience for youth.

Mr. Goldwater loses no opportunity to emphasize that he has a "deep concern" about poverty, but almost everything else he says on the subject makes it plain that he believes most of the poor are poor because they are too stupid or too lacking in ambition to make anything of themselves. He regards the antipoverty program as a "worthless nostrum," and he insists that the country must choose between "Santa Claus dreams and rolled-up sleeves."

The Johnson program, in its present dimensions, is far short of measuring up to the President's assurance that "the days of the dole in our country are numbered." But, for all its limitations, the compound of idealism and realism it embodies is much more reflective of the American spirit than the lack of understanding that makes Mr. Goldwater blame the poor for so much of their own poverty.

FIGURE 4.1 The war on poverty

Source: *New York Times (1857–Current file)*; October 19, 1964; ProQuest Historical Newspapers The New York Times (1851–2005) pg 32. Reproduced with permission of the copyright owner.

classic liberalism, **neoliberalism** is a popular market-oriented form of political domination. As a way of governing, it consists of a set of practices that aim to prioritize economic growth; increase the role of the free market; encourage flexibility in labour markets; and reform state welfare activities through an emphasis on privatization, deregulation of state control over industry, marketization, decentralization, and fiscal austerity (see also: Little and Marks 2010; Willis, Smith, and Stenning 2008). These practices do not form a coherent framework, nor do they have the same transformative effects or impacts on particular groups of people. In this regard, we believe it is worthwhile to conceive of neoliberal agendas as involving "a migrating set of practices" (Ong 2007: 3) that is taken up in varying social, economic, and political contexts and that link to everyday lives and livelihoods in diverse ways.

Rather than being unified and having the same effects on people's lives in Canada and in other places around the world, neoliberal agendas tend to exist alongside other state and social formations, such as neoconservatism or authoritarianism (see Dean 2010; Peck, Theodore, and Brenner 2009). In response to the breakdown of accumulation regimes and established systems of governance, national and local states throughout the older industrialized world slowly began to dismantle the basic institutional components of postwar settlement and to mobilize policies designed to extend market discipline, competition, and commodification. In this context, according to Peck, Theodore, and Brenner, neoliberal practices were used to justify "the deregulation of state control over industry, assaults on organized labor, the reduction of corporate taxes, the downsizing and/or privatization of public services and assets, the dismantling of welfare programs, the enhancement of international capital mobility, and the intensification of interlocality competition" (2009: 50). Thus, through such neoliberal and other related practices, there has been a move away from the social dimension of liberal social government—from various rights, entitlements, obligations, and public-order and security practices of the welfare state (see Table 4.1).

In fact, the last two decades have seen an escalating rollback of states joined with a roll forward of new forms of regulation. This has facilitated such things as new contractual relations between government departments and agencies in the private and not-for-profit sectors; a new emphasis on the personal responsibilities of individuals, their families, their neighbourhoods, and their communities for their own wellbeing (see, for example, Harvey 2005); the increasing development of private interests, private–public partnerships; and the privatization of public services (see Barlow and Clarke 2004; Ilcan 2009; Peck and Tickell 2002) such as healthcare, transportation, and water. The privatization of water provides an important example in this regard.

Water is an essential natural resource for living populations. Today about 1.4 billion people do not have direct access to drinking water, and more than half of these live in areas where there are no water purification systems.

Table 4.1 Welfare and Neoliberal Approaches

Benefits	Welfare Approach	Neoliberal Approach
Employment Regulations	• regulations on hiring and firing • protection against unemployment and the imposition of arbitrary dismissal through employment regulations	• reduced regulations on hiring and firing • employment costs shared between employers and state
Work Benefits	• protection against accidents and illness at work through health and safey regulations • state support for paid health benefits	• limited protection against accidents and illnesses at work • reduction in provisions for sick pay • increasing individualization
Skills	• opportunities for skills enhancement through state programs for employment training	• limited opportunities to gain skills through employment training • increasing emphasis on helping oneself and being entrepreneurial
Income	• protection of income through comprehensive social security mimimum wage protocols and pension benefits	• limited protection of income through minimum wage legislation • decrease in permanent employment for many sectors • for those underemployed, increasing emphasis on working more than one job

Source: Adapted in part from Standing (1997) in Vincent Pattison (2008), "Neoliberalization and its discontents: The experience of working poverty in Manchester" in A. Smith et al., *Social Justice and Neoliberalism: Global Perspectives*, p. 93.

According to the World Health Organization, some 30 million annual deaths in developing countries are caused by diseases related to water pollution, such as cholera, hepatitis, dengue fever, and malaria (Mayor and Binde 2001:196–7). Even though access to safe drinking water is a major challenge for many people, especially the poor, in developing countries, in recent years the World Bank has been imposing a for-profit system of water delivery that is leaving millions of people without access to water. According to Maude Barlow and Tony Clarke (2004), "The Bank is taking advantage of the 'Washington Consensus' model of development now adopted by its donor countries and promoting the interests of a handful of transnational water corporations. Instead of using its massive funds to promote expertise in the public sector, thereby acknowledging that water is a human right and an essential public service, the Bank is forcing many countries to commodify their water resources and put them on sale to the highest bidder." Privatizing water is a highly profitable activity and there are major corporate players that deliver fresh water services for profit. Some of the largest players, such as the Suez and Vivendi [now called Veolia Environment] of France and the RWE-AG of Germany, deliver water and wastewater services to almost 300 million customers in over 100 countries and are expanding to many other parts around the globe. Although less than 10 percent of the world's water systems are under private control, the top three corporations will, according to Barlow and Clarke (2004), control over 70 percent of the water systems in Europe and North America in a decade (www.globalpolicy.org/component/content/article/209/43398.html).

For some social justice organizations and agencies, such as the Council of Canadians, it is not simply enough to make the claim that water is vital to people's health and livelihoods unless there are sustainable policies dealing with water protection and addressing urgent water issues. Canada's Federal Water Policy, for example, is over 20 years old and lacks federal leadership to conserve and protect the water in the country. In the words of the Council, "Our freshwater faces crises including contamination, shortages and pressure to export water to the United States through pipelines and diversions" (www.canadians.org/water/). The Council's water campaign calls for a national water policy that protects Canada's water from bulk exports and privatization. In this campaign, it recognizes that public water is safer, cleaner, and more affordable, and that water is essential for people and nature. However, it also acknowledges that Canada's water supply is limited, that the free market does not guarantee access to water, and that bulk exports could unlock the floodgates to trade challenges under neoliberal policy platforms and agendas.

Flowing from contemporary neoliberal agendas are many other developments that have, among other things, resulted in new patterns of income distribution. For example, since the mid-1970s, there have been dramatic reversals in patterns of income distribution in the United States. According to Fine, the average income of 90 percent of the population has stagnated and the share of income of the top 1 percent has increased from well below 10 percent to around double that. Alongside these reversals there has been the huge remuneration accruing to those occupying "management" functions, with the rewards from finance being particularly significant, as well as growing consumption levels that have been sustained by the speculative and mortgaged rewards deriving from property ownership. The decreasing expenditure on private health, education, and consumption has been associated with the growing US trade deficit and accumulation of dollar reserves across the world, with China's new role especially prominent (Fine 2009). In Canada, income inequality has been increasing as well, as Figures 4.2, 4.3, and 4.4 clearly indicate.

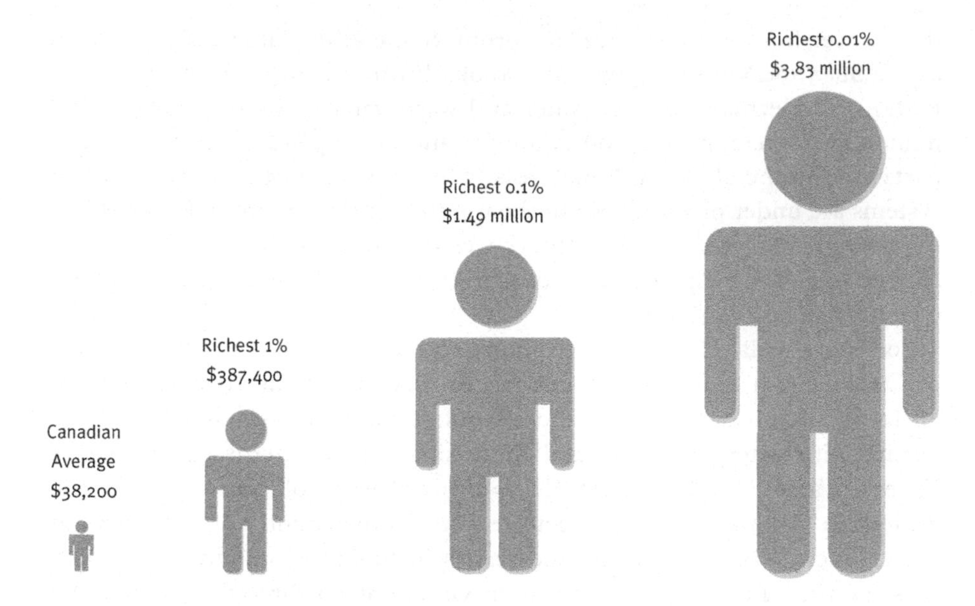

FIGURE 4.2 Average earned incomes, 2007
Source: www.policyalternatives.ca/publications/commentary/infographic-99

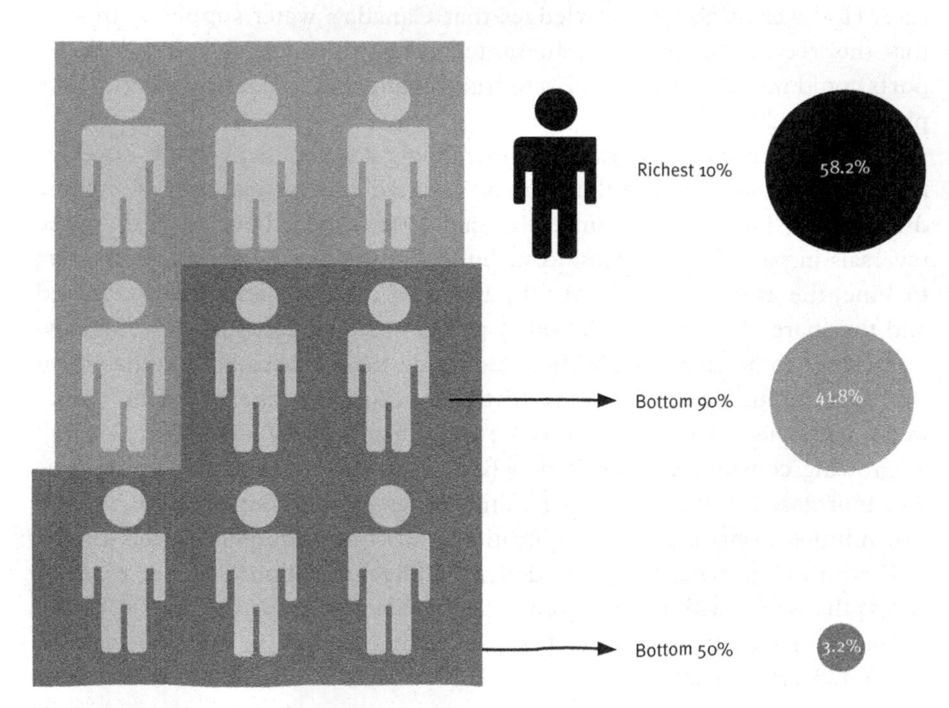

FIGURE 4.3 Canadians' net worth, 2005
Source: www.policyalternatives.ca/publications/commentary/infographic-99

Market incomes are household incomes from all sources before government income supports and income taxes are taken into account.

Between 1980 and 2009 . . .

. . . the top 20% saw their household market income increase by **+ 38.4%** ↗

. . . while the middle 20% saw their household market income decrease by **−0.3%** ↙

. . . and the bottom 20% saw their household market income decrease by **−11.4%** ↙

FIGURE 4.4 Household income inequalities, 1980–2009
Source: www.policyalternatives.ca/publications/commentary/infographic-99

Toward New Responsibilities and New Service Providers?

One of the institutional logics supporting neoliberalization is the devolution, retraction, and retrenchment of the welfare state apparatus. These changes involve a process in which certain responsibilities previously held by the state are redistributed among non-state actors, such as individuals, families, schools, hospitals, private firms, and the voluntary sector (see Chapter 5 for a discussion of the latter). Through such decentralized approaches to governance, the state can "enable, inspire, and assist citizens to take responsibility for social problems in their communities and formulate appropriate orientations and rationalities for their actions" (Ilcan and Basok 2004: 132). However, state efforts to "enable" and "assist" in the voluntary sector can pose a threat to this sector's autonomy and existence. In a case study of immigrant- and refugee-serving non-profit organizations in Minneapolis-St. Paul, Minnesota, Trudeau (2008) convincingly illustrates this threat in the context of the decline of the welfare state. According to Trudeau, the process of state restructuring has involved the decentralization of political decision making via three processes: the dismantlement of public programmes; the devolution of public responsibility to lower levels of government; and the privatization of responsibility for public service. In this context Trudeau notes that "many states opted to sign service contracts with non-profit organizations in order to limit the size of the public payroll, minimize bureaucratic red tape and offer a way to generate responsive and 'innovative solutions to pervasive policy problems'" (2008: 1578). Coupled with the 1996 welfare reforms, which placed limits on who could receive public assistance and for how long, state restructuring processes have, according to Trudeau, increased non-profit organizations' access to government funding while introducing new administrative responsibilities and restrictions on service delivery.

As states move away from direct service provision toward a more administrative function, non-state actors can take on the role of service provider. For example, in response to the privatization of waste management in South Africa, discussed in Box 4.1, a number of municipalities began to call upon poor residents who could not afford to pay the full cost of services to minimize service delivery costs by volunteering free labour. Volunteerism in the waste management sector had been reported in cities and towns across the

BOX 4.1 ❊ PRIVATIZING COLLECTIVE PUBLIC GOODS: A CASE STUDY OF STREET CLEANING IN JOHANNESBURG, SOUTH AFRICA

The *iGoli* 2002 plan was developed under the pretext of responding to a financial crisis within the municipality. It is overtly based on implanting market logic into the heart of the municipality, and grounded within the contracting model of the local state. Waste management was targeted for transformation into a utility and on 1 January 2001, previously independent waste management units were dissolved and merged to form Pikitup Pty Ltd. In converting its waste management departments into Pikitup, the Council created the largest private waste management company in Africa.

To increase profitability, Pikitup adopted a sophisticated strategy to minimize expenditure on nonrevenue-generating activities and maximize income and profits from revenue-generating activities. In order to boost income, Pikitup actively marketed new commercial waste management services and sought to regain lost market share in the provision of bulk business services. With respect to minimizing expenditure, Pikitup focused on street cleaning, which was by far the largest budget item in this category. The utility employed two key strategies to cut costs in providing this service. First, it dramatically reduced its own staff. Second, Pikitup subcontracted private companies to deliver services on its behalf.

Although Pikitup managed to reduce expenditure, it was still required to pay for these services. For Pikitup, the ideal scenario would therefore be to replace the provision of street cleaning as a collective public good with a commodified, fee-for-service alternative, or at the very least to find a way to ensure that the main beneficiaries of the collective public good directly financed its delivery. Reducing the level of service provision created the conditions for other parties concerned with city cleanliness to undertake initiatives that would shift shifting service provision outside of the public sector and refragmented service delivery along class lines. For example, in bourgeois and commercial areas, service delivery was shifted to the private sector via the development of city improvement districts (CIDs), yet in working class areas privatized delivery was provided within the voluntary and development sectors. (Source: Samson 2007: 119–43).

country, particularly in Black townships. These initiatives fell into three categories. First, together with Council, the private waste management company, Pikitup, had conducted several high-profile, short-term, volunteer cleanup campaigns in which politicians and citizens volunteered for one or two days to pick up litter and clean the streets. Second, ward committees, residents' groups, and schools in both wealthy and working-class areas organized smaller scale, short-term cleanup initiatives. Pikitup collected the waste and sometimes provided volunteers with bags, caps, and t-shirts. The third kind of volunteer work was conducted exclusively in the working-class townships. These volunteers cleaned the street and illegal dumping sites, worked five days a week for no pay, and received no protective clothing or equipment (Samson 2007).

Non-state actors often provide voluntary services in partnership with the state. For example, when President Clinton signed the Personal Responsibility Work Opportunity Reconciliation Act (PRWORA) in 1996, twenty years of changes in federal programs for poor families won by social liberals from the 1950s through the early 1970s were eliminated and the door closed on efforts to make cash assistance a social right within the United States. By removing the entitlement to welfare benefits and implementing a new federal block grant, federal policy-makers authorized state and local governments to require parents—overwhelmingly single mothers—to submit to new government regulation of their domestic lives and to work or engage in work-related activities in order to receive assistance (Mayer 2008: 155). According to Stryker and Wald (2009), "actors promoting the PRWORA deployed perversity rhetoric to argue that the welfare system caused poverty by encouraging welfare dependency and associated behavioral ills of crime, illegitimacy, and idleness" (2009: 522). The idea that historically instituted welfare systems caused undesirable dependency was, according to the authors, a hallmark of neoliberal discourses across advanced capitalism more generally.

Various kinds of anti-social efforts and policies fit into the broader conceptualizations of the decline of the welfare state under neoliberal agendas. Like many other nations, Canada has been reducing the availability and accessibility of social programs, privatizing government ("crown") corporations, contracting out some public service work to the for-profit sector, and producing greater responsibilities for non-profit agencies and certain kinds of citizenship groups to engage in service delivery (see, for example, Armstrong and Armstrong 2002; Brock and Banting 2001; Isin and Wood 1999; McDaniel 2003; O'Connor and Ilcan 2005). For example, federal governments and international organizations, such as the World Bank, have been identifying non-governmental and non-profit organizations as playing a partnership role in the service delivery of social programs (Basok and Ilcan 2004; Fyfe 2005). Indeed, as Brodie stresses, "social programs are progressively abandoned as all nation-states are forced to engage in a competitive race to the bottom, while citizens are released from social entitlements and obligations as they maximize their choice and capacities for self-sufficiency" (2008a, 39). Steeply rising demands are increasingly being placed on people to find "biographic solutions" or personal causes and responses to what are, in effect, collective social problems. Janine Brodie calls this process "individualization" (2008: 41). This process is not simply equated with *laissez-fair* lifestyle options; it also involves viewing individualization as a discourse which in turn allows better insight into the relations of knowledge and power that produce individuals as entrepreneurial selves (Horschelmann 2008: 143). Addressing the erosion of the social movements–based collective notion of citizenship under neoliberalism in Brazil, Dagnino points out a "perverse confluence" between two forms of participation: one that relates to the extension of citizenship and the deepening of democracy (discussed in Box 3.8) and another that is associated with the reconfiguration of the state, the shrinking of its social responsibilities, and its progressive exemption from the role of guarantor of rights (2005: 158).

Changes to social welfare programs, such as Canada's income security policy and Britain's welfare system, have generally rendered women more marginalized in the workplace, economically precarious, and even poor as they attempt to balance their responsibilities at home and at work. In Canada, (im)migrant women are particularly marginalized by neoliberal immigration policies that prioritize the economic (im)migrant (typically male) as the primary applicant. Declining immigration service delivery due to budget cuts and the non-recognition of professionals' foreign credentials also marginalize these women. In Britain, racial tensions and changes to immigration policy have also compounded the effects of welfare reforms for (im)migrant women and female asylum-seekers. Despite their low incomes and greater difficulties in securing employment and adequate housing, these women have seen relatively less state support than other women in recent years when it comes to maternity payments, milk tokens, Jobseekers' Allowance, and Income Support to Child Benefit and Disability Allowance. Women's ability to claim citizenship rights and needs in these countries has also diminished under neoliberal agendas and policies. The "time crunch" stemming from the universal breadwinner model has compromised women's capacity for formal and informal political participation. At the same time, women's advocacy is challenged by structural inequalities based on class, race, ethnicity, and gender, and by major barriers to full citizenship. In Canada, for example, women's groups and other equality rights–seeking groups have been discredited as "special interest" groups. Such discrediting efforts have led to cuts in funding for advocacy and reductions in federal programs such as the Status of Women of Canada (Dobrowolsky 2008; Dobrowolsky and Lister 2006; Jenson and Phillips 2001).

Neoliberal welfare reforms in Great Britain have resulted in a transformation of those in need of assistance into "'aspirational citizens' [who will] . . .

'better' themselves and become more like an imagined social 'mainstream'" (Raco 2009: 436). This practice legitimizes state action and intervention in order to create individuals who are eager and responsible, and able to take care of themselves and their communities. In this sense, "states and governments actively define, categorise, and institutionalise the essential characteristics of human nature, well-being, responsibility, and virtue" in order to implement reform policies (2009: 436). In order to be considered an exemplary citizen of the state, individuals are encouraged to be more responsible and entrepreneurial, a process Raco refers to as an "institutionalisation of citizenship boundaries" (2009: 437). This institutionalisation implements "complex and highly politicized citizenship-building processes" that are, according to Raco, "founded on dominant conceptions of what roles and responsibilities individuals, communities, and the state could and should possess" (2009: 437).

These and other changes to social welfare approaches have moved the basis of citizenship from collectively respected social rights (Lazar 2007; Molz 2005)—which provided language for the systemically disadvantaged to mandate the state to regulate and avert the structural undermining of individual and collective well-being (Brodie 2007)—to a focus on the erosion of citizenship rights and on individual and citizenship-based entrepreneurial responsibilities. Neoliberal transformations thus pose a challenge to T.H. Marshall's portrayal of evolutionary citizenship rights as expressed in his *Crafting a New Conservative Consensus on Welfare Reform*. In this book he defined social citizenship to mean "the whole range from the right to a modicum of economic welfare and security to the right to share to the full in the social heritage and to live the life of a civilized being according to the standards prevailing in the society" (1964: 72). However, this definition does not account for the manner in which citizenship rights can be expanded and eroded in that they can be won or lost for different groups over time and space. Contemporary feminist scholars, for example, have taken up Marshall's concept of social citizenship but point out that citizenship identities are multiple, infused with both racialized and gendered meaning, and have been mobilized politically to expand and to circumscribe opportunities afforded to different social groups (Orloff 1993; Fraser 1989).

While many excluded groups have struggled to expand the applications of citizenship (as discussed in Chapter 3), certain political developments have made citizenship more exclusive. For example, existing empirical studies of gender equity and health sector reform suggest that market-oriented health reforms tend to create or intensify gender inequities. For example, market reforms attempt to reduce the costs of healthcare by transferring a greater share of healthcare provision from state or private providers to individuals, and especially to women within families, as a result of shorter hospital stays or greater reliance on home-based primary care. Markets also tend to view women as higher "risks" due to their reproductive health needs and related greater healthcare usage rates. Moreover, in systems organized around an individual's capacity to pay, women are the least likely to be covered by health insurance and the least likely to be able to pay fees for health services—reflecting broader patterns of gender discrimination in labour markets, women's greater levels of poverty, and intra-familial power dynamics. The impact of healthcare reforms on gender equity in Columbia provides an illustration of these kinds of trends (discussed in Box 4.2). Furthermore, with the decline of the welfare state under neoliberal agendas the emphasis on "rights talk" is increasingly being displaced by discourses that emphasize the duties and obligations of an active citizenship.

BOX 4.2 ❊ GENDER EQUITY AND HEALTH SECTOR REFORM IN COLOMBIA: MIXED STATE-MARKET MODEL YIELDS MIXED RESULTS

On December 23, 1993, Colombia passed Law 100 on Social Security Reform which constituted a sweeping national health and pension reform. The health reforms of Law 100 were hailed by the World Bank and the World Health Organization as an international model. Colombia utilized a combination of market mechanisms and state intervention; its "managed competition" approach pairs the belief that market competition will increase efficiency with the belief that government regulation is necessary to ensure equity.

The key health components of Law 100 were individual insurance, regulated competition between health providers, consumer choice, state subsidies for the poorest, and a guarantee to benefits contained in a package of services determined by the state. Although the Constitution required the creation of a universal insurance system, as the reform progressed beneficiaries were divided into two groups served by separate health regimes: contributory beneficiaries (those with ability to pay) and subsidized beneficiaries (the poor). Another group remains uninsured, some of whom are poor and use the public system, and others are wealthy enough to pay for healthcare privately. Although insurers initially were to serve both regimes, due to profitability concerns insurers divided themselves into two groups, one serving the contributory regime and the other the subsidized regime. Beneficiaries of the subsidized regime are selected based on a targeting instrument designed to identify the poorest and most vulnerable, including pregnant women and single female heads of households. These policies have had an impact on gender equity in areas such as financial equity, gender stratification, and women's health needs. For example, in terms of financial equity, the Colombian reforms would suggest improved financial gender equity, such as the incorporation of dependents and the creation of a subsidized system for the poor that also targets pregnant women and single female heads of households. Law 100 dictated that the state system provide complete health insurance to dependents. While women have increased their workforce participation over time, more than half of these working women are concentrated in the informal sector and thus not eligible for the contributory regime. Insurance coverage for dependents has led to substantial increases in healthcare coverage in general and for women in particular; however, the concentration of women as dependents places a greater proportion of women in a more precarious state as regards health insurance. Dependent coverage is more precarious than coverage gained by employment or coverage as a citizenship right because it depends upon the coverage gained through the marriage partner or parent. If dependent relationships become strained or dissolve, or if the contributing partner loses work or dies, dependents may lose their rights to healthcare as well. Overall, the fragmentation of the Colombian health system into one system for those who can pay (the contributory system) and another for those who cannot (the subsidized system) has led to stratification between men and women where women are concentrated in the lesser-quality subsidized health system. (Source: Ewig and Hernandez Bello 2009: 1145–52).

Policies that promote social rights are increasingly being undermined through welfare reforms that involve social-spending cuts and reallocations, as well as the modification of eligibility criteria for social services support (discussed in Box 4.3 in terms of the decline of children's entitlements). Such changes are embedded in neoliberal orientations that require certain populations to be self-managing and self-enterprising individuals in different spheres of everyday life, including access to healthcare, educational training, and professional development. It is here that the neoliberal subject is no longer a citizen with claims on the state but rather a self-enterprising citizen-subject who is obligated to become an entrepreneur him- or herself (Bondi and Laurie 2005; Ilcan 2009; Ong 2006). What makes neoliberal practices so powerfully transformative, such as in the creation of neoliberal subjects, is their ability to move through, across, and beyond the political agendas of nation-states. Jamie Peck (2009) views the power of neoliberalism in terms of its ability to transform itself by initially working against the "social state, social entitlements, and social collectivities" as well as working "from dogmatic deregulation to market-friendly reregulation, from structural adjustment to good governance, from budget cuts to regulation-by-audit, from welfare retrenchment to active social policy, from privatization to public–private partnership, from greed-is-good to markets with- morals" (2009: 106). Ideas of neoliberalism travel not only from one geographic location to another or from one state to another but they also tend to mutate as they come into contact with other ideas, and are enacted under specific conditions (see May et al. 2008: 64; Ong 2007) and within commercial environments.

BOX 4.3 ❁ THE MEANING AND MAKING OF CHILDHOOD IN THE ERA OF GLOBALIZATION: CHALLENGES FOR SOCIAL WORKS

Over the past two decades, advocates for neoliberal globalization have argued that support for free markets, privatization of state enterprises, and welfare retrenchment would lead to growth and expansion that will trickle down to the poorest across the globe. What has not been fully recognized is the way in which reform movements that celebrated individual responsibility and pathologized dependency also marginalized concern for children. The widely touted process of "ending welfare as we know it" in the US, resulting in passage of the Personal Responsibility and Work Opportunity Reconciliation Act (PRWORA) in 1996, provides a critical example of the translation of neoliberal ideas into public policy. In the process, children's entitlement to a minimal level of income support (Aid to Dependent Children) was eliminated as the spotlight focused on the "work effort" of their parents. Under the dramatically altered welfare rules, only one-quarter of poor children were receiving benefits under its provisions yet the program was widely heralded as a success. However, the current economic recession places welfare reform in a new light as forecasts predict that the number of poor children will increase to between 2.6 and 3.9 million children and the number of children in deep poverty will rise to between 1.5 and 2.4 million children. It is predicted that poverty rates among all US children will jump from 18 percent in 2007 to 27 percent in 2010, and among Black children it will rise from 27 percent (2007) to more than 50 percent (2010) if predicted levels of unemployment materialize. At the same time, there has been a growing trend in the US toward the privatization and corporatization of public institutions for children including schools, social services, and correctional facilities. For example, there has been an increasing trend toward the corporate sponsorship of schools and the transformation of community schools into quasi-business structures that evidences a growing infatuation with the socialization of children by private, often for-profit interests. (Source: Finn and Shook 2010: 246–254).

There is no doubt that alterations in social welfare schemes have re-emphasized the entrepreneurialism of individuals and their ability to invest in themselves and to meet new kinds of obligations. This emphasis has been growing alongside other commercial appeals, such as those of business, which Walters (2000: 132–3) identifies in the popularization in Britain and North America since the early 1990s of such concepts as "corporate citizenship," "the new corporate philanthropy," and "corporate social responsibility." These terms emphasize the participation of private businesses in various aspects of society through, for example, the donation of money to a charitable organization, financial assistance for the building of an arts centre or a sporting event, or indirect contributions that aim to reduce poverty and unemployment. Vis-à-vis the history of the governing of unemployment, Walters (2000) also reveals the growing number of networks, institutes, and centres that deliberate and transmit principles of corporate citizenship among business people and the public. Similarly, there are sustained efforts to mobilize vulnerable citizens, such as the poor, into entrepreneurial actors and have them meet new types of obligations. The World Bank, for example, has established a consortium of thirty-three public and private development agencies—the Consultative Group to Assist the Poorest (CGAP)—to expand access to financial services for the poor. Its work is to implement international financial programs, such as microcredit, and enable the poor in the developing world to act in entrepreneurial, responsible ways, which would, it is believed, connect them to the global market and lift them out of poverty. Such programs not only promote partnerships between citizens, government departments, private businesses, and international and nongovernmental organizations but they also emphasize new ways of shaping the actions and conduct of vulnerable groups (Ilcan and Lacey 2011), such as the sick, the elderly, women, and the poor (see Box 4.4 on welfare reform and the poor).

BOX 4.4 ❊ PUNISHING THE POOR: THE NEOLIBERAL GOVERNMENT OF SOCIAL INSECURITY

In the case of the poor and indigent populations in Western Europe and North America, the retrenchment and devolution of the welfare state as well as the moral and punitive logics of neoliberal agendas have worked to criminalize and make invisible the poorest factions of society. Löic Wacquant illustrates this critical point in his book *Punishing the Poor: The Neoliberal Government of Social Insecurity*. In this book he examines the emergence and implementation of the United States' 1996 welfare reforms and their effects on the poor. He argues that the various measures connected to these reforms ultimately "converge to treat—and in turn constitute—the dependent poor as a troublesome population to be subdued and "corrected" through stern behavioural controls and paternalistic sanctions, thus fostering a programmatic convergence with penal policy" (2009: 79).

The aim of the US welfare reform's Personal Responsibility and Work Opportunity Reconciliation Act (PRWORA) was to reduce "an alleged *dependency* of families on public aid" (Wacquant 2009: 80) which, in turn, meant reducing the numbers of women, children, elderly, and indigent on the welfare rolls. This legislative reform is based on four principles: 1) the withdrawal of the right to assistance (included in the Social Security Act of 1935) and the introduction the obligation for parents on assistance to work within two years and receive no more than five years of assistance; 2) the devolution of public assistance responsibilities (i.e., eligibility criteria, payment dispersal, and program creation) to the lower levels of government; 3) the establishment of "block grants" or permanent welfare budgets, regardless of inflation, unemployment, or any other socially variable factors; and 4) the exclusion of many people from the welfare rolls, including foreign residents with less than six years in the country, persons convicted of federal drug offenses, children with disabilities, and teenage mothers who did not reside with their parents, among others. According to Wacquant, these four principles "cast persistent poverty as an outlaw status to be dealt with through paternalist supervision and deterrence, and effectively shift the burden of coping with destitution onto the most deprived individuals and their families" (2009: 88).

In broad terms, Wacquant views welfare reform in the United States as both an economic project to promote labour flexibility and a political project of statecraft. On one hand, he claims that the reform has reshaped welfare recipients' dispositions through what he calls an "intensive moral armament." It has also forced them into the unskilled and deregulated labour market by legislating the duty to work while on assistance and placing lifetime caps on individuals' public assistance benefits. On the other hand, he explains, PRWORA has "recalibrate[d] public authority at three levels: its internal organization (bureaucratic segmentation and differentiation through devolution), its external boundary (redrawing the division of labour between the public and private sectors), and its functional loading (via the penalization of welfare and the shift from the assistantial to the penal treatment of the more disruptive correlates of poverty)" (2009: 103). (Source: Wacquant 2009: 76–109).

There have been challenges to the decline of the welfare state and to neoliberal initiatives. For example, as part of "roll-out neoliberalism," policies to combat social exclusion were often included (see Brenner and Theodore 2002) which may indeed be related to an ethical commitment to equity or greater fairness, as in the concept of "Adjustment with a Human Face" or to the inclusion of policies promoting justice and ethics (Smith, Stenning, and Willis 2008: 9). Furthermore, there have been challenges to neoliberal agendas and policies, such as protests, the formation of economic collectives, and the development of new forms of resistance efforts that aimed to create more liberated forms of economic life, such as barter networks (North 2008: 18; also see Chapter 7). For example, alternative strategies to challenge neoliberalism are evident in a study by Mahon and MacDonald (2010) that focuses on Toronto and Mexico City. While these two cities have two different welfare regimes (one liberal and the other corporatist) and political structures, they face similar challenges in the form of national poverty reduction strategies which, according to the authors, do little to meet the needs of their inhabitants. In response to this issue, both cities provide a site for mobilizing resources that support alternative anti-poverty policies and are inspired by the principles of social citizenship (2010: 210). In this regard, leaders in both municipalities defy the dominant neoliberal strategies adopted by their federal counterparts and design innovative and creative responses to poverty rooted in the values of inclusion, universalism, and social citizenship. These strategies may be insufficient to tackle the diverse issues related to poverty in their respective locations, but they do raise critical questions around the significance of "progressive post-neoliberal politics" (2010: 215).

Conclusion

It is important not to romanticize the era of the burgeoning welfare state as one that is compatible with achieving social justice since it produced exclusions, inequalities, and social divisions. Yet, under neoliberalism, new forms of exclusion, inequality, and social cleavages have emerged. Indeed, there is an urgency to keep problematizing neoliberal and other similar initiatives that work to undermine democratic practices. David Harvey (2006) argues that "internationally the lack of elementary accountability let alone democratic control over institutions such as the IMF, the WTO and the World Bank, to say nothing of the overwhelming private power of financial institutions, makes a mockery of any serious concern for democratization" (2006: 25). He reminds us that to bring back the demands for democratic governance, including economic, political, and cultural equality and justice, it is necessary to re-invent each of the meanings in each instance in order to cope with current conditions as well as find new potentialities.

Key Terms

neoliberalism market-oriented form of governing consisting of a set of practices that aim to prioritize economic growth; increase the role of the free market; encourage flexibility in labour markets; and reform state welfare activities through an emphasis on privatization, deregulation of state control over industry, marketization, decentralization, and fiscal austerity.

welfare state a social system based on the assumption by a political state of primary responsibility for the individual and social welfare of its citizens

Questions for Critical Thought

1. What do you understand by the term "the social"? How might this term reveal an understanding of the relationship some groups have with the welfare state?
2. How did the social welfare approach get assembled and for what specific reasons? In what ways did the approach presume that citizens would understand themselves in particular kinds of ways?
3. What is meant by the term "individualization" and what are its implications for understanding the social or economic changes taking place in people's lives today? Can you identify any of these changes in the neighbourhood, community, or region where you live?
4. What kinds of processes are linked to the "institutionalization of citizenship boundaries"?
5. How have alterations in social welfare schemes re-emphasized the entrepreneurialism of individuals and thereby re-defined certain people's responsibilities for themselves or others?

Annotated Additional Readings

Keith Banting and Will Kymlicka. 2006. *Multiculturalism and the Welfare State: Recognition and Redistribution in Contemporary Democracies*. Oxford University Press. This book focuses on the adoption of multiculturalism policies for immigrant groups, the acceptance of territorial autonomy and language rights for national minorities, and the recognition of land claims and self-government rights for indigenous peoples. In this context, the authors ask whether the fears of a conflict between a "politics of recognition" and a "politics of redistribution" are compelling. Their findings shed light on debates about the social and political foundations of the welfare state, and on basic concepts of citizenship and national identity.

Gunnar Broberg and Nils Roll-Hansen. 2005. *Eugenics and the Welfare State: Sterilization Policy in Denmark, Sweden, Norway, and Finland*. Ann Arbor: Michigan State University. This book examines eugenics practices in European countries and the United States, and offers a critical analysis of the history and politics that led to mass sterilization programs in Norway, Sweden, Denmark, and Finland before the rise of Nazism in Germany.

Anne Lise Ellingsaeter, Arnlaug Leira, Jon Kvist,, Johan Fritzell, Bjorn Hvinden, and Olli Kangas, Eds. 2011. *Politicising Parenthood in Scandinavia: Gender Relations in Welfare States*. Policy Press. The collection of essays in this book examines the differences and similarities in recent developments in the social, economic, and employment policies for supporting parenthood within the four Scandinavian countries.

Silja Häusermann. 2010. *The Politics of Welfare State Reform in Continental Europe: Modernization in Hard Times*. London: Cambridge University Press. This book identifies and investigates the new political cleavages formed during the reform of existing welfare states and the institutional conditions that facilitate policy compromises both among political parties and among social actors. It challenges existing theories of welfare state change by analyzing pension reforms in France, Germany, and Switzerland between 1970 and 2004. Through its analysis of lines of conflict, configurations of political actors, and coalitional dynamics over time, the book argues that socio-structural change has led to a multidimensional pension reform agenda.

Shirley Tillotson. 2009. *Contributing Citizens: Modern Charitable Fundraising and the Making of the Welfare State, 1920–66*. Vancouver: University of British Columbia Press. This book focuses on the social, cultural, and political history of Community Chests, the forerunners of today's United Way, to provide a new perspective on the development of professional fundraising, private charity, and the emergence of the welfare state. Through the use of case studies, the author reveals that fundraising work in the 1940s and 1950s used the language of welfare state reform which helped institute the notion of universal contribution from which key social policies grew.

Related Websites

Canadian Department of Social Services
www.cdss.ca.gov/cdssweb/PG141.htm

Canadian Social Research Links
www.canadiansocialresearch.net/welfare.htm#historical

Childcarecanada.org
http://childcarecanada.org/documents/child-care-news/11/07/latest-oecd-figures-confirm-canada-public-health-laggard

Ministry of Social Justice and Empowerment, Government of Idea
http://socialjustice.nic.in

Organization for Economic Co-operation and Development (OECD), Social and Welfare Statistics
www.oecd.org/topicstatsportal/0,3398,en_2825_497118_1_1_1_1_1,00.html

Welfare State Reform over the (Very) Long-run, The London School of Economics and Political Science (public lectures and events)
www2.lse.ac.uk/newsAndMedia/videoAndAudio/channels/publicLecturesAndEvents/player.aspx?id=790

5 Voluntary Organizations: Delivering Public Services to Marginalized Groups

Learning Objectives

- Explore the concept of voluntary organizations
- Understand the role of post–World War II voluntary organizations
- Identify the changes that influenced the role of voluntary organizations in western, democratic countries
- Recognize the links between the non-profit voluntary sector and marginalized and disadvantaged groups
- Explain the ways in which voluntary organizations work in partnership with states
- Identify the impact of these partnerships on the ability of voluntary organizations to meet the needs of disadvantaged groups, to provide homecare, and to protect the environment

Introduction

Governments, the private sector, and international organizations are identifying non-governmental, non-profit, and community organizations, including voluntary organizations, as playing a critical role in supporting marginalized and disadvantaged groups. While national and international efforts that identify these organizations as providing solutions to certain kinds of problems, such as unemployment, poverty, or illness, may be viewed as achieving social justice, in many cases these organizations are faced with limits in terms of their ability to bring about sustainable change for vulnerable groups.

This chapter examines the voluntary sector in an effort to reveal that organizations operating in this sector have been constrained in terms of how they work and carry out their service provisions and their potential impact on improving marginalized and disadvantaged groups. We employ the term voluntary sector to designate an assemblage of groups characterized by non-coercive membership that aims to engage in unconstrained participation and activity. This sector involves groups, associations, and organizations that commonly participate in work-related education, health and home care, and social welfare, and can range from small, community and human service organizations such as homeless shelters or arts centres, to large, federated organizations like the Canadian Red Cross or the Salvation Army. The voluntary sector is also known as the "third sector" which includes voluntary organizations offering assistance to marginalized and disadvantaged groups not to gain profit but to provide services that the state no longer offers fully or adequately. The chapter begins by providing a brief history of voluntary organizations and their activities in western democratic countries after World War II. In light of the decline of the welfare state, the chapter then focuses on a selection of voluntary organizations working in the area of environmental protection and home care for the elderly within and outside of Canada, their provision of services to disadvantaged groups, and the extent to which these services meet the needs of marginalized and disadvantaged groups.

A Brief History: Post–World War II Voluntary Organizations

Prior to the establishment of welfare states, during and immediately following World War II, diverse aid and philanthropic participants and organizations played a critical role in assisting disadvantaged groups, such as the poor, the unemployed, and the sick and dying (see Figures 5.1 and 5.2).

During and following World War II, voluntary organizations included community-based organizations that would engage in self-help and welfare

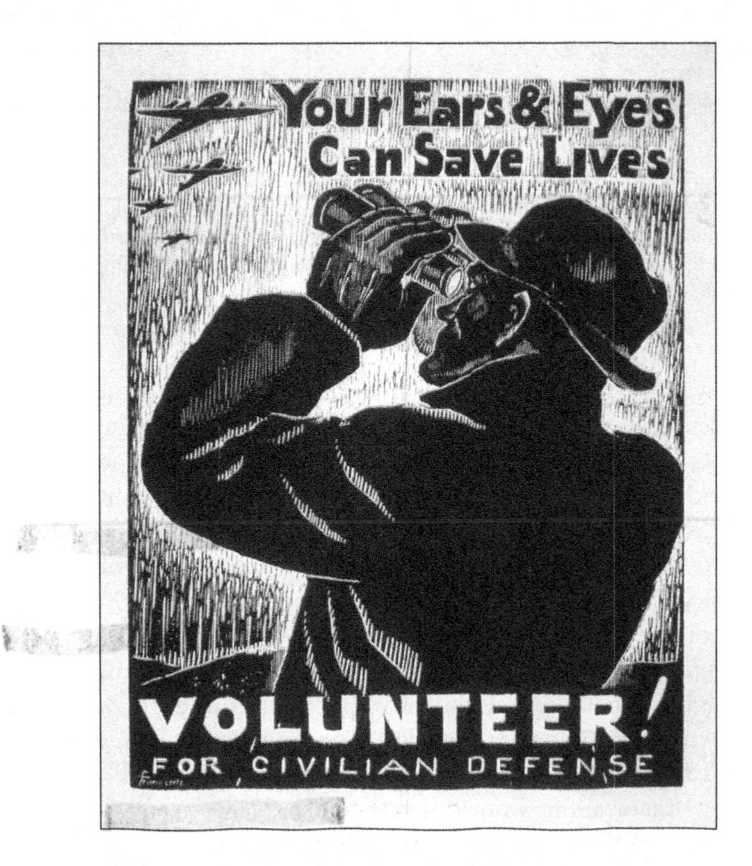

FIGURE 5.1 World War II Poster: "Volunteer! For Civilian Defense"

Source: http://research.archives.gov/description/513614; National Archives Identifier: 514614; Local Identifier: 44-PA-168

FIGURE 5.2 On the Home Front: The Red Cross in Toronto During World War II. The familiar Red Cross symbol was everywhere during the war, and the Canadian Red Cross Corps eventually numbered 15,000 women, of whom 641 volunteers served overseas to bring food and medical supplies. At home, they waged vigorous fundraising campaigns.
Source: Toronto Archives; Fonds 1257, Series 1057, Item 2691A

activities as well as private voluntary organizations such as CARE, Catholic Relief Services, Oxfam, and World Vision. These and other related organizations often directed their actions towards the needs of the poor and were notable providers of healthcare and welfare in national economies around the world. They engaged in what was referred to as "voluntary action" or what came to be understood as activities aimed for social advancement in the community. This definition of the term "voluntary action" is taken from the founder of the British welfare state, William Beveridge. In his 1948 report on *Voluntary Action*, Beveridge argued that it was crucial that voluntary action, through mutual aid and philanthropy, be permitted to co-exist with the newly formed welfare state that was developing at the time. From his perspective, an environment had to be created in which the state, individuals, and voluntary organizations worked together for "social advance" (Beveridge in Oppenheimer 2005: 82.3). The term voluntary action is closely associated with the concepts of civil society and social capital (practices that facilitate the coordinated action of particular group membership) that have been used to explore contemporary ideas of democratic practices and social networks within local communities as identified in the scholarly work of Pierre Bourdieu (1986) and Robert Putnam (1993). For example, Putman (1993) defined social capital as the "features of social organization, such as trust, norms, and networks, that can improve the efficiency of society by facilitating coordinated action" (35). Yet various place-based differences in the social capital approach raise questions about the utility of this approach for analyzing the relationship between voluntarism and the development of civil society. Xu and Ngai (2011) note, for example, that volunteer groups may be delimited by race, social background, or ethnicity, and may aim to enhance the social capital or solidarity of their members rather than facilitate public engagement.

Since the end of World War II, significant changes came to characterize the operating environment of voluntary organizations in many western, democratic countries. One of the most important shifts was increased statutory action in social welfare, that is, the application of welfare state provisions that typically aimed to provide certain levels of healthcare, education, housing, cultural enjoyment, and social well-being to national citizens. For example, the Commonwealth enacted legislation to make voluntary organizations eligible for subsidies for aged care in 1954, for homecare nursing in 1956, and for marriage guidance in 1960. This enacted legislation followed the Commonwealth's engagement in other areas of social welfare through the administration of grants to the States, such as the supply of free milk for primary school children (1950), the development of emergency housekeeping (1951), and the blood transfusion services of the Australian Red Cross in 1953 (Oppenheimer 2005, 82.9).

At this time it was widely believed that the introduction and operation of welfare state provisions had substantially reduced poverty for particular groups, though it was recognized that considerable gaps characterized the entire terrain of welfare provision. In the mid-1960s in Britain, for example, large-scale poverty, especially among children and large families, was "rediscovered" by researchers at the London School of Economics. This rediscovery stimulated a new breed of professionalized, media-aware campaigning organizations that focused mainly on pressing for more effective state action. Organizations in Britain, such as the Child Poverty Action Group, founded in 1965, and Shelter, founded in 1966, were products of this new awareness of escalating poverty in an increasingly affluent society. These organizations formed alongside the growing numbers of trained social scientists graduating from universities who were keen to participate in efforts to change the world (Thane 2010). And generally, in both Britain and Canada, established voluntary organizations reconfigured their activities to fill the gaps in welfare provision, while other organizations continued in their social justice advocacy roles. The latter often demanded changes in state policy for the recognition and treatment of vulnerable groups.

The international economic crisis of the mid-1970s led to attempts to reduce state welfare in a wide number of liberal states, albeit to varying extents, and encourage and subsidize NGOs, including voluntary organizations, to replace it. As discussed in Chapter 4, the transformation of the welfare state was especially apparent under the Conservative governments of the 1980s. The Thatcher, Reagan, and Mulroney governments in Britain, the United States, and Canada, respectively, were recognized as the enforcers of neoliberal orientations and agendas that aimed to persuade citizens that it was unreasonable to support public sector services through taxation and to abandon their support for the public sector (Coulter 2009: 31). Such orientations upheld privatization and contracting-out efforts, public–private partnerships, and individual responsibility while omitting critical discussions of social inequities and the marginalization of specific groups, such as the unemployed, women, the elderly, and the poor[1]. Under the Harris reforms in Canada, Jenson and Phillips (2000) observe that "the historically privileged position of nonprofit organizations in service delivery has been replaced by an open, competitive bidding process in which large for-profit companies are increasingly successful" (44). Particularly over the last 30 years, with the decline of the welfare state, there has been the concurrent decentralization of states, the privatization of public services (e.g., Appadurai 2001; Armstrong and Armstrong 2002; Smith, Stenning and Willis 2008), and the devolution of federal responsibilities to regional and local governments (Evans and Shields 2002), private organizations (Isin and Wood 1999), citizenship groups, voluntary organizations, and NGOs (Basok, Ilcan and Noonan 2008; Laforest and Orsini 2005; MacDonald 2001; Weber 2004). This situation has resulted in strategic and financial insecurity for non-profit and voluntary organizations as well as concerns over the quality of service these organizations are able to provide to vulnerable and disadvantaged groups. Increasingly, voluntary organizations today are allocating resources to diversify their funding base, cutting costs substantially, and restructuring their boards of directors. Reducing the number of board members and shifting from an administrative to a policy governance model has been a common practice for voluntary organizations in their attempts to be more strategic in their planning efforts and more secure in their financial undertakings (Imagine Canada 2005: 9–10).

In the lead-up to the reform of welfare in the United States, community-based organizations, including voluntary organizations, demanded that individuals be able to take more control of and assume greater responsibility for their lives and their families' welfare. As Staeheli (2008) notes, members of these organizations argued that government regulations and the inadequacies of provision "kept low-income families in poverty and perpetuated behaviours that were destructive of families and individuals." In making their case for a larger family role in ensuring welfare, they were not, however, advancing the elimination of state support. Yet, "the suite of reforms that have been part of state restructuring has taken that language of obligation and responsibility in order to shift care more firmly into the private spaces of the home and onto families and communities" (2008, 14). The move towards community responsibility for social welfare provision not only highlights the links between individuals, communities, and the state, but it also emphasizes that certain citizenship groups, such as volunteer organizations and their volunteers, can become increasingly responsible for service provision through the introduction of state initiatives and policies. What has become ever more visible since the decline of the welfare state and the shift towards "free trade" and "economic freedom" in many liberal democratic countries (see Chapter 4) is the rise in non-profit voluntary organizations and, more broadly, non-governmental organizations (NGOs) that rely on volunteers for carrying out their tasks. By the end of the 1980s, for example, the World Bank announced that "NGOs have been heralded as new agents with the capacity and commitment to make up for the shortcomings of the state and the market in reducing poverty." It was believed that these organizations would offer elements of "comparative advantage" in relation to government and business, with these elements including cost-effectiveness, administrative flexibility, and an ability to work closely with the poor (Lewis 2010: 338).

A New Face for the Non-Profit Sector?

With the increasing growth of the non-profit voluntary sector, many voluntary organizations today aim to deliver services to marginalized and disadvantaged groups. For example, social justice–oriented voluntary agencies in Ontario, Canada, reveal that the voluntary sector is invested indirectly by local, provincial, and federal governments with the task of training volunteers to become responsible citizens by providing social services to disadvantaged groups. With the decline of the Canadian welfare state and the restructuring of public services, the activities of these voluntary agencies involve delivering services to relieve the state of some of its obligations to plan and steer from the centre, and address social and economic problems. Canadian voluntary agencies have been and continue to be transformed into "community government," a form of rule that works to define, shape, and orient various communities by making citizens responsible for service provision that was formerly undertaken by the state (Ilcan and Basok 2004). Canadian welfare state reform and public sector restructuring have resulted in, among other things, the undermining of the advocacy work of voluntary agencies. As forming part of this reform agenda, the Canadian Income Tax Act, which allows a registered charity to devote only up to ten percent of its resources to advocacy, has made it more and more difficult for many voluntary agencies to engage in social justice activism (Basok and Ilcan 2003). The downloading of services from the state to the voluntary sector and the subsequent decline in political activism on the part of this sector occurs not only in Canada and the United States, but in other countries around the world. Box 5.1 provides an illustration of how a Hungarian voluntary organization, Periferia Association, which originally hoped to engage in a dialogue with political decision makers, was made responsible for the provision of services to marginalized and vulnerable groups.

The reduction or elimination of various state provided public services facilitates a new face for the non-profit voluntary sector. The sector is increasingly serving as a significant service provider through favourable funding conditions that, as Trudeau suggests, has led to "a threefold increase in the size of the nonprofit sector in Canada" (2009: 1121). Many citizens work as unpaid volunteers in these NGOs. The Canadian trend shows that about half of citizens participated in voluntary organizations in 1997, with this trend remaining

BOX 5.1 ❋ THE PERIFERIA ASSOCIATION

Forming part of the Hungarian Voluntary Community Organizations (VCO), the "Periferia Association" in Nyiregyhaza, Hungary, uses "the alternative paradigm" approach to influence public policy, an approach that develops its own policy alternatives and dialogues with political decision makers. Many local examples, ranging from non-profit psychiatric hospitals to shelters and victims services, demonstrate the success of the approach in the Hungarian context where "direct lobbying often proves to be futile" (2008: 338).

The Periferia Association was founded in 1995 by a group of volunteers who had graduated from social work programs. Its main goal was to support homeless people in Nyiregyhaza. Two highly publicized deaths of homeless people, however, gained attention and resulted in its first local government funding of 60,000HUF for one year. One of the founding members of Periferia stated that "if [Periferia] gets government money then we have to do what [the donor] wants. . . . . [T]he government defines the contract" (Osborne et al. 2008: 339). Additional pressure emerged from this embryonic institutional relationship with local government and resulted in diversification of tasks performed. The local government began to pressure Periferia to handle issues beyond homelessness and to work with child protection and prostitution. By 2003, Periferia Association was transformed from a community organization interested in influencing polity to a critical service provider to the homeless community in Nyiregyhaza. It was perceived by local government as an organization that could be trusted to perform its services to marginalized and vulnerable groups. Instead of challenging the structural issues of homelessness to local government, many VCOs try to survive through negotiation and "nurturing" networks. [Source: Osborne et al. 2008].

constant until 2000. Over the past decade, membership in voluntary organizations increased by about 20 percent and this growth in participation is evident in fields ranging from homeless shelters to healthcare and elderly care (Ferguson et al. 2009: 81). In these contexts, citizens are increasingly being forced to seek alternative ways of accessing diverse public services that were formerly provided by the state.

The changes that have been emerging in the neoliberal era of contracting out work from the public sector to the private and not-for-profit sectors are transforming the very basis of the voluntary sector and undermining its independence (Smillie 1995: 3). Such changes are reflected in terms that emphasize the work of voluntary organizations along the lines of their "performance," "outcomes," "missions," or "prevention" and in the use of a language of business where users and citizens are viewed as "stakeholders," "partners," "consumers," or "clients." The stress on monitoring the service performance of voluntary and other non-profit organizations, for example, has been increasing over the last few decades and follows from the broader emphasis on measurement systems which began with the of rise of large formal organizations in the early part of the twentieth century, and continues to the present day. These formal organizations provided not only new challenges for management and administrative control but also, according to Michel Power (2004), new sites for micro-economic measurement systems capable of classifying, representing, and intervening in organizational activities. These instruments for performance assessment and control have been subject to waves of innovation and fashion at the organizational level, and acted out by accountants, actuaries, economists, consultants, and financial and non-financial analysts—which continues to stimulate demands for the measurement of everything (Power 2004: 466–77). The application of performance measurement frameworks or audit practices is increasingly shaping the activities of the voluntary sector today.

Despite its increasing influence and responsibility, the voluntary sector continues to be scrutinized by government agencies and shaped by neoliberal orientations that focus on monitoring service performance, enforcing eligibility requirements, and implementing sanctions (Trudeau 2008b: 671). According to the UK Labour government's strategy, the voluntary sector must comply with accountability requirements that are premised on the idea that once governments subsidize this sector using public funds there is an obligation on the part of voluntary organizations to keep track of their performance and have their performance evaluated by other governing authorities. While the use of performance measurements attempts to ensure accountability for public money expenditures by both public and voluntary organizations, Moxham and Boaden note the obstacles to measuring the effectiveness of voluntary organizations. The voluntary sector provides the majority of social services and, they emphasize that government bodies expect that this sector will "deliver and demonstrate value for money" (2007: 827). Yet demands for accountability stem from outside the UK government, from non-government funders, donors, volunteers, employees, users, and beneficiaries, just to name a few, and play an important role in sustaining public trust and confidence. Due to the contextual specificity of the services provided by voluntary organizations, it is important to remember that there can be no "one size fits all" approach for measuring impact. The voluntary sector faces key challenges and, for Moxham and Boaden, these include: insecure short-term contracts; inefficient and bureaucratic procedures within the funding bodies; and little guarantee from the public sector that the voluntary organization will recover the full cost of the services it provides (2007: 833–839). Additionally, auditing practices detract from the organization's activities since considerable resources are required to administer them.

In light of the increasing role of the voluntary sector, the following section focuses on a selection of voluntary organizations that engage in the delivery of public service provision and demonstrate the importance of their work and contribution to assisting disadvantaged groups and protecting the environment. These voluntary organizations are numerous and include, for example, those that focus on issues of the environment, healthcare, gender, the elderly, poverty, and ethnicity. Our analysis highlights some of these kinds of voluntary organizations and pays particular attention to the ways in which, rather than being separate from the state and challenging government policies and agendas, they are increasingly drawn into partnerships with the state and sometimes the private sector. As a result of these partnerships, we emphasize the downsizing of the public sector and the downloading of responsibility to the voluntary sector, and the depoliticization of voluntary organizations (i.e., the move away from advocacy and political dialogues into the sphere of service delivery). Our analysis draws upon specific case studies to show that the practices of volunteering are constrained in terms of their social justice efforts and associated with particular approaches to work, communities, and changing times under neoliberal orientations.

Downsizing the Public Sector and Downloading Responsibility

Due to the downsizing of the public sector under neoliberal agendas (see Chapter 4), there has been a subsequent reliance on voluntary organizations and volunteers to perform tasks that were formerly done by the state. Many examples demonstrate the implications that this situation can have on the voluntary sector.

There have been a number of healthcare initiatives that have demanded the labour of volunteers, such as in drug treatment services. A study by Mold and Berridge (2007), for example, examines the development of a national British heroin "problem" in the 1980s through a focus on the Central Funding

Initiative (CFI)[2] for drug services. Through the CFI, less emphasis was placed on treatment alone and greater attention was given to the social and medical consequences of drug use. This attention was to be achieved by voluntary organizations because they were regarded as more flexible than statutory bodies and thus better equipped to respond in new ways to the rapidly developing drug problem. The authors suggest that the involvement of the voluntary sector in the provision of services for drug users reflected wider shifts within health and welfare in Britain during the 1980s led by Prime Minister Margaret Thatcher. Alongside the numerous initiatives, CFIs provide improved services for children under five years old, better services for mentally ill elderly people, enhanced services for children with mental disabilities, and more general initiatives such as Opportunities for Volunteering and Helping the Community to Care. A Department of Health and Social Services (DHSS) official noted that funding is deliberately limited in duration to preserve their development and catalyst role. Health and local authorities were expected to find the money for continuing schemes from within their regular sources of funding, and voluntary bodies were required to continue raising their own funds. The central funding initiatives thus encapsulated a key aspect of the Thatcherite policy of "rolling back the state" which involved reducing direct statutory involvement in welfare provision by transforming the functions of the state. The policy created an internal market within health and social care by establishing a divide between the "purchasers" of services and the "providers" of services. Local authorities, for example, were able to "purchase" a particular service, such as a needle exchange for intravenous drug users, from a local "provider." The provider could be a statutory, voluntary, or private organization; these providers were expected to "compete" within the internal market for the custom of the purchaser. The argument advanced here was that services would be more cost effective and responsive to consumer demand if they were competitive which in effect involved replacing "welfare statism" with "welfare pluralism" (Mold and Berridge 2007).[3]

The paradox is that as statutory support for voluntary organizations increased, and was formalized during the 1990s with the introduction of contracts between purchasers and providers, voluntary organizations were transformed into *de facto* agencies of the state that financed them and indirectly determined their policy. It was not politics initially that put the matter on the policy agenda but rather, as Mold and Berridge (2007) suggest, the new forces emergent in drug policy, particularly the new "policy community" of the 1980s. A new "policy community" began to form within the drugs field. There was a shift from a primarily medically oriented policy community to one that included voluntary organizations, researchers, civil servants, and politicians. In the early 1980s, the Standing Conference on Drug Abuse (SCODA) was reporting that while the number of drug users continued to grow, services had failed to expand, which resulted in additional pressure on existing facilities. SCODA and the Advisory Council on the Misuse of Drugs (ACMD) led the body to call for intervention from central government. Thus, in 1982, the Secretary of State for Social Services, Norman Fowler, announced that £2 million would be made available for grants to local authorities and voluntary bodies to provide services for drug users. Initially, the CFI was designed to provide £6 million over three years, but the program was extended in January 1986, partly in response to the discovery of HIV/AIDS among injecting drug users. What was significant about the CFI was the way funds were issued. Grants were made on a pump-priming basis: agencies in receipt of a grant were expected to find alternative sources of funding once the grant came to an end. For voluntary agencies, this meant securing the support of the relevant local authority at the time of application as a way to ensure that when the fixed period of central funding finished, services would not disappear. All of the 14 Regional Health Authorities received some funds, but not equally. Areas thought to have the most extensive drug use (for example, the Thames region and Merseyside) received the most money.

The CFI was a product of "the developing drug problem" in the 1980s but it also exemplified broader changes in health and welfare policy. The CFI prefigured many of its key aspects: central government as the funder but not the provider of services, the increased devolution to local authorities as purchasers of services, and the growing use of nonstatutory organizations in service provision. By encouraging voluntary organizations to deliver the program and shifting the responsibility to evaluate the program to local authorities, the central government reduced its role in the provision of drug services. At the same time, the central government continued to shape and direct the drug policy through its unilateral decisions on the funding for these services. For Mold and Berridge (2007: 44), this is analagous to the so-called "command-and-control tendencies of the Thatcher administration, where the rhetoric of enhancing freedom and choice actually masked a significant degree of centralization." Through their partnership arrangements with the state, voluntary organizations would carry out drug service delivery tasks and secure funding for these services. Their time focused on training volunteers about and getting them involved in the "the drug problem" in a climate of public sector downsizing where more and more responsibilities were shifted onto voluntary organizations.

In one case study on the environment, Perkins (2009) examines three organizations in Milwaukee, namely The Lisbon Avenue Neighborhood Development Corporation (LAND), Greening Milwaukee, and Friends of the Milwaukee River Wisconsin to demonstrate that civil sector groups are stepping up as service providers in face of the downsizing of local government and its municipal environmental labour. According to Perkins, neoliberal orientations to the environment, such as through market deregulation or market expansion, can further exploit and commodify the environment

(2009: 395) and thereby affect the geographies of inner-city environments, such as parks and forests. For example, Milwaukee's Forestry Bureau has become a large bureaucracy within the Department of Public Works; it is composed of managers and skilled and unskilled manual labourers directly accountable to City Hall. Milwaukee County, specifically the Milwaukee Country Park Director, is now in charge of city parks, along with the contributions provided by many skilled and unskilled labourers. These bureaucracies have used tax revenue to produce nearly 6000 hectares of public parks, approximately 200,000 street trees, and 200 kilometres of flowering boulevards during the last 50 years. These public amenities have long contributed to the care and social reproduction of workers and their families by enhancing their living environment. However, like many state restructuring programs, government provisions for forestry and parks programs in Milwaukee are breaking down. There is now less opportunity for public programs to employ municipal labour to maintain urban trees and park spaces, and, over the last decade, there has been a renegotiation concerning government provision for parks and trees. According to the Milwaukee Forestry Bureau manager, the Mayor's Office has cut the Department of Public Works budget to the point where the Forestry Bureau has lost 40 percent of its operating capital since 2003—a reduction of $300,000 annually. The manager has subsequently cut jobs through layoffs and retiree attrition and reduced tree maintenance and plantings.

In Milwaukee, the Forestry Bureau, Parks Department, and other government agencies are frequently assisted by non-profit, voluntary organizations to plan and coordinate green projects in the inner city; they shoulder a considerable amount of responsibility for environmental work. For example, Greening Milwaukee works directly with Milwaukee's Forestry Bureau to extend its ability to enhance tree canopy throughout the city. Park People of Milwaukee County helps to maintain parks and negotiates with the Milwaukee County Parks Department to increase the non-profit's input in parks management. Friends of Milwaukee's Rivers have largely taken over monitoring water quality in Milwaukee from the Wisconsin Department of Natural Resources (Perkins 2009: 395). Although these groups do not hold formal government contracts, their volunteer work is relied upon to get the work done. Members of these groups acknowledge that their reliance on unpaid volunteerism is in part based on the refusal of government agencies to grant them formal, paid contracts. In order to make up for the lack of labourers, voluntary, non-profit organizations are partnering with government agencies to work as unpaid volunteers on environmental projects with paid public employees. Such unpaid volunteerism can supplant the municipal labour force. According to Perkins, partnerships emerge when government diminishes its own municipal labour market and simultaneously generates new market spaces for non-profits and their unpaid volunteer labourers. This exchange is legitimated through the apparent inevitability of neoliberal market rationalities as costly government employees are "necessarily" replaced by non-profit experts and volunteer workers. But the neoliberal downsizing of government is also a material process in that non-profits and volunteers are empowered to negotiate some of the terms under which they contribute to a renewed basis for social and environmental reproduction. For Perkins, consent to neoliberal hegemony through shared governance arrangements fosters two activities: one the one hand, it transfers the cost of environmental service provision away from government; on the other hand, it advocates a neoliberalized basis for social and environmental reproduction through the promotion of active citizenship (2009: 395).

In this study, Perkins examines the role that non-profit organizations play within the region of Walnut Hill, Washington Park, and Midtown. This region is predominantly African-American and, according to the latest census, nearly 43 percent of the neighbourhoods' families live in poverty. LAND is particularly active within the region and its key purpose is to facilitate citizens' committees that work to improve community health. It assists grassroots coalitions as they work toward ameliorating social injustices like crime and hunger and the environmental injustices resulting from exposure to environmental hazards. According to one of the directors for LAND, one must consider the debilitating obstacles to potential greening efforts in these neighbourhoods (i.e., socio-economic constraints) (2009: 399). The effect of a lack of local grassroots activism is compounded by the fact that the city government is withdrawing its direct support for social and environmental service provision in these poor neighbourhoods.

A program put forth by Greening Milwaukee is Urban Nurseries Implementing Training and Education (UNITE). Organized in 1986, the non-profit works with the Forestry Bureau to find ways to enhance canopy cover on public and private property. Greening Milwaukee leases vacant lots in the Lisbon Avenue area from the city for its urban nurseries, which are used to educate and train inner-city and underserved citizens to accomplish the work of planting trees in an urban environment. Greening Milwaukee purchases young trees and its paid coordinator and inner-city volunteers are trained to plant and care for young trees on the lots until the saplings are adopted by residents approximately a year later. The same volunteers then transplant the young trees to their new homes for the residents, and through this process hundreds of well-cared-for trees have been planted on private properties throughout the city. UNITE staff seek to provide residents with life and employment skills that will enable them not only to green their local environment, but also to become more employable within the urban political economy. The program focuses specifically upon inner-city youth becoming voluntary, self-serving agents of change. According to Perkins, the program is an example of professional forms of voluntarism that attempt to steer volunteers away from dependence on public assistance and toward wage labour markets (2009: 401–2). In this regard, partnerships do not promote or encourage volunteers to question the political or economic context from which the organization originated. Citizenship in UNITE, for example, is construed through working hard while not questioning the reasons behind the urban disinvestment they seek to overcome. Such voluntary efforts increasingly "absolve the government from direct intervention in social and environmental service provision for society's poorest citizens" at the same time that they reproduce, according to Perkins, "the culture of human and environmental marginalization via personal accountability" (2009: 403; see Box 5.2 on accountability).

Over the past few decades, various changes to healthcare in liberal, democratic countries, including a reduction in state healthcare workers, continue to create both a higher demand for volunteers and challenges to the voluntary sector. In Canada, the Ontario Health Reform, for example, has created heavy burdens on the voluntary sector which in turn affects disadvantaged groups. Daly (2007) discusses two reforms in Ontario's long-term care provision. The first is the commercialization of home care as a result of the implementation of a "managed competition" delivery model that was market oriented and tied the award of home care contracts to a competitive "request for proposal" The second is the Ministry of Health and Long-Term Care's privileging of "healthcare" over "social care" by mandating which types of home care and home support services meet eligibility requirements for public funding. The current role of non-profits in delivering home care and home support has diminished significantly compared to the previous decade when they were primarily responsible for delivery of non-family supports. By contrast, the state's role has expanded, not only in providing more funding to the sector, but also in determining which organizations can perform what services, mandating the types and nature of services, and reducing the relationship with non-profits from partner to contractor status. With these changes, an increasing number of people are no longer eligible to receive publicly funded home care services and are forced to seek other alternatives, such as drawing on family and friend networks, relying on and hiring private companies, leaving their homes, or entering into a homecare institution.

Beginning in 1990, the government consolidated the administration and funding for long-term care in the Ministry of Health and Long-Term Care, which enabled it to make funding and regulatory changes that reflected its overall goals for the sector. The government created a joint MCSS/MOH Integrated Homemaker Program. It also consolidated MCSS and MOH responsibility for long-term care into a single centralized administrative structure with local area offices. By switching the lead ministry from MCSS to MOH, it reallocated responsibility for long-term care from the municipality to the province. Finally, it created a single ministerial point of access for home and social care services that facilitates multiple regulatory and funding changes. As a result of these efforts, there has been a change in the quantity and type of support available to vulnerable adults and people with disabilities, reflecting a cultural shift away from a social care to a healthcare philosophy. For Daly (2007), basic elements of an individual's social self—cooking, grooming, and

BOX 5.2 ❊ MAKING THE VOLUNTARY SECTOR ACCOUNTABLE

The practices of audit associated with neoliberal restructuring programs within the voluntary sector are particularly evident in various organizations. The Lao Family Community (LFC) in Minneapolis–Saint Paul serves as a good example. This organization receives government funding to provide services to and for the Laotian community. Welfare state restructuring has led to the "offloading" of responsibilities of the state onto the voluntary sector, a process that occurred through the "purchase-of-service contracts" that transfer the responsibility of service provision to non-profit organizations. However, while non-profits have increasingly become responsible for certain provisions, the state continues to control who can receive services, how much they can receive, and for how long they can receive the services. This offloading of responsibility "fosters a leaner state" and enables the development of services that are responsive to local communities' preferences and circumstances. In order for non-profit organizations to monitor service performance, enforce eligibility requirements, and implement sanctions, Trudeau suggests that with these mandates in mind, many organizations draw on business management techniques and employ staff with professional credentials and technical skills specific to organization management and service delivery. These processes of accountability are clearly evident in the LFC case. The organization was encouraged to become a critical part of a larger planned network of social service providers by adopting record-keeping practices that would both allow the organization's work to be evaluated and enable LFC to share information about refugee clients with other social service providers, and by observing its place in the wider network of social service organizations working with refugees. Forming part of a larger network of social service providers meant that the organization would provide services to individuals who were considered eligible according to criteria specified in its service contract. It also meant that the organization would serve a limited part of the refugee population and recruit people to other organizations to receive services. Overall, such mandates call into question the capacity of non-profit organizations, including voluntary organizations, to pursue their charitable agendas and serve as institutions of civil society, and to integrate people as citizens. [Source: Trudeau 2008b].

maintaining a home—are compromised by service cutbacks, redefinitions, and changes. It is an environment of time constraints, increased workloads, and reduced hours of care, despite clients' assessed need, and this contributes to the prioritization of a certain view of health over social care. The upkeep of the home space of the frail elderly and people with disabilities is downloaded to private individual and family responsibility.

As a consequence of Community Care Access Centres (CCAC) expenditure controls imposed in 2003, the levels of service to individuals have dropped. Non-profits note they are facing higher demand and pressure for their services as a result of more CCAC referrals, particularly for individuals on CCAC waiting lists and as a result of existing clients with greater health needs and a higher level of acuity. One interviewee representing Home Support agency, a non-profit organization, expresses how she must make choices: "The people we have couldn't get on [public transportation]. . . . I'd like to be able to . . . take people to more than just doctor appointments. . Like tak[ing] them to the hairdresser or to the . . . cemeteries, or wherever they wanted to go." While overall funding has increased, more demand and higher program costs deflate the benefits of the increases. Furthermore, the voluntary nature of the service requires staff administration to recruit and train volunteers. In addition, the number of volunteers willing to provide an escorted trip to a doctor's office is limited by the uncertain amount of time that people will be required to wait to see the doctor, which in turn restricts the number of available volunteers. In other instances, particularly in rural areas where public transportation is non-existent, drivers, who routinely use their own vehicles, are unable to escort anyone who is not mobile enough to get in and out of the vehicle without assistance (Daly 2007).

A study by Chouinard and Crooks (2008) elucidates a case by Dunway (2004) that demonstrates that British Columbia's deep cuts to home care and home support services starting in 1994 led to ignoring the needs of the elderly population. "People with disabilities, chronically ill, and seniors denied housekeeping assistance are at serious risk of living in unhygienic, unsafe conditions" (Chouinard and Crooks 2008: 177).[4] The authors also illustrate that the restructuring of social programmes by the Ontario Harris government included cutting welfare services by 21.6 percent in 1995 and enforcing tighter restrictions on gaining disability income. The provision of fewer publicly funded home care and home support services translates into higher personal and familial costs and makes it difficult for individuals to continue to live in their communities (Chouinard and Crooks 2008: 177). The result is the recruitment of unpaid work for coordinating, funding, and delivering home care and home support to family and friends. Those left most vulnerable are the ones for whom preventive home care and home supports enabled them to remain in their own homes. Without this kind of assistance, there is often little choice but to leave one's home or become institutionalized in a private care facility; these facilities which are often filled with "chronic home care users" who tend to be older, isolated, and female (Daly 2007).

Using the example of healthcare, Jenkins (2009) problematizes the widespread move towards an increased reliance on voluntary sector provision. In studying women's long-term voluntarism in community development in Lima, Peru, she conceptualizes the privatization of healthcare in two ways: healthcare as a commercial, private sector enterprise, and healthcare to be provided within the private sphere of the home (principally by women) in the face of the introduction of user fees. Using the case study of a Peruvian health promotion project which the author refers to as "Integra," she investigates the long-term voluntary activity of health promoters by studying a clinic in the community of Barrio Alegre. There, voluntary health promoters are responsible for running the clinic, providing medical consultations and laboratory tests, and dispensing drugs from a small pharmacy. Their work is overseen by workers from the NGO, but it is the health promoters who are in charge of the daily operations of the clinic. The promoters also go out into the community to give workshops to groups of women on issues pertaining to sexual and reproductive healthcare. Depending on their responsibilities, the health promoters work between 20 and 40 hours a week and often their work is under-recognized and undervalued (2009: 22–6). While their knowledge, skills, and embeddedness in local networks are vital in ensuring the success of the work they do in the community, these attributes are not framed as valuable or marketable skills, but are instead taken for granted as being naturally the preserve of women. This view therefore facilitates the continued categorization of women's labour as volunteering (as opposed to "work") and the associated lack of remuneration that this labour entails. These issues illustrate a link between voluntarism and gendered critiques of social capital in that there is a tendency for poor women to assume responsibility for social development in the face of government failure to adequately provide welfare services. NGO development projects such as Integra rely on women's long-term, largely voluntary, participation, effectively embracing neoliberal strategies based on self-help and minimal government intervention, and often exploiting the energies of the poorest in society (Jenkins 2009: 26).

Depoliticizing the Voluntary Sector

A "partnership" strategy has been hailed by government and private sectors as a way to influence their ties to voluntary and non-profit organizations and to shape how these organizations operate, implement policies, and carry out their tasks. Voluntary organizations working in such partnerships often face the depoliticization of their social justice activities. For example, the Asia-Pacific Partnership on Clean Development and Climate (APP) was established between the United States and Asian-Pacific states and can be seen as a pioneer of the climate partnership movement. Its partnership was announced in 2005 with seven members (Australia, Canada, China, India, Japan, the Republic of South Korea, and the United States) that include business and civil society actors. The central activity of APP focuses on developing greenhouse gas abatement and clean coal technology (Backstrand 2008: 91), energy efficiency, carbon capture and storage, civilian nuclear power, bio-energy, wind power, and solar power. Another group is The Methane to Market Partnership (M2M) that the US Environmental Protection Agency (EPA) announced in 2004. The purpose of this partnership is to reduce global methane emissions, enhance economic growth, promote energy security, improve air quality, and reduce greenhouse gas emissions. The twenty governments involved in the M2M form a partnership designed to promote public–private collaboration on methane recovery and use, develop methane emission estimates, and identify cost-effective means of receiving methane from energy production. Like APP, M2M extends beyond government partners and builds on the involvement of the private sector, voluntary organizations, NGOs, multilateral development banks, and scientists (Backstrand 2008). The idea of such partnerships is to ensure that participants are thinking in market-oriented terms and working towards a common market goal for energy production; this, in effect, depoliticizes the work of voluntary organizations and their ability to challenge neoliberal orientations to private–public partnerships, and to engage in social justice advocacy and political dialogues.

The influence of neoliberal orientations to and restructuring practices on the environment is critical today. In the field of environmental politics, the line between public and private is becoming increasingly blurred as shifts from state-led implementation of environmental policies to conservation plans are implemented and managed by multi-sectoral networks of governments, the private sector, and environmental non-governmental organizations (ENGOs). Logan and Wekerle examine the privatization and neoliberalization of nature through an examination of land trusts as private conservation initiatives have become part of neoliberal arrangements and partnerships (2008: 2097). According to the Ontario Land Trust Alliance, an umbrella organization for land trusts across Ontario, land trusts are "non-profit, charitable organizations which have as one of their core activities the acquisition of land or interests in land (like conservation easements)" for the purpose of conservation (Logan and Werkele 2008: 2098). Through a case study on the Oak Ridges Moraine in southern Ontario, the authors analyze forms of environmental governance, illustrate the gradual adoption of a discourse of private conservation by government, business, and ENGOs, and examine the multiple contradictions embedded within an approach to ecosystem conservation that relies on partnerships and collaboration among the private, non-profit, and state sectors. In this study, the authors emphasize the forging of relationships between land trusts, environmentalists, private property owners, and state agencies. They reveal how powerful private and state actors utilize concerns for ecological preservation and engage in discourses of partnership to control environmental politics and the establishment of environmental policies (Wekerle 2008: 2098). Thus, such partnerships contribute to the depoliticization of those non-profit voluntary organizations involved in ecosystem conservation as these organizations can find themselves embedded in neoliberal orientations that lean towards the privatization of conservation initiatives.

Advocacy and reform, long an integral part of the voluntary *raison d'être*, are now frequently unwanted or even feared by governments, and efforts to minimize or subvert them are sought through legislation and contractualization. Nevertheless, it is crucial to recognize the importance of spaces occupied by voluntary organizations and their volunteers to campaign for social justice while simultaneously being drawn into neoliberal agendas and related partnerships.

Conclusion

What has been under-recognized in writings on the voluntary sector is how the sector has been forced to take on more and more responsibility for delivering services to disadvantaged groups, compelled to sacrifice its social justice advocacy work and its political dialogue efforts, and bound to operate through partnership relations with the state or private sectors. Under neoliberal public sector downsizing initiatives and downloading of services to the voluntary sector, the transformations in the work of voluntary organizations tells us about how this sector is being shaped by other governing bodies to engage in new ways of developing and delivering its programs and new ways of interacting with disadvantaged and vulnerable groups. These transformations reveal that voluntary organizations are no longer disconnected from the state and not always challenging the government's neoliberal plans and initiatives but are increasingly being brought into forms of service provision.

In this chapter, we have demonstrated that voluntary organizations have provided and continue to provide key services for marginalized and disadvantaged groups throughout the era of neoliberal restructuring and agenda-setting. From the examples presented in this chapter, ranging from environment issues to home care for vulnerable groups, it is evident that voluntary organizations rely very much on stable funding and resources from donors and local or government authorities. Our analysis pays particular attention to the ways in which these organizations are drawn into partnerships with the state and how these partnership relations can encourage more and more voluntary organizations to take on service provision, which can in turn result in the depoliticization of the work of voluntary organizations. Particularly as liberal, western states continue to retreat from the provision of social services, volunteers and voluntary organizations are increasingly called upon by these very same states to deliver a plethora of services. Individual citizens, such as volunteers, are thus made increasingly responsible for the welfare of others. Furthermore, considering the trend of budget cuts and the recent continuation of neoliberal reforms in many countries, several non-profit voluntary organizations will be further weakened by the influential practices of market performance frameworks as discussed in this chapter. These and other similar changes to the voluntary sector raise questions about the ability of this sector to provide key services for marginalized and disadvantaged groups while also engaging in social justice advocacy work.

Notes

1. In 1995, for example, the Canadian right-wing conservative party under the leadership of Mike Harris blamed the welfare state, government regulation, and public spending as contributing to the problem of unemployment. Similar to other conservative governments at the time, the Conservative government in Canada cut back social assistance by 21 percent, reduced municipal grants by 35 percent, eliminated the building of affordable housing units, curtailed support for women's shelters by 30 percent, and disparaged the poor by stating that "welfare recipients would no longer be allowed to shoot their cheques up their arms" (Coulter 2009: 30).
2. This is a multi-million-pound program dedicated toward the provision of services for drug users, particularly those in areas away from London and the Southeast.
3. Historically, voluntary groups had been involved in providing assistance to drug users since the 1960s. While this funding was offered under Section 64 of the Public Health Services and Public Health Act of 1968, it was generally limited to nation-based voluntary bodies. Both SCODA and the Institute for the Study of Drug Dependence (a drugs information service and library), received funding in this fashion. However, in this context, Mold and Berridge (2007: 39) emphasize there were smaller local agencies that often obtained funds on an ad hoc basis but most of them "were chronically underfunded and under the threat of financial collapse."
4. Much like the elderly who are further marginalized through neoliberal reforms, the physically challenged populations have been "forced to try to subsist on the substantially lower rates of income assistance [and] freezes on provincial disability income support rates meant that even those who succeeded in qualifying have faced increasing difficulty purchasing necessities such as shelter and food" (Chouinard and Crooks 2008: 176). Thus, an increasing number of physically challenged people are expected to find employment on their own, simultaneously needing community-based services and support.

Questions for Critical Thought

1. Discuss and explain the key factors that contribute to the decline of the welfare state and thereby to transformations in the lives of particular groups.
2. How did the voluntary sector, including the work of volunteers, change after the decline of the welfare state? Do you view these changes to the voluntary sector as short-term in duration? If so, why? If not, why not?
3. What has been the impact of the voluntary sector on marginalized populations? In what ways can you identify the role that this sector plays in your area or district?
4. Under neoliberal conditions, what kinds of constraints does the voluntary sector face in terms of its ability to advocate on behalf of, or provide services to, disadvantaged groups? Can you identify any disadvantaged groups in your neighbourhood, community, or region that receive assistance or benefit from the advocacy work of voluntary organizations? If so, from your point of view discuss the social justice relevance of this type of advocacy work.
5. From your standpoint, what role do you see public servants, professional experts, and practitioners playing in the discussions of issues relevant to the voluntary sector in Canada?

Annotated Additional Readings

Rachel Laforest, ed. 2009. *The New Federal Policy Agenda and the Voluntary Sector: On the Cutting Edge* (Public Policy and the Third Sector). Kingston: School of Policy Studies Queen's University. This book brings together contributions by Canadian experts to examine the shifting relationship between the federal government and the voluntary sector. Taking into account the new policy context set by the Conservatives after a decade of the Liberals in power, it discusses how the role of the voluntary sector in policy is being reassessed, and how the funding and organization of services and of political representation is being transformed. Topics include debates in key policy areas such as: relationship building, funding infrastructure, citizenship building, urban issues, and social economy. This collection of papers is based on the Seventh Annual National Forum of the Initiative, held 20–21 October 2006, which brought together public servants, experts, and practitioners to discuss the place of the voluntary sector in the New Federal Policy Agenda.

Susan Phillips and Steven R. Smith, eds. 2011. *Governance and Regulation in the Third Sector: International Perspectives*. London: Routledge. The book brings together scholars and experienced practitioners from different countries to investigate the relationship between regulation and relational governance for the third sector in a comparative context. Each chapter reviews recent regulatory changes in the country in question. The book reveals the gap between theory and reality, and the chapters explore critical challenges for regulatory reform for the third sector.

Related Websites

CUSO-VSO North America
www.cuso-vso.org/about-cuso-vso

International Volunteer Day for Economic and Social Development
www.timeanddate.com/holidays/un/international-volunteer-day

The Alliance of European Voluntary Service Organizations
www.alliance-network.eu

Voluntary Sector Initiative Impact Evaluation: Lessons Learned from the Voluntary Sector Initiative (2000–2005)
www.hrsdc.gc.ca/eng/publications_resources/evaluation/2009/sp_946_04_10e/page05.shtml

6 Human Rights: The Challenge of Universal Protection

Learning Objectives

- Understand similarities and differences between citizenship rights and human rights
- Explore human rights principles and instruments
- Question the presumed universality of human rights
- Assess the power of the human rights regime to influence change at the national level
- Recognize how human rights norms inspire, legitimize, and advance social activism

Introduction

> At one end of the complex continuum, we can see international human rights being manipulated by the world's most powerful states and economic actors to their own ends while, at the other end, we find social movements using the international system of human rights in attempts to open up new challenges to power in all sorts of different ways, all over the world. Between these lie a range of practices which are complex, multifaceted and ambiguous (Stammers 2009: 116).

In the previous chapters we have discussed how citizenship, as an expression and practice of social inclusion, ends up excluding certain groups of people "from within" and "from without." We have also discussed how social citizenship has been eroded under neoliberal agendas and policies. Finally, we have examined the extent to which voluntary organizations can address the needs of disadvantaged people and advance their rights. In this chapter, we turn our critical gaze to human rights norms and institutions. The main question we ask in this section is whether the human rights regime is capable of addressing the protection gaps (re)created by national states.

Like Western conceptions of citizenship rights, the notions of human rights are rooted in the idea of natural rights as "inalienable rights of man," as first elaborated by the Enlightenment era philosophers. As discussed in Chapter 3, with the advance of nation-states in the Western world, these ideals were translated into the concept of citizenship. As the notions of rights, citizenship, and nation-state became interwoven, the state assumed the responsibility of defining rights eligibility and content, as well as the specific ways these rights were to be guaranteed. In other words, it was up to nation-states to define who was eligible for what kinds of rights and which institutions were to deliver specific rights and protect citizens from their denial and abuse. However, by the end of the Second World War, it had become clear that in many instances the nation-state had failed to protect its citizens from rights violations perpetrated by other states or citizens and, in other instances, that nation-states had been responsible for these violations. Much of the impetus behind the establishment of the principles of universal human rights at the international level can be attributed to the world's outrage over the Nazi regime's perpetration of such atrocities as enslavement, torture, and genocide. In an effort to protect the world from such crimes against humanity, the UN Charter, also known as the Charter of the United Nations, was drawn up in 1945. This Charter is the international community's written constitution and, as such, it outlines the basic principles that promote international cooperation and a commitment to respecting the human rights and fundamental freedoms of all members of humankind. A few years later, on 9 December 1948, the UN General Assembly approved the Convention on the Prevention and Punishment of the Crime of Genocide. On the very next day, the UN General Assembly adopted and proclaimed the Universal Declaration of Human Rights (Kallen 2004: 14).

Like citizenship rights discussed in Chapter 3, the human rights elaborated in the Universal Declaration on Human Rights (hereafter UDHR), and the treaties and declarations that followed it, identify **civil**, **political**, and **social rights** (see Table 6.1 for a list of the nine core UN human rights treaties). In addition, labour rights are addressed by International Labour Office (ILO) conventions (see Table 6.2 for a list of major ILO conventions). The **rights to culture** (or "the set of distinctive spiritual, material, intellectual and emotional features of society or a social group" that encompass "in addition to art and literature, lifestyles, ways of living together, value systems, traditions and beliefs") are enshrined in the 2001 UNESCO Universal Declaration on Cultural Diversity, although the defence of cultural diversity is subordinated to other human rights (Goodale 2009: 79). As can be seen, human rights principles address all three aspects of social inclusion discussed in Chapter 2, namely, provision of protections, benefits, and rights; political participation, and respect for cultural diversity.

While the content of rights is, in many ways, the same for citizenship and human rights, the rules of inclusion in the community of people who can claim these rights (or frames of representation, to use Fraser's terminology as discussed in Chapter 2) are different. The set of principles expressed in UDHR and its related treaties is meant to apply universally to all human beings merely by virtue of their membership in humankind. The significance of UDHR is that it represents "the first international authoritative affirmation that all humans are human" (Teeple 2005: 139). In comparison with citizenship rights, which apply to those persons recognized as members of nation-states, universal human rights intend to be all-inclusive. Such intentions are, however, not always practised on the ground in the same way. In this chapter we will question whether UN treaties offer universal protections. First, we will discuss

THE UNIVERSAL DECLARATION OF Human Rights

WHEREAS *recognition of the inherent dignity and of the equal and inalienable rights of all members of the human family is the foundation of freedom, justice and peace in the world,*

WHEREAS *disregard and contempt for human rights have resulted in barbarous acts which have outraged the conscience of mankind, and the advent of a world in which human beings shall enjoy freedom of speech and belief and freedom from fear and want has been proclaimed as the highest aspiration of the common people,*

WHEREAS *it is essential, if man is not to be compelled to have recourse, as a last resort, to rebellion against tyranny and oppression, that human rights should be protected by the rule of law,*

WHEREAS *it is essential to promote the development of friendly relations among nations,*

WHEREAS *the peoples of the United Nations have in the Charter reaffirmed their faith in fundamental human rights, in the dignity and worth of the human person and in the equal rights of men and women and have determined to promote social progress and better standards of life in larger freedom,*

WHEREAS *Member States have pledged themselves to achieve, in co-operation with the United Nations, the promotion of universal respect for and observance of human rights and fundamental freedoms,*

WHEREAS *a common understanding of these rights and freedoms is of the greatest importance for the full realisation of this pledge,*

NOW THEREFORE THE GENERAL ASSEMBLY

PROCLAIMS *this Universal Declaration of Human Rights as a common standard of achievement for all peoples and all nations, to the end that every individual and every organ of society, keeping this Declaration constantly in mind, shall strive by teaching and education to promote respect for these rights and freedoms and by progressive measures, national and international, to secure their universal and effective recognition and observance, both among the peoples of Member States themselves and among the peoples of territories under their jurisdiction.*

ARTICLE 1 —All human beings are born free and equal in dignity and rights. They are endowed with reason and conscience and should act towards one another in a spirit of brotherhood.

ARTICLE 2 —1. Everyone is entitled to all the rights and freedoms set forth in this Declaration, without distinction of any kind, such as race, colour, sex, language, religion, political or other opinion, national or social origin, property, birth or other status.

2. Furthermore, no distinction shall be made on the basis of the political, jurisdictional or international status of the country or territory to which a person belongs, whether this territory be an independent, Trust or Non-Self-Governing territory, or under any other limitation of sovereignty.

ARTICLE 3 —Everyone has the right to life, liberty and the security of person.

ARTICLE 4 —No one shall be held in slavery or servitude; slavery and the slave trade shall be prohibited in all their forms.

ARTICLE 5 —No one shall be subjected to torture or to cruel, inhuman or degrading treatment or punishment.

ARTICLE 6 —Everyone has the right to recognition everywhere as a person before the law.

ARTICLE 7 —All are equal before the law and are entitled without any discrimination to equal protection of the law. All are entitled to equal protection against any discrimination in violation of this Declaration and against any incitement to such discrimination.

ARTICLE 8 —Everyone has the right to an effective remedy by the competent national tribunals for acts violating the fundamental rights granted him by the constitution or by law.

ARTICLE 9 —No one shall be subjected to arbitrary arrest, detention or exile.

ARTICLE 10 —Everyone is entitled in full equality to a fair and public hearing by an independent and impartial tribunal, in the determination of his rights and obligations and of any criminal charge against him.

ARTICLE 11 —1. Everyone charged with a penal offence has the right to be presumed innocent until proved guilty according to law in a public trial at which he has had all the guarantees necessary for his defence.

2. No one shall be held guilty of any penal offence on account of any act or omission which did not constitute a penal offence, under national or international law, at the time when it was committed. Nor shall a heavier penalty be imposed than the one that was applicable at the time the penal offence was committed.

ARTICLE 12 —No one shall be subjected to arbitrary interference with his privacy, family, home or correspondence, nor to attacks upon his honour and reputation. Everyone has the right to the protection of the law against such interference or attacks.

ARTICLE 13 —1. Everyone has the right to freedom of movement and residence within the borders of each state.

2. Everyone has the right to leave any country, including his own, and to return to his country.

ARTICLE 14 —1. Everyone has the right to seek and to enjoy in other countries asylum from persecution.

2. This right may not be invoked in the case of prosecutions genuinely arising from non-political crimes or from acts contrary to the purposes and principles of the United Nations.

ARTICLE 15 —1. Everyone has the right to a nationality.

2. No one shall be arbitrarily deprived of his nationality nor denied the right to change his nationality.

ARTICLE 16 —1. Men and women of full age, without any limitation due to race, nationality or religion, have the right to marry and to found a family. They are entitled to equal rights as to marriage, during marriage and at its dissolution.

2. Marriage shall be entered into only with the free and full consent of the intending spouses.

3. The family is the natural and fundamental group unit of society and is entitled to protection by society and the State.

ARTICLE 17 —1. Everyone has the right to own property alone as well as in association with others.

2. No one shall be arbitrarily deprived of his property.

ARTICLE 18 —Everyone has the right to freedom of thought, conscience and religion; this right includes freedom to change his religion or belief, and freedom, either alone or in community with others and in public or private, to manifest his religion or belief in teaching, practice, worship and observance.

ARTICLE 19 —Everyone has the right to freedom of opinion and expression; this right includes freedom to hold opinions without interference and to seek, receive and impart information and ideas through any media and regardless of frontiers.

ARTICLE 20 —1. Everyone has the right to freedom of peaceful assembly and association.

2. No one may be compelled to belong to an association.

ARTICLE 21 —1. Everyone has the right to take part in the government of his country, directly or through freely chosen representatives.

2. Everyone has the right of equal access to public service in his country.

3. The will of the people shall be the basis of the authority of government; this will shall be expressed in periodic and genuine elections which shall be by universal and equal suffrage and shall be held by secret vote or by equivalent free voting procedures.

ARTICLE 22 —Everyone, as a member of society, has the right to social security and is entitled to realisation, through national effort and international co-operation and in accordance with the organisation and resources of each State, of the economic, social and cultural rights indispensable for his dignity and the free development of his personality.

ARTICLE 23 —1. Everyone has the right to work, to free choice of employment, to just and favourable conditions of work and to protection against unemployment.

2. Everyone, without any discrimination, has the right to equal pay for equal work.

3. Everyone who works has the right to just and favourable remuneration insuring for himself and his family an existence worthy of human dignity, and supplemented, if necessary, by other means of social protection.

4. Everyone has the right to form and to join trade unions for the protection of his interests.

ARTICLE 24 —Everyone has the right to rest and leisure, including reasonable limitation of working hours and periodic holidays with pay.

ARTICLE 25 —1. Everyone has the right to a standard of living adequate for the health and well-being of himself and of his family, including food, clothing, housing and medical care and necessary social services, and the right to security in the event of unemployment, sickness, disability, widowhood, old age or other lack of livelihood in circumstances beyond his control.

2. Motherhood and childhood are entitled to special care and assistance. All children, whether born in or out of wedlock, shall enjoy the same social protection.

ARTICLE 26 —1. Everyone has the right to education. Education shall be free, at least in the elementary and fundamental stages. Elementary education shall be compulsory. Technical and professional education shall be made generally available and higher education shall be equally accessible to all on the basis of merit.

2. Education shall be directed to the full development of the human personality and to the strengthening of respect for human rights and fundamental freedoms. It shall promote understanding, tolerance and friendship among all nations, racial or religious groups, and shall further the activities of the United Nations for the maintenance of peace.

3. Parents have a prior right to choose the kind of education that shall be given to their children.

ARTICLE 27 —1. Everyone has the right freely to participate in the cultural life of the community, to enjoy the arts and to share in scientific advancement and its benefits.

2. Everyone has the right to the protection of the moral and material interests resulting from any scientific, literary or artistic production of which he is the author.

ARTICLE 28 —Everyone is entitled to a social and international order in which the rights and freedoms set forth in this Declaration can be fully realized.

ARTICLE 29 —1. Everyone has duties to the community in which alone the free and full development of his personality is possible.

2. In the exercise of his rights and freedoms, everyone shall be subject only to such limitations as are determined by law solely for the purpose of securing due recognition and respect for the rights and freedoms of others and of meeting the just requirements of morality, public order and the general welfare in a democratic society.

3. These rights and freedoms may in no case be exercised contrary to the purposes and principles of the United Nations.

ARTICLE 30 —Nothing in this Declaration may be interpreted as implying for any State, group or person any right to engage in any activity or to perform any act aimed at the destruction of any of the rights and freedoms set forth herein.

UNITED NATIONS

FIGURE 6.1 The Universal Declaration of Human Rights

Source: T/K

Table 6.1 United Nations Core Human Rights Conventions and Parties: 1950–2011

Name of Convention	Treaty-based Monitoring Bodies	Date Established	Status
International Convention on the Elimination of All Forms of Racial Discrimination (ICERD)	Committee on the Elimination of Racial Discrimination (CERD)	7 Mar 1966	174 parties
International Covenant on Civil and Political Rights (ICCPR)	Human Rights Committee (CCPR)	16 Dec 1966	167 parties
International Covenant on Economic, Social and Cultural Rights (ICESCR)	Committee on Economic, Social and Cultural Rights (CESCR)	16 Dec 1966	160 parties
Convention on the Elimination of All Forms of Discrimination against Women (CEDAW)	Committee on the Elimination of Discrimination against Women (CEDAW)	18 Dec 1979	816 parties
Convention against Torture and Other Cruel, Inhuman or Degrading Treatment or Punishment (CAT)	Committee against Torture (CAT)	10 Dec 1984	147 parties
Convention on the Rights of the Child (CRC)	Committee on the Rights of the Child (CRC)	20 Nov 1989	193 parties
International Convention on the Protection of the Rights of All Migrant Workers and Members of Their Families (ICRMW)	Committee on Migrant Workers (CMW)	18 Dec 1990	44 parties
Convention on the Rights of Persons with Disabilities (CRPD)	Committee on the Rights of Persons with Disabilities (CRPD)	13 Dec 2006	99 parties
International Convention for the Protection of All Persons from Enforced Disappearance (CPED)	Committee on Enforced Disappearance (CED)	20 Dec 2006	27 parties

Source: http://treaties.un.org/pages/ParticipationStatus.aspx, accessed online 31 March 2011; and www2.ohchr.org/english/law/index.htm, accessed online 17 June 2011.

Note: **"Parties"** refers to states (and other entities) with treaty-making capacity that have agreed to be bound by a treaty that is in force and applies to them.

Table 6.2 International Labour Organization (ILO): Fundamental Conventions: 1919–2011

Name of Convention	Year Adopted	Countries Ratified
Forced Labour Convention (no. 29)	1930	175
Freedom of Association and Protection of the Right to Organise Convention (no. 87)	1948	150
Right to Organise and Collective Bargaining Convention (no. 98)	1949	160
Equal Remuneration Convention (no. 100)	1951	168
Abolition of Forced Labour Convention (no. 105)	1957	169
Discrimination (Employment and Occupation) Convention (no. 111)	1958	169
Minimum Age Convention (no. 138)	1973	160
Worst Forms of Child Labour Convention (no. 182)	1999	174

Source: This elaboration is based on: www.ilo.org/ilolex/english/subjectE.htm and www.ilo.org/ilolex/english/index.htm, accessed on 17 June 2011.

exclusions "from within" the human rights regime. We will ask the following questions: Are the rights of workers and economically disadvantaged people protected as much as the rights of the corporate elites? Stated differently, are social and economic rights accorded the same status as civil and political rights? Are cultural differences recognized by so-called "universal" human rights standards? Are the rights of women protected as equally as men's? Are children's rights fully acknowledged? Are the collective rights of Aboriginal peoples recognized on par with the individual rights enshrined in core human rights instruments? Then we will explore exclusions "from without" by asking whether the rights of non-status people (or those persons found to reside without authorization in the territories of nation-states) are protected. Finally, we will explore the extent to which the principles and institutions of human rights can be employed to address and correct deficiencies in the provision and protection of **citizenship rights**. In other words, we will examine the power of the human rights regime to institute change at the national level. We will draw particular attention to the role of social activism, inspired by and drawing from the language of human rights, in bringing about social change.

Protecting the "Social" in Human Rights?

Since its inception, the human rights regime has been plagued by an unresolved tension between social and economic rights, on the one hand, and civic and political rights on the other. In the negotiation of the principles of the UDHR, the former Soviet Union insisted on the inclusion of economic and social rights (such as the right to fair employment and social provisions). While Western capitalist countries were primarily interested in the protection of civil rights (such as the rights of private property and the freedom of expression) as well as political rights (the right to participate in democratically run political processes), they did not resist the inclusion of social and economic rights in the UDHR. After all, the Declaration was meant to be more of a guide than an enforceable agreement to action (Teeple 2007: 139; see also Basok, Ilcan, and Noonan 2006). Consequently, UDHR contains Article 25, which states, "Everyone has the right to a standard of living adequate for the health and well-being of himself and of his family, including food, clothing, housing and medical care and necessary social services, and the right to security in the event of unemployment, sickness, disability, widowhood, old age or other lack of livelihood in circumstances beyond his control." This right is particularly important for economically disadvantaged people who, without state support, would not have access to these valuable protections and provisions. Workers' rights (such as the right to work and have just and favourable conditions of work, protection against unemployment, equal pay for equal work, just and favourable remuneration, and the right to form and join trade unions) are protected in Article 22 (www.un.org/en/documents/udhr).

While the UDHR itself is not designed to be enacted and enforced, but rather to be recognized and referred to as a declaration of intention and a reference, the treaties that followed, such as the International Covenant on Civil and Political Rights and the International Covenant on Economic, Social and Cultural Rights, on the other hand, were designed for enactment and enforcement by those countries that ratify them (Teeple 2007: 139). Thus, it may appear that the international law recognizes both social and economic rights as well as civil and political rights. This recognition, however, is deceptive. From the very onset, social and economic rights have been assigned a second-class status despite resistance from former socialist countries and some countries of the Global South (Teeple 2005; Evans 2011; Chong 2009). Under US pressure, more concrete normative obligations and stronger monitoring mechanisms have been reserved for civil and political rights. For example, the ICCPR envisioned the immediate enforcement of civil and political rights, creating a dedicated UN committee to monitor compliance (under Article 28). At the same time, the ICESCR merely required states to "take steps" with their "available resources" to "progressively" realize these rights. Civil and political rights have been adopted in dozens of national constitutions while economic and social rights have been ignored or downgraded in national constitutions as more vague "directive principles" (Chong 2009: 112–13). Thus, as can be clearly seen, social and economic rights of workers and economically disadvantaged people are subordinated to civil and political rights.

Moreover, certain civil rights (such as the protection of private property) lead to the violation of social and economic rights. For example, civil rights protect the right of corporations to move freely across borders and to engage in practices that pollute environments and exploit and repress labour or, in other words, violate social rights (Teeple 2007). Under the conditions of neoliberalism, global market expansion has resulted in the deterioration of social and economic rights of workers and disadvantaged people (Falk 2002). As a result of neoliberal policies adopted by countries of the Global South, women and girls, in particular, have lost jobs, pensions, health insurance and maternity rights, the right to rest and leisure, the right to adequate standards of living, and the right to education despite the fact that these rights are recognized in Articles 23, 24, 25, and 26 of the Universal Declaration (Elson 2002).

Today states find it increasingly difficult to guarantee the social and economic rights of workers and the poor in a globalized era in which transnational corporations and supranational frameworks hold so much power (Teeple 2005 and 2007; Evans 2011; De Gaay Fortman 2011). Instead of exercising their sovereign right to legislate according to citizens' and national interests, national states have succumbed to demands, conditions, recommendations, and rules and regulations from supra-national bodies, such as the World Trade Organization (WTO), the International Monetary Fund (IMF), the World Bank (WB), and multi-national trade agreements such as the North American

Free Trade Agreement (NAFTA). Gary Teeple (2005) draws attention to the challenges ordinary citizens face in resisting the disproportionate power of transnational corporations (TNCs):

> With limited political, economic, or legal leverage against the pre-eminence of global corporate rights, the non-corporate sectors do not have the same means of exacting countervailing social rights or civil and political rights that they have at the national level. And there is no reason why TNCs, with assets and revenues many times greater than most of the world's national states, would agree to share power and the global social product via a politically determined means that would include representation of the interests of subordinate groups (Teeple 2005: 153).

Tony Evans (2011) goes as far as to argue that under neoliberal globalization, the human rights architecture has lost its relevance. He observes that the interests of the global political economy (e.g., freedoms associated with property, including intellectual and investment rights) are consistently privileged over humanitarian objectives:

> Within the context of economic globalization, the central policy objectives of economic growth and development cannot be achieved without the state cooperating with the private interests of non-state actors, including large transnational corporations and international trade and financial institutions. Given the focus of economic development that these new relationships are supposed to foster, and the potential for a state's human rights obligations to be compromised, it remains unclear whether humanitarian interests can be secured within this context (Evans 2011: 92).

Pessimistically, Evans concludes that human rights are embraced only insofar as they support the economic objectives of corporations (2011: 100). The recently developed partnership between the UN and global corporations illustrates how the human rights regime has been employed by corporations to pursue their economic interests. In an address to the World Economic Forum in Davos, Switzerland, on 31 January 1999, the former Secretary-General (SG) of the United Nations, Kofi Annan, invited business leaders to join an international initiative, the Global Compact. The Global Compact brings companies together with UN agencies, labour organizations, and civil society groups to support universal environmental and social principles. Following Annan's speech, the UN established the Office for the Global Compact. The aim of the Global Compact is the promotion of "responsible global corporate citizenship." It is premised on ten principles including human rights, labour issues, the environment, and anticorruption. To register its membership with the Global Compact Office, a corporation has to commit itself to filing an annual report that details actions taken by this corporation to satisfy these principles during the preceding twelve months. Advocates of the Global Compact see this initiative as an opportunity for global corporations to demonstrate their concern for human rights publicly. Yet, critics are pessimistic of the role of global corporations in this regard. They point out that as long as corporations provide evidence of some concern for the environment and commitment to promote some human rights, then injustices, violations of other human rights, and gross inequalities are tolerated. This concern is seen as a means for corporations to conceal their poor record of complicity in human rights violations by legitimating their actions through the offices of the United Nations (Evans 2011: 108). Critics call this practice "blue-washing" (referring to the colour of the UN flag).

One of the critics of Global Compact is the Alliance for a Corporate-Free UN, a global network of human rights, environment, and development groups that work to address "undue corporate influence" in the UN and to hold corporations accountable on issues of human rights, labour rights, and the environment. Corpwatch serves as the Alliance secretariat. It openly questions this new relationship between the UN and corporations, and expresses concern that the Global Compact may be "threatening the integrity of the UN." CorpWatch finds it particularly disturbing that leaders of corporations that are known for fostering exploitative working conditions in sweatshops, environmental pollution, and supporting political repression, sat at the same table as the UN Secretary-General. It is concerned that there is no mechanism to enforce adherence to the Compact's principles and that this arrangement undermines the UN's potential for demanding corporate accountability (Gasser 2007: 16).

Respect for Cultural Diversity?

One of the concerns raised by the critics of the human rights regime has been its Western bias. It has been suggested that if applied to non-Western countries, human rights principles may destroy local cultures. While some of these claims may have been overstated, they have helped raise awareness about the cultural dimensions of human rights. The cultural critique of the presumed "universality" of human rights has come from different camps, including some non-Western countries and some anthropologists. Although their arguments (and the rationale behind them) have been different, their main premises are shared. They maintain that UDHR and other treaties reflect Western values that leave out important cultural traditions of the non-Western world; likewise, they argue that moral standards cannot be universal but should be relative to cultural values and practices.

Some leaders of Southeast Asian and South Asian countries (particularly Singapore, the People's Republic of China, and Malaysia) have asserted that "Asian values" (inspired by Asian religions) are incompatible with the supposedly universal framework of human rights, particularly with regard to family matters (Kallen 2004: 23). Yet other analysts of international human rights have responded to this position with a degree of scepticism. It has been pointed out that these countries often use cultural arguments to justify political repression and violation of the rights of disadvantaged groups. Of particular concern to many human rights analysts is the fact that women's rights are often disputed by those who claim to defend "culture" in nationalistic terms. Those who stand to lose patriarchal privileges fear that if women are guaranteed certain rights then established hierarchies will be destabilized. As Merry observes, "thinking of culture as national essence provides governments with an excuse not to intervene more energetically to protect human rights since they can defend their resistance as the protection of the national identity" (Merry 2006: 14). Many analysts also contend that the argument in favour of the uniqueness of "Asian values" was used by repressive states to justify authoritarianism and the denial of rights to workers and other activists (Goodale 2009: 53; Teeple 2005: 28–9; Evans 2011: 78–80). Still, today, some of these states use the "Asian values" argument to stifle and constrain claims to human rights advanced by some activists (see, for example, Elias 2008). Furthermore, it has been noted that such critics of the West as Gandhi, Nkrumah, Ho Chi Minh, and the leaders of a number of non-Western states were among the strongest supporters of the inclusion of the commitment to human rights in the UN Charter. In addition, several Latin American states contributed to the UDHR and their delegates were among strong supporters of the social and economic provisions of this declaration (Stammers 2009: 117).

Some anthropologists (known as "relativists") also reject the universalism of values and insist that the tolerance of cultural differences is more important than the imposition of universal standards (discussed in Merry 2006: 8–9; Goodale 2009; see also Chapter 3). In response to this position, other anthropologists point out that the relativists view culture as static and inflexible. They insist that if culture is understood as "historically produced in particular locations under the influence of local, national, and global forces and events" (Merry 2006: 11), it is not incompatible with human rights. According to this conception, cultures consist of repertoires of ideas, values, and beliefs, as well as practices, habits, institutional arrangements, political structures, and legal regulations. These ideas and practices are not homogeneous but rather reflect many contradictions. They are constantly changing as old ideas and practices are replaced by new ones. They reflect power relations in a society and are used to justify and perpetuate them. In turn, these cultural discourses and practices are contested by those who feel disadvantaged. In addition, they are open to new ideas and influences from other cultures (Merry 2006: 11, 15). When the notion of culture is seen as contested and as a mode of legitimating claims to power and authority, arguments made against human rights in favour of the preservation of "cultural values" are no longer compelling (Cowan, Dembour, and Wilson 2001: 4–15).

Despite the critique of the "Asian values" and "cultural relativist" positions, for many writers local cultures play a very important role in the definition and application of human rights. Cultures can be viewed as a context that defines and constrains the possibilities of action (Merry 2006: 9; Goodale 2009: 90). Thus, to be effective, human rights norms and principles have to be "translated" into the local language or "vernacularized" (Merry 2006). The human rights framework that ignores cultural differences may end up doing more harm than good. Box 6.1, for example, illustrates the importance of locally relevant framing in the human rights campaign to end "female genital mutilation" (FGM). As discussed in this box, in several African countries, a health frame has been found to be more effective than a human rights frame for anti-FGM campaigns because of local customs; as such, both types of discourses have often been combined by local activists.

Gender Bias: A Feminist Critique

Since the end of the Second World War, women's rights have received increasing recognition and acceptance as a human rights issue. More than 20 international declarations and conventions specific to women have been established and ratified over the past six decades, the most significant of which include the 1979 Convention on the Elimination of Discrimination against Women (CEDAW) and the 1993 Vienna Declaration on the Elimination of All Forms of Violence against Women. Since the signing of these two instruments, UN human rights agencies have demonstrated a greater awareness of the gender dimensions of human rights violations in general, and violence against women, in particular, in the work of their treaty bodies. Women's participation in UN human rights review and reporting mechanisms (Gaer 2001: 101–104) has also increased. This progress can be largely attributed to the tireless work of the UN Commission on the Status of Women (see Box 6.2) and international activists.

In spite of these important achievements, many analysts argue that international human rights instruments do not guarantee equity for women. Recognizing that language plays a fundamental role in shaping our visions and practices, gender equity cannot be achieved if international law continues to use gendered language. Despite the efforts of women's rights advocates to ensure that the UDHR and the UN Charter were drafted using gender-inclusive language (Teeple 2005), feminists continue to criticize universal human rights as possessing a dominant discourse which is (and always has been) male centred (Kaufman and Lindquist 1995). Gendered language is used in many human rights instruments, such as the UDHR, in such a way that it augments the interests of men and assumes a subservient social, economic, or political

BOX 6.1 ❊ THE LOCAL-GLOBAL NEXUS IN THE "ANTI-FEMALE GENITAL MUTILATION" CAMPAIGN

Since the 1970s, international activists, primarily Western feminists, have worked to eliminate Female Genital Mutilation (FGM), which they see as violence against women, as well as women's lack of control over their own bodies, and women's social and sexual disempowerment. The international anti-FGM human rights campaign has been fuelled by discussions, resolutions, and declarations advanced at the UN level. In 1990, the UN Committee on the Elimination of Discrimination against Women adopted General Recommendation no. 14 which formally expressed concern over Female Genital Mutilation and called for its eradication. This position was reaffirmed in 1993 when the UN Declaration on the Elimination of Violence against Women made an explicit reference to FGM as a form of violence against women. However, this human rights frame clashed with the discourses advanced by local activists.

In Africa, local activists have traditionally preferred to organize their anti-FGM campaigns around a health frame which educates people about FGM's short- and long-term health consequences for women and girls, including extreme pain, bleeding, shock, tetanus, sepsis, infections, scarring, infertility, and an increased risk of infant and maternal mortality in childbirth. The human rights anti-FGM advocacy was resisted locally in the name of cultural tradition, as well as suspicion of cultural and religious imperialism. However, while the health frame avoided issues of cultural and religious imperialism, it also led to the medicalization of the practice in some cases, leaving the underlying gender discrimination issue unchallenged.

Because of these tensions, a mixed health and human rights frame for anti-FGM campaigns has been used more widely since the late 1990s in an effort to appeal to the international community without alienating local people. Generally, such mixed campaigns include a non-coercive and nonjudgmental approach, calling attention to the harmfulness of FGM to women's health and encouraging collective commitments and public declarations to abandon the practice. (Source: Baer and Brysk 2009).

role for women in relation to men (Evans 2011). Article 1 of the UDHR, for example, calls for human beings to "act towards one another in the spirit of *brotherhood*"; Article 11.1 provides that "he has had all the guarantees necessary for his defence" during trials; and Article 5 excludes women from protection under the national constitution when it says that "the right to an effective remedy by the competent national tribunal for acts violating the fundamental

Box 6.2 ❋ The UN Commission on the Status of Women: Advancing Women's Rights

Much of the progress with respect to women's human rights can be traced back to the establishment of the UN Commission of the Status of Women (CSW) in 1946. Since its inception, this full, free-standing women's commission was given the power to make recommendations on women's rights and submit these directly to the UN Economic and Social Council (ECOSOC) and the UN General Assembly. During the drafting of the Universal Declaration of Human Rights (UDHR), CSW members, delegates, and female activists made their voices heard on the wording which was to be used. They insisted that the "rights of men" and use of the term "men" in the document was outdated and could be interpreted to exclude women. As a result, the relatively gender-neutral term "everyone" was used extensively (though not exclusively) throughout the UDHR.

CSW has also promoted a series of World Women's Conferences, such as the 1975 International Women's Year Conference in Mexico City (followed by the UN the Decade for Women), the 1980 UN World Women's Conference in Copenhagen, the 1985 Third World Women's Conference in Nairobi, Kenya, and the 1995 World Conference on Women in Beijing, China. All of these conferences have been central to raising international awareness about women's equality rights and sex discrimination. Likewise, they stimulated the establishment of local and international networks of women interested in rights advocacy. (Sources: Fraser 2001; Merry 2006; Gaer 2001; Teeple, 2005).

rights granted him by the constitution of the law" (emphasis added, cited in Evans 2011: 33). Furthermore, the Declaration assigns women a subservient role to men in social, economic, and political life when it repeatedly talks of the rights of men and *their families*, thus turning women into the appendages of their husbands in a family. It should be noted that the family—defined as a heterosexual couple and their children—is presented by UDHR as the "national and fundamental group unit of society" (Evans 2011: 33).

The second fundamental problem is the distinction made in international law between the **public sphere** (such as work and politics), dominated by men and protected by human rights instruments, and the **private sphere** (or family), reserved for women and left legally unprotected (see, for example, Kaufman and Lindquist 1995; Teeple 2005; Evans 2011). This public-sphere bias has led some feminists to consider international law to be an active participant in women's oppression (Evans 2011: 34). It is in this way, then, that human rights frameworks contradict proclamations of women's equality of human rights when the nuclear family, as "a social unit outside of economic relations but dependent on those relations—the site of exploitation of unpaid labour and of women's dependence on men, and the source of the rationale for unequal pay and treatment in the workforce—is deemed natural and to be protected" (Teeple 2005: 57). Finally, there is a fundamental contradiction in the fact that, by protecting the institution of the family, cultural autonomy, and **state sovereignty** (the right and power of national states to regulate their internal affairs without foreign interference), international human rights law upholds local customs, religious canons, and national laws, all of which commonly violate women's rights (see, for example: Nash 2002; Merry 2006; Molyneux and Razavi 2002; Teeple 2005).

Are Children's Rights Fully Protected?

The idea of children's human rights is a relatively new development in the expansion of the human rights framework. Although a non-binding UN Declaration of the Rights of the Child was created in 1959, it wasn't until the drafting and broad ratification of the UN Convention on the Rights of the Child (CRC) in 1989, followed by the adoption of the International Labour Organization's Convention on the Elimination of the Worst Forms of Child Labour in 1999 (see Tables 6.1 and 6.2), that persons under the age of eighteen became legally recognized as rights-holding individuals and were no longer considered the legal possession of their parents, guardians, or the state (Teeple 2005: 59–60, 62; Grugel and Piper 2007: 112).

Under CRC, children are entitled to a name, nationality, culture, identity, shelter, education, adequate food and clean water, expression, and association. They are also entitled to develop and participate in decisions which affect their well-being and to receive state protection from exploitation, abuse, neglect, and violence. In laying out children's well-being and welfare as a question of objective entitlements, CRC contributed to limiting the wide range of definitions and levels of will among parents, caregivers, or charity groups. Although the family is still privileged as the principal source of protection for children, the notion that children are persons in possession of inherent and inalienable rights undermines the authority that parents, guardians, and states have over them (Grugel and Piper 2007: 112–13).

Although in many respects the Convention represents an achievement with regard to guaranteeing children's human rights, it does have its limitations. First of all, it applies only to children who are under the guardianship of a (primarily, nuclear) family or state authority. The Convention therefore does not take into account those children who have been abandoned, trafficked, or orphaned by disease, war, or natural disaster. It also excludes children who have chosen life on the streets over a violent or dysfunctional family or state institutional environment (Teeple 2005: 64). Likewise, the Convention does little to recognize the unique needs of particularly vulnerable categories of children, such as those who are born as a result of war-time rape and, as a consequence, are highly susceptible to infanticide, abuse, neglect, abandonment, and widespread discrimination in conflict and post-conflict societies (Carpenter 2009).

Second, Article 18 of CRC establishes that it is the parents that have the "primary" responsibility for providing for the "best interests of the child." Yet, in a free-market society, the nuclear family is increasingly unable to meet the minimum obligations for children's rights. At the same time, states have been shifting toward neoliberal policies which seek to minimize or reduce state responsibilities (as discussed in Chapters 4 and 5). So, if families are unable to guarantee children's entitlements and the state is increasingly unwilling to intervene, who will guarantee children's human rights? In addition, even if the state is willing to take on this responsibility when families are unable to, the assumption that all states are benevolent and act in the best interests of children is questionable given the amount of evidence that demonstrates widespread state sanction and perpetration of children's rights violations via economic exploitation, the use of children in armed conflict, and child abuse and neglect by state institutions (Teeple 2005: 66–7). A final limitation of existing children's rights frameworks relates to accountability. Neither the ILO Convention on the Elimination of the Worst Forms of Child Labour, nor the UN Convention on the Rights of the Child, have time frames or defined objectives or goals that can be evaluated upon implementation (Teeple 2005: 66).

Are Aboriginal Rights Compatible with Human Rights?

Until recently, the international human rights system had effectively left out Aboriginal rights. The 1948 Universal Declaration of Human Rights contains no explicit reference to Aboriginal (or indigenous) peoples and their rights. Early international rights frameworks concerning Aboriginals, such as the International Labour Organization's 1957 Convention on Indigenous People, were developed with the aim of assimilating Aboriginal peoples by integrating them into industrialized, modern societies (Engle 2011: 156; Teeple 2005: 93). This Convention thus denied Aboriginal peoples the right to autonomy and the pursuit of Aboriginal cultures. It is no wonder that Aboriginal rights advocates generally viewed such frameworks as instruments of oppression and rejected them (Engle 2011).

Nevertheless, in the 1970s, the United Nations began commissioning studies on Aboriginal rights through bodies such as the UN Subcommittee on the Protection of Minorities and the Prevention of Discrimination and the UN Working Group on Indigenous Populations. These efforts ultimately brought to light widespread instances of discrimination and marginalization, as well as the intentional usurpation of land and the purposeful destruction of indigenous languages and cultures (Teeple 2005: 92). These studies helped set the stage for the fundamental shift that came in the 1980s and 1990s when the international community started to look more closely at Aboriginal rights and indigenous movements began to consider the human rights frame for their claims, particularly in relation to cultural rights (Engle 2011).

In 1989, the ILO revised its 1957 Convention on Indigenous People, removing some of its earlier assimilationist objectives and including the term "peoples" (in plural) and other language which opened up the possibility of interpreting indigenous rights claims in a collective sense, and not solely on an individual basis. This has since been used by indigenous rights advocates to force states who have signed it to "guarantee a wide range of indigenous rights, including the right to prior consultation by the state on development initiatives that affect the lands they use or occupy" (Engle 2011: 157). Also, beginning in 1995, the United Nations declared two concurrent International Decades of the World's Indigenous Peoples (Engle 2011). In 2000, a UN Permanent Forum on Indigenous Issues was created and, in 2007, the United Nations General Assembly adopted the UN Declaration on the Rights of Indigenous Peoples (UNDRIP). This latest UN Declaration represents perhaps the most important achievement in indigenous rights over the past 50 years because it recognizes indigenous people's right to culture and self-determination, and it considers the possibility of collective rights.

Despite these achievements, there are significant gaps in this framework. While UNDRIP and other recent frameworks have essentially expanded the rights granted to indigenous groups, they have also provided the legal "loopholes" for the denial of these same rights. For example, customary rights linked to collective property as exercised by Aboriginal peoples remain subordinated to individual property rights enshrined in mainstream human rights instruments. Furthermore, the ILO's 1989 revision of the Convention on Indigenous Peoples grants Aboriginal peoples the right to retain their customs and institutions so long as these are *compatible* with the fundamental rights established in previously recognized national and international frameworks. This Convention provides the rationale for states to restrict certain indigenous rights, especially those collective rights which are thought to threaten the individual rights that underpin the human rights frameworks (Teeple 2005: 90; Engle 2011: 162). Another major issue, particularly for those indigenous peoples seeking national autonomy, is the restricted notion of self-determination. Paragraphs 2 and 3 of UNDRIP's Article 46 restrict the meaning of self-determination so as to eliminate the possibility of seceding from the state with a purpose of forming an independent state. These paragraphs subject the right to self-determination to mainstream international human rights obligations and the mainstream "principles of justice, democracy, respect for human rights, equality, non-discrimination, good governance, and good faith" (Engle 2011: 150).

Persons with Disabilities: Challenging Exclusions

Despite their noble intentions, such international law instruments as UDHR, ICCPR, and ICESCR denied humanity and basic rights to people with disabilities (Mégret 2008). Disability rights advocates realized that many of these acts could occur because these Conventions did not explicitly prohibit discrimination on the grounds of disability or provide special rights to persons with disabilities (Lord 2009). The ICCPR, for example, prohibits discrimination on several grounds, including sex, colour, language, religion, political or other opinion, origin or "other status." Yet, it does not explicitly refer to persons with disabilities. This abstract language and omission essentially allowed for the exclusion of persons with disabilities (Mégret 2008). Prior to the adoption of Convention on the Rights of Persons with Disabilities in 2006 (see Table 6.1), international law only recognized specific disability rights in a series of "soft" (non-binding) legal instruments, such as the Standard Rules on the Equalization of Opportunities for Persons with Disabilities and the World Program on Action; the UN Declarations on the Rights of Mentally Retarded Persons and on the Rights of Disabled Persons; and the Principles for the Protection of Persons with Mental Illness and the Improvement of Mental Health Care. These instruments emphasized some social and economic rights and omitted the civil and political rights of persons with disabilities (Dhanda 2008). Nevertheless, even the social and economic rights were contingent on the availability of economic resources. Furthermore, in the absence of civil and political rights, persons with disabilities were unable to assertively claim their rights (Dhanda 2008: 46).

Recognizing these limitations around disability, the International Disability Alliance, with the support of Human Rights Watch and Amnesty International, advocated for the adoption of a convention that would address these gaps. As a result of this campaign, the United Nations Convention on the Rights of Persons with Disabilities (CRPD) was adopted in December 2006 by the UN General Assembly. Its aim is to embrace "a social model of disability and articulate the full range of civil, political, economic, social, and cultural rights with specific application to disability" (Lord 2009: 91).

The CRPD attempts to recognize both "sameness" and difference in its notion of equality by affirming disabled persons' right to the same respect and dignity as the rest of the population and by providing an additional entitlement of reasonable accommodation in order to guarantee their inclusion and full participation (Dhanda 2008). The inclusion of civil and political rights in the CRPD underpins a fundamental shift from a "welfarist" (provision of aid) to a rights-based approach to the claims of persons with disabilities (Dhanda 2008). The CRPD has given voice to persons with disabilities, thereby turning them into an integral part of political decision making. The Convention has done this by recognizing disabled persons as "persons before the law" and as persons with the agency to "manage their own affairs." It recognizes that disabled persons have contractual capacity even if they may need support in exercising it (Dhanda 2008). CRPD reformulates the rights outlined in other conventions and specifies how the rights are to be implemented and guaranteed. These points were overlooked in the major human rights instruments. For example, even though UDHR and the ICCPR recognized rights to equality before the law, the CRPD reformulated these rights. It states that the right to be equal before the law means that persons with disabilities must have access to "the support they may require in exercising their legal capacity" and that this legal capacity must be protected by "appropriate and effective safeguards to prevent abuse in accordance with international human rights law." It then spells out in detail what sorts of considerations these safeguards should take into account (Mégret 2008: 503). In addition to clarifying the pre-existing rights language which might be abstract or ambiguous, the Convention also guides the implementation of these rights by specifically referring to states' obligation to enable persons with disabilities to exercise their rights, facilitate their lives and employment; repeal or adopt certain laws; and launch public awareness campaigns (Mégret 2008). The Convention on the Rights of Persons with Disabilities should be lauded for its ability to redress the exclusions (although the full extent of its impact is too early to assess).

Exclusions from "Without": Protecting "Non-Citizens"?

Some ILO and UN Conventions address the rights of international migrants. However, these human rights instruments apply mostly to *legal* migrants and leave out the migrants whose arrival or stay in the country is unauthorized. Thus, to use Nancy Fraser's language, unauthorized migrants are "misrepresented" in the human rights regime. The labour rights of migrants were first addressed by two ILO conventions. The 1949 Convention 97 on Migration for Employment and the 1975 Convention 143 on Migrants in Abusive Conditions and the Promotion of Equality of Opportunity and Treatment of Migrant Workers set principles of non-discrimination for legally admitted migrant workers in such areas as employment security, the provision of alternative employment, relief work, and retraining. Shortly after Convention 143 was adopted, a working group was established to draft a UN convention on migrants' rights. With about half of the UN member states participating in this process, the International Convention on the Protection of the Rights of All Migrant Workers and Members of Their Families was adopted on 18 December 1990 (Pécoud and de Guchteneire 2006). The Convention distinguishes between migrant workers with regular and irregular status, however. Some rights in the convention on migrants' rights are accorded to all migrant workers, regardless of their immigration status. These are fundamental civil and political rights, including freedom from torture and forced labour; the rights to life, due process, and the security of the person; and freedom of opinion and religion. Some economic, social, and cultural rights are also afforded to all migrant workers, including emergency medical care and access to education for children of migrant workers. At the same time, only legal migrants are extended such rights as family reunification, equal treatment in the workplace, and the right to join a trade union (GCIM 2005). Thus, for Dauvergne, the Convention ends up widening the gap between authorized and unauthorized migrants (2008: 26).

Some analysts argue that all migrants—whether they have been legally admitted or have entered or remained in a national territory in an unauthorized manner—by virtue of their humanity are covered by universal human rights. However, international law does not make it clear which state (or supra-state organization) is responsible for implementing and/or enforcing the respect and protection of these rights. In fact, even though international human rights are meant to be applied universally, it is membership in a national community of citizens that makes the realization of human rights possible. The denial of citizenship strips an individual of a "right to have rights" (Arendt 1979 [1951]; Somers and Roberts 2008: 395). As Alfredson observes, "the reality of noncitizens' situation epitomizes the fundamental paradox of human rights: human rights are meant to transcend states, while relying precisely on states, which typically care only for their citizens, for implementation" (2009: 238–9). States can be pressured to provide better protection for their own citizens, yet they are not obligated to protect individuals who are not their national members (Alfredson 2009: 238; Goldston 2006).

Similar to migrants, many refugees often find themselves outside the human rights framework. Refugee protection is defined by two UN documents: the 1951 Convention Relating to the Status of Refugee and the 1967 Protocol. The two key features of these documents include a definition of a refugee and the principle of **non-refoulement**. According to the 1951 Refugee convention, a refugee is "any person who is outside their country of origin and unable or unwilling to return there or to avail themselves of its protection, on account of a well-founded fear of persecution for reasons of race, religion, nationality, membership of a particular group, or political opinion." The principle of *non-refoulement* prescribes broadly that no refugee shall be returned in any manner whatsoever to any country where he or she would be at risk of persecution or torture. In addition, Article 31 of the 1951 Refugee Convention also prescribes freedom from penalties for illegal entry (www.unhcr.org). As of 1 April 2011, 144 states were party to the Convention and 142 had made commitments to both instruments (see www.unhcr.org).

Even countries that are party to the Convention and the Protocol retain, however, a high degree of freedom to act in their own interests. Regulations outlined by the UNHCR Convention and Protocol apply only to those who are recognized as genuine refugees. Governments may decide to consider certain migrants as refugees who are entitled to receive protection and others as "economic immigrants" who are subject to deportation. The Convention does not lay out procedures for deciding whether someone is a refugee or not. It is left to the discretion of each individual state to design procedures—open or restrictive—to determine the legitimacy of refugee claims. Research on refugee policies throughout the world provides ample evidence of inconsistencies in state decisions to grant asylum to one group of migrants but not to other groups (see Basok 1996 for further discussion of inconsistencies in the Canadian refugee policy).

In the last two decades, there has been an observable trend towards restricting the opportunities for refugees to claim and receive asylum. The global crackdown on illegal migration has made it more difficult even for *genuine* refugees (those fleeing violence and persecution) to receive safe asylum (Dauvergne 2008; Goodwin-Gill and McAdam 2007). While Article 14(1) of UDHR provides the right to claim and enjoy asylum, it does not guarantee a right to receive it. National states are not obligated to grant asylum to refugee claimants (or asylum seekers). Denial of access is the objective for many states anxious to avoid the requirement to abide by such obligations as *non-refoulement*. Asylum seekers are directly "interdicted" while outside territorial jurisdiction. Their movements are increasingly controlled indirectly through the application of restrictive visa policies and/or carrier sanctions. Those who arrive in the territory of the state may be denied access to a procedure for the determination of asylum or refugee status or to courts and tribunals that would determine their rights. They also lack information they require to make informed decisions (Goodwin-Gill and McAdam 2007: 370–80). The trend towards increasingly restrictive asylum policies is not new. However, after the 11 September 2001 terrorist attacks in New York, countries around the globe have adopted tougher security measures vis-à-vis refugees and migrants: "(d)etention grounds have been expanded, exclusion clauses have been applied more broadly than international law stipulates, and stronger links have been forged between immigration, intelligence services, and criminal law enforcement" (Goodwin-Gill and McAdam 2007: 372).

The *Tampa* affair (discussed in Box 6.3) illustrates how the Australian government avoided its international responsibility to provide a safe haven to refugees. Since the Tampa affair, a number of other states have also taken measures to curtail their intake of asylum seekers. Similar to Australia, the UK has circulated proposals to process asylum claims outside their territory. Canada has introduced legislation that expands exclusion from the Refugee Convention on the basis of criminality (Dauvergne 2008: 59). Canada and the US have also passed the *Agreement Between the Government of Canada and the Government of the United States of America for Cooperation in the Examination*

BOX 6.3 ❋ THE TAMPA REFUGEE CRISIS IN AUSTRALIA

On 26 August 2001 the Norwegian vessel *MV Tampa* was called on to assist a boat in distress off the coast of Australia. The *Tampa* was ordered to return the 450 (mostly) Afghan refugees on board to Indonesia. Nevertheless, it headed for Australian shores because some of the asylum seekers were in need of medical attention and others were so adamant about not returning to Indonesia that they threatened suicide if the boat was returned. Four miles off Christmas Island (Australian territory), the *Tampa* was detained by Australian authorities and prevented from reaching the island. A standoff ensued, during which the refugees on board were prevented from receiving legal counsel, medical attention, or information relating to their situation. On 29 August, the boat's Captain decided to move forward without permission from authorities and was stopped by Australian troops, who then proceeded to occupy the boat. Several days later, the *MV Tampa* refugees were transferred to Nauru and later Manus Island (Papua New Guinea) where their claims for a refugee status were processed.

Politically, the Australian government, which was in the middle of elections, justified its decision to turn away the *MV Tampa* by citing the need to crack down on an "influx" of migrant "queue jumpers," stem the abuse of Australia's asylum system, and protect would-be migrants from human traffickers and smugglers. Legally, it defended its actions by citing its right to sovereignty and its capacity to decide who enters national territory. While the Australian government insisted that it had abided by the 1951 Refugee Convention to the letter, critics contended that it had failed to meet some of its obligations. For example, by denying these refugees access to legal counsel, the Government had clearly violated Article 16 of the Convention, which provides that refugees have free access to courts. Furthermore, following the *Tampa* affair, the Australian government passed a series of pieces of legislation, known as the "Pacific solution," aimed at preventing people without proper travel documents from landing on the Australian territory for the purpose of claiming asylum. In addition to the Pacific solution, the Australian government introduced enhanced interception and interdiction policies to prevent would-be refugee claimants from reaching Australian waters. Under these policies, vessels carrying asylum seekers or undocumented migrants arriving from Indonesia or Malaysia were stopped and seized by the Australian navy. (Sources: Dauvergne 2008; Inder 2011).

of Refugee Status Claims From Nationals of Third Countries (known as the Safe Third Country Agreement), which was implemented on 29 December 2004 (see www.cic.gc.ca/english/department/laws-policy/safe-third.asp).

The Safe Third Country Agreement made it possible for border officials from each country to refuse entry to individuals entering from Canada or the US and seeking to make a refugee claim. This refusal is based on the assumption that the claimants were already in a safe country. Canadian critics of this policy contended that this agreement denied an opportunity for a fair status determination process to those refugee claimants who travel via the United States, a country known for its refusal to grant refugee status to many victims of persecution. In 2007, the Federal Court of Canada declared that the operation of the Safe Third Country Agreement was unconstitutional and contrary to the Charter of Rights and Freedoms (www.cpj.ca/en/content/dismantling-safe-third-country-agreement). This decision has been appealed (Dauvergne 2008: 41, 59).

The Power of Human Rights

So far, we have discussed groups of people whose rights are not protected, either fully or partially, by UN treaties. We have looked at the half of the glass that is empty. However, let us examine the other half of the glass that is full. UN treaties do offer protection from physical violence and torture. They defend freedom of speech and political organization. They assert freedom from want. They call for protection from discrimination. In many cases they go beyond protections provided by national states to their citizens. UN treaties and covenants are *moral guidelines* or universal standards to which all national laws and practices are expected to conform. They are designed for enactment and enforcement by those countries that ratify them. As such they are meant to be *above national law*. They are meant to challenge states to revise their laws and practices if these laws and practices violate the rights of their citizens (Kallen 2004: 13; Teeple 2007). Figure 6.2 illustrates how the UN human rights system encourages individual citizens, civil society organizations, and nation-states to abide by human rights principles and report non-compliance. But how effective are human rights principles and instruments in challenging the limitations of citizenship rights regimes?

The power of human rights treaties to bring about change is limited by *national sovereignty*, on the one hand, and the lack of authority and resources within the UN, on the other. It was never the intention of the UN Charter and the treaties to undermine national sovereignty. The right of nation-states to rule over domestic affairs without external interference was clearly affirmed by all states during the discussions that preceded the creation of UDHR (Evans 2011: 10–11; Goodale 2009). States may choose not to ratify any convention. States can also seek exemptions from specific

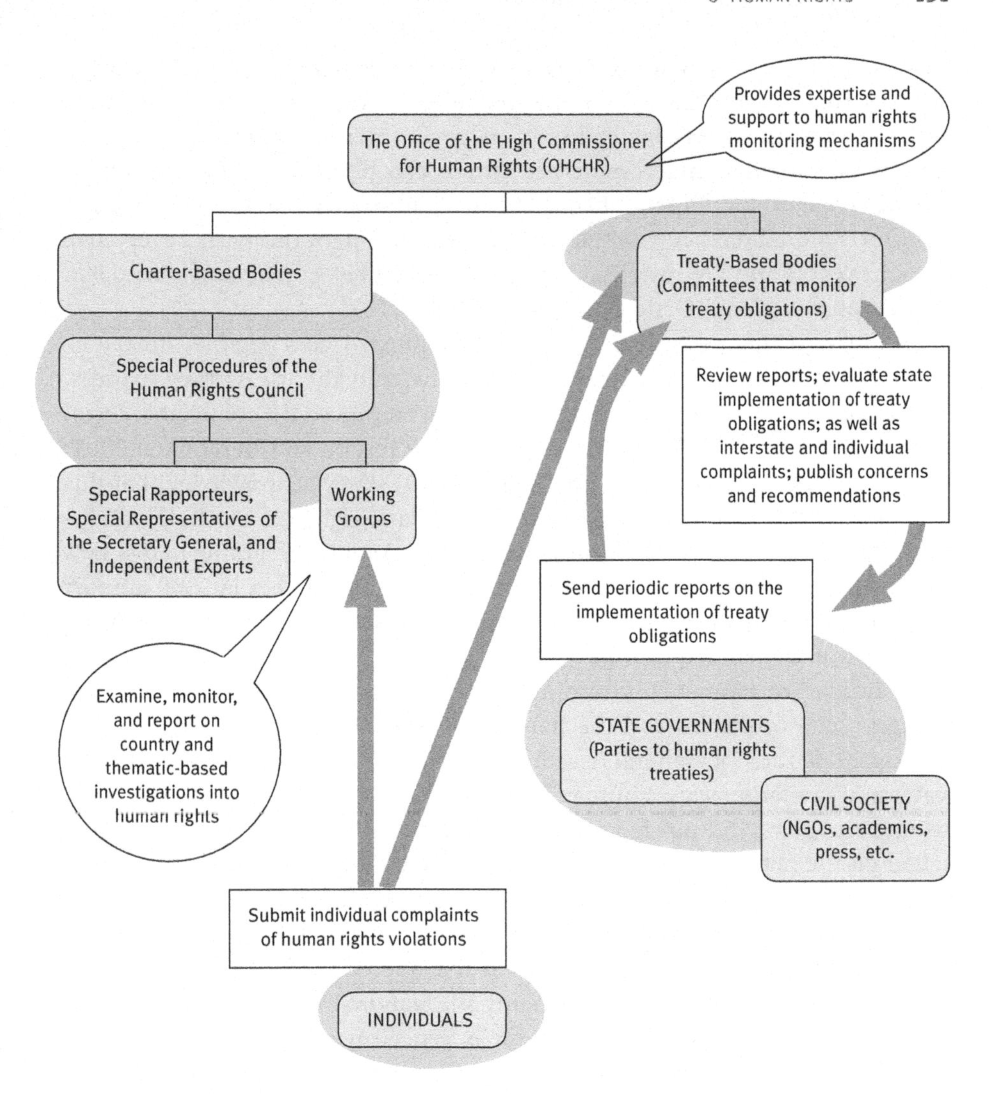

FIGURE 6.2 United Nations Human Rights Monitoring Systems
Source: Prepared by Victoria Simmons on the basis of information provided on http://www.ohchr.org/en/hrbodies/Pages/HumanRightsBodies.aspx

clauses and/or broadly define their compliance since some of the articles are very loosely defined. Moreover, the UN system is unable to defend human rights effectively because it lacks the autonomy and authority needed to do so. There are no sanctions or penalties for non-compliance and therefore states can sign a convention for political or diplomatic reasons without much risk (Grugel and Piper 2007). As such, the UN agencies that are dedicated to monitoring and defending human rights are limited to "naming and shaming" those states that do not meet their international human rights obligations. Agencies such as the Office of the High Commissioner for Human Rights (OHCHR), for example, have no independent investigative authority and must rely instead on non-governmental organization (NGO) reports of human rights compliance which can be incomplete and inconsistent (Grugel and Piper 2007: 116). In addition, the OHCHR can only monitor state adherence to their obligations on a periodic basis (every five to eight years) and are restricted to "supportive-like" constructive criticism in their observations (Grugel and Piper 2007: 116).

Contrary to this pessimistic view of the human rights regime, other analysts contend that human rights conventions, and the ideals they express, have become a valuable political and legal tool employed by politicians, social movements, and NGOs for demanding change (Gordon and Berkovitch 2007; Grugel and Piper 2007; Risse and Sikkink 1999). They acknowledge that this discourse assists different struggles to uphold basic rights; it also helps subjugated peoples to express their discontent and supplies the authoritative language to their claims. Box 6.4, for example, illustrates how a lack of support for people living with HIV/AIDS was defined as a violation of human rights by activists who demanded change.

In addition to treaties, UN resolutions urge nation-states to adopt certain human rights principles and mechanisms to uphold them. For instance, on 28 July 2010, the UN General Assembly declared that safe and clean drinking water and sanitation were a human right. Recognizing that 900 million people around the globe did not have access to clean water, the General Assembly called on the nation-states to "offer funding, technology and other resources to help poorer countries scale up their efforts to provide clean, accessible and affordable drinking water and sanitation for everyone" (UN News Centre 2010). Even though Canada was one of the 41 countries that chose to abstain from the vote, Meera Karunananthan, National Water Campaigner for the Council of Canadians, asserted: "It is crucial now that communities in Canada use this opportunity to hold our government accountable to the international commitment to recognize water and sanitation as human rights. We must demand legislation at home to ensure that these rights are enjoyed by all peoples of Canada without discrimination. It is time for Canada to do something about the deplorable conditions on First Nations reserves that have lacked access to safe drinking water and adequate sanitation for generations" (Council of Canadians 2010; see also Chapter 4 on the privatization of water). At the same time, the human rights system, and particularly the Human Right Committee, can be used to address individual complaints. Countries that ratify the International Covenant on Civil and Political Rights can also sign the Nations Optional Protocol that would allow individual citizens to bring complaints to the United Nations Human Rights Committee. Canada is one of the countries that have ratified this Protocol. A significant number of complaints have been filed by Canadian citizens against Canada under

BOX 6.4 DEFINING THE HIV/AIDS CRISIS AS A HUMAN RIGHTS ISSUE

Since the late 1980s, many activists and key public officials have addressed the HIV/AIDS crisis from a human rights perspective. This has meant framing their campaigns and programs around one central argument, namely that the battle against the HIV/AIDS epidemic requires that state governments respect human rights. Using this angle, activists have appealed to UDHR and ICCPR principles, such as "freedom from arbitrary detention" and "restriction of movement," for example, in order to address the detention, quarantine, and isolation to which people living with HIV/AIDS (PLWHA) have been subjected, especially in the early days of the epidemic. The reasoning is that, by detaining and isolating PLWHA, the disease will not be contained but rather exacerbated since these measures cause people to fear and resist testing and counselling. Activists have also invoked the rights to information and education in order to overcome societal taboos on the discussion of certain topics, such as sexuality and intravenous drug use, and to facilitate the dissemination of basic information on the disease and its treatment.

In more recent years, activists and officials have referred to broader socio-economic rights in their battle against HIV/AIDS. In Brazil, for example, during the late 1980s, AIDS activists successfully lobbied government for the constitutional recognition of the human right to health. This right was subsequently invoked by activists during the 1990s in order to demand free and universal access to antiretroviral drugs (ARVs), a treatment that, at that time, had been proven fundamental in prolonging and enhancing the quality of life of PLWHA but was not financially accessible to all sectors of the population.

Similarly, in South Africa, activists involved in the Treatment Action Campaign (TAC) have brought legal cases against the government, charging it with violating its obligation to guarantee the individual rights to equality, dignity, and health care that are outlined in the South African Constitution and Bill of Rights. TAC has also referred to international human rights treaties, such as the right to an adequate standard of living for health and well-being, for example, outlined in Article 25 of UDHR, and the Rome Statute of International Criminal Court on crimes against humanity and the denial of medicines, in order to pressure the South African government for a comprehensive AIDS program that would include greater access to ARVs and to education about rights in the context of HIV/AIDS. (Source: Youde 2009).

BOX 6.5 ❋ THE UN HUMAN RIGHTS COMMISSION IN LOVELACE VS. CANADA (1980)

Sandra Lovelace was born and raised as a Maliseet Indian on a reserve in eastern Canada. In 1970, she married a non-Indian. As a result, she lost her Indian status and her right to live on a reserve. With the dissolution of her marriage, however, Ms. Lovelace decided to return to live on the reserve where she grew up, but she was prevented from doing so due to her loss of status under Canada's Indian Act.

In 1977, Sandra Lovelace filed a complaint against the Government of Canada. She argued that, by not allowing her to live on the reserve, the government was violating its obligations to uphold Article 27 of the International Covenant on Civil and Political Rights, which states that "[i]n those States in which ethnic, religious or linguistic minorities exist, persons belonging to such minorities shall not be denied the right, in community with the other members of their group, to enjoy their own culture, to profess and practise their own religion, or to use their own language."

Although Canada's Indian Act no longer recognized Ms. Lovelace as a status Indian, the Human Rights Committee decided that her lifelong connection to the Maliseet ethnic community should be considered "belonging." The Committee underlined the differences between those protections offered to groups under the Indian Act and those offered under the Covenant and ruled that, by preventing Ms Lovelace from living on the Tobique Reserve, the only space where her ethnic community could be found, Canada's legislation concerning the right to live on a reserve interfered with her right to practise her language and culture in community. As a consequence of this international ruling, Canada amended the Indian Act and removed the discriminatory clause in 1985. (Sources: Kallen 2004: 179; International Covenant on Civil and Political Rights. Accessed online 18 May 2011 at www2.ohchr.org/english/law/ccpr.htm#art27 and www.lawsite.ca/WLSC/Lovelace_w.htm).

BOX 6.6 ❋ INTERNATIONAL LAW AND COLLECTIVE BARGAINING RIGHTS IN CANADA

In 2002, the Government of British Columbia passed the *Health and Social Services Delivery Improvement Act*. Part 2 of this legislation effectively invalidated existing collective agreements and precluded collective bargaining on specific issues relating to the workplace; it gave employers the ability to contract out and lay off employees, and to unilaterally change their worksites and/or areas of responsibility. Labour unions and individuals responded by challenging the legislation in the courts on the grounds that it violated several guarantees under the *Canadian Charter of Rights and Freedoms*, including the right to freedom of association (sections 2(d)); the right to life, liberty, and security of the person (section 7); and the right to equality and non-discrimination (section 15). In particular, the trial lawyers argued that the law excluded specific groups from their right to join a union (association); that it would cause the workers financial and emotional distress; and that it constituted gender discrimination because the majority of the employees affected were women.

Initial court decisions ruled in favour of the government legislation. Nevertheless, following a series of union-led appeals, in June 2007, the Supreme Court overturned its earlier decisions, ruling that the right to collective bargaining was in fact an integral element of freedom of association covered in a number of international conventions to which Canada is a party and that these international norms should inform the interpretation of the guarantees outlined in the *Canadian Charter of Rights and Freedoms*. In pronouncing its decision, the Supreme Court referred to three international instruments that Canada has acceded to and ratified and that, according to the Court, reflect principles that Canada embraces: *The International Covenant on Economic, Social, and Cultural Rights*; the *International Covenant on Civil and Political Rights*; and the *International Labour Organization's (ILO's) Convention (No. 87) Concerning Freedom of Association and Protection of the Right to Organize*. The Court pointed out that the interpretation of these Conventions supports the proposition that there is a right to collective bargaining in international law and suggests that such a right should be recognized in the Canadian context under the Charter. (Sources: Basok and Carasco 2010; Centre for Constitutional Studies 2011).

this protocol (Kallen 2004: 178–9). The first one among them was Lovelace vs. Canada (1980), discussed in Box 6.5. Finally, values expressed in human rights treaties have influenced the understanding of rights that are debated in the court of law. Box 6.6 illustrates how UN and ILO Conventions were used in the court decision to award collective bargaining rights to Canadian nurses.

Conclusion

Recognizing the failures of nation-states to protect their citizens from rights violations, the international community adopted certain principles and norms to protect the rights of humankind worldwide. The UN Charter, the Universal Declaration of Human Rights, and other treaties that followed clearly expressed a set of principles to be endorsed, accepted, and translated into national policies by nation-states. These principles emphasized universal respect for the civil, political, and social rights of human beings. Yet, the realization of such universal principles remains a dream to this day despite certain achievements by activists in advancing the rights of people with disabilities, women, children, Aboriginal peoples, migrants, and refugees. As we have seen in this chapter, the rights of workers and economically disadvantaged people are subordinated to the rights of corporations; human rights principles are at times blind to cultural diversity; women are afforded less protection than men; not all children's rights are fully protected; Aboriginal rights are granted no more than lip service by the human rights regime; and, finally, many refugees and unauthorized migrants are completely left out of the human rights framework.

Furthermore, the power of the human rights regime to enforce these norms is limited by national sovereignty. It is left to the discretion of nation-states whether to endorse these principles (with or without reservations) and devise ways to turn them into national laws and practices. The UN does not have the power to enforce human rights norms. Yet, despite its limitations, the human rights regime does have merit. As numerous examples illustrate, the human rights framework has been employed by social movements around the globe to frame and claim rights for people who have been dispossessed, marginalized, and downgraded.

Key Terms

citizenship rights rights granted by nation-states

civil rights rights to individual freedoms

non-refoulement prohibition to expel or return refugees

political rights rights to political organization and participation

private sphere a set of activities the correspond to unpaid work, household relations, and informal (community-based) politics

public sphere a set of activities that embrace paid employment and participation in formal politics (e.g., voting, serving as a members of government)

rights to culture rights to preserve and practice a set of distinctive spiritual, material, intellectual and emotional features of society or a social group

social rights rights to such social protections as unemployment insurance, and access to education and healthcare

state sovereignty the right and power of national states to regulate their internal affairs without foreign interference

Questions for Critical Thought

1. How and to what extent is it possible to protect the human rights of workers and economically disadvantaged people in the era of neoliberal globalization? Identify some of the challenges that you see facing disadvantaged peoples in this regard.
2. Is it feasible to have universal human rights in a culturally diverse world? Why or why not?
3. Is it possible to reconcile collective and individual rights? If so, what would be the benefits or limitations of such a reconciliation?
4. How can the rights of non-citizens be protected? From your point of view, can you identify any non-citizens in your neighbourhood, community, or region who are in need of human rights protection? If so, how might these non-citizens benefit from such protection?
5. Discuss how and to what extent human rights principles can be enforced in a political system that upholds the principles of national sovereignty.

Annotated Additional Readings

Clifford Bob, ed. 2009. *The International Struggle for New Human Rights.* Philadelphia: University of Pennsylvania Press. This collection of essays offers an important framework for understanding key conflicts and strategies involved in the struggle to expand human rights concerns, advocacy, and entitlements beyond the traditional realm of civil and political rights.

Jane K. Cowan, Marie-Benedict Dembour, and Richard Wilson, eds. 2001. *Culture and Rights.* Cambridge: Cambridge University Press. This edited volume offers a much more complex understanding of the universalism/cultural relativity debate surrounding human rights by providing an interdisciplinary look at the concrete effects of human rights discourse and practice in a variety of settings around the world.

Evelyn Kallen. 2004. *Social Inequality and Social Injustice: A Human Rights Perspective,* New York: Palgrave Macmillan. Diverse case studies are presented in this book to illustrate how the injustices facing particular social groups are socially constructed and sustained through human rights violations and how human rights legislation can offer restitution for those groups which are marginalized.

Sally E. Merry. 2006. *Human Rights & Gender Violence: Translating International Law into Local Justice,* Chicago: Chicago University Press. This volume draws on extensive ethnographic field research in order analyze how local cultures assume and ordain international human rights law with respect to gender violence.

Gary Teeple. 2005. *The Riddle of Human Rights.* Canada: Merlin Press (UK) and Garamond Press Ltd. This volume challenges prevailing conceptualizations of human rights as "universal" and "absolute," suggesting instead that they are time bound and relative to a capitalist mode of production whose conflicts and contradictions underpin pervasive human rights violations.

Related Websites

United Nations Human Rights Commission
www.un.org/en/rights/index.shtml

University of Minnesota Human Rights Library
www1.umn.edu/humanrts/instree/ainstlsa2.html

7 Transnational Activism and Struggles

Learning Objectives

- Distinguish between transnational activism from above and from below
- Explore the link between transnational activism from above and neoliberal rationalities
- Critically assess specific activities of transnational organizations such as Oxfam International, the International Organization for Migration, and the United Nations High Commissioner for Refugees
- Understand how Transnational Advocacy Networks work and what makes them effective
- Critically assess gaps in the scholarly analyses of transnational advocacy networks
- Explore the early development of the Global Justice Movement and identify its strengths and weaknesses

Introduction

In previous chapters we have discussed how certain nation-based programs, such as welfare reform, enact a diversity of strategies to exclude particular groups from access to rights and political participation. In this regard, we recognize that national programs of reform and nation-states themselves can trigger reactions not only from populations and groups living within a national territory but also from populations and groups that are located across and beyond the national territory and are involved in transnational activism and struggles that demand change. As with other researchers and activists, we recognize that transnational activism—including activism by participants engaged in local and regional groups as well as national and international organizations—is becoming increasingly important in bringing about change at social, economic, and political levels. For example, transnational activist organizations such as Amnesty International and Human Rights Watch have pushed human rights issues onto state agendas and international platforms. It was through this kind of activism that the Universal Declaration of Human Rights (UDHR), adopted by the United Nations in 1948, became one of the key reference points for local struggles for justice and equality around the globe (see Mihr and Schmitz 2007). These and other forms of activism often involve struggles that can push social justice demands for human rights, gender equity relations, or poverty reduction onto the transnational public agenda despite resistance or opposing pressures from particular states, private agencies, and international organizations.

While transnational activism and struggles have been characterized by both successes and limitations, we believe it is essential to be sensitive to the conditions that shape transnational activism: to the role of powerful organizations and states in these processes (see also Olesen 2011: 5; Routledge and Cumbers 2009), to how such activism can produce short- or long-term change, and to the potential for enlarging the social and political spaces of transnational activism. From our perspective, transnational activism and struggles are bound up in various kinds of activities that are fluid and characterized by unstable relations and networks rather than by relations that are territorialized at the level of the nation-state.

In this chapter our analysis centres on certain forms of activism and struggle that operate within, across, and beyond the nation-state and through initiatives from inter-governmental and international organizations and activist networks alike. While we recognize that there is a diversity of transnational forms of activism, our specific focus is on those forms that operate "from above" and "from below" and involve social justice issues such as rights, humanitarianism, and political participation. **Transnational forms of activism from above** refers to advocacy efforts by organizations at the international level that operate on the behalf of others and use the language of rights, protection, or humanitarianism to bring about change for marginalized or vulnerable groups. In this chapter we explore specifically three such organizations: Oxfam International, the International Organization for Migration (IOM), and the United Nations High Commissioner for Refugees (UNHCR). We recognize that while their efforts may have noble intentions, these often end up being undermined as these organizations engage in excessive control measures or in neoliberal governing agendas. **Transnational forms of activism from below** refers to the advocacy efforts of diverse **transnational activist networks** (TANs) that operate on the ground in local and national circles and that have a global reach, including those critical of neoliberal policies, practices, and organizations. In this chapter we explore not only how TANs operate but what makes them successful. We recognize that not all TANs are critical of neoliberalism. In fact, many accept it as legitimate, while critiquing certain state practices. In contrast, the Global Justice Movement, analyzed in this chapter, questions the very rationalities and practices of the neoliberal order. We assess both the strengths and weaknesses of this movement.

These two forms of activism invite us to ask a range of critical questions that speak to the effects of transnational activism on human lives and conditions, in terms of shaping and changing values and agendas, and of transforming public debates. They also enable an exploration of both the light and dark sides of transnational activism as we illustrate in this chapter through empirical cases. How and to what extent is meaningful change brought about for those demanding social justice on behalf of others or for themselves through transnational activism? This question guides our discussions in this chapter.

Transnational Activism "from Above"

There are many transnational activist organizations that operate from above and attempt to act on behalf of others by engaging in advocacy work, including those organizations that use, for example, the language of human rights, protection, international civil society, or humanitarianism for the purposes of aiding vulnerable, marginal, and marginalized groups. These organizations engage in processes that involve developing solutions to identified problems, fostering partnerships or agreements with other organizations and participants, and expanding, contracting, or reconfiguring themselves while simultaneously being embedded in wider social and political relations. In varying degrees, transnational activist organizations from above support a kind of activism that is partnership oriented, such as involving public–private sector arrangements, that includes a commitment to change that may foster new social relations and divisions, but that often supports, directly or indirectly, excessive controls over particular groups and neoliberal policies and agendas. Through their advocacy programs and initiatives, such organizations encompass, for example, inter-governmental organizations such as the International Organization for Migration (IOM); international non-governmental organizations such as Oxfam and Save the Children, United Nations agencies such as the UNHCR, UNDP, and UNESCO (see Table 7.1 for a list of UN agencies and their mandates); the World Health Organization (WHO); and other international organizations.

Transnational activist organizations from above address a wide spectrum of social justice issues that can range from demands for fair trade, fair treatment, and human rights for vulnerable groups to the eradication of poverty and violence. These issues are discussed in numerous documents, programs, forums, speeches, and media communications that extend beyond the territory of a nation, and can be fuelled by the powerful actions of other organizations. For example, the World Bank, the International Monetary Fund, and the World Trade Organization have long defended a system of "global free trade" as a way to move developing economies "forward" in an open world economy consisting of agricultural commodities, manufactured goods, artisanal projects, and other consumer goods originating in diverse geographies. With the expansion of neoliberal agendas, such a free trade economy would, it is believed, improve economic growth, reduce global poverty, and advance living standards, such as wages and work conditions. The push for global free trade has been met by diverse forms of transnational activism, including anti-globalization movements, that recognize the unequal relations characterizing the world economy. Such movements have been known to speak out against the injustices of transnational corporations (Routledge and Cumbers 2009) and neoliberal institutions and governments, such as the "global days of action" that took place in Seattle, Genoa, Gleneagles, and elsewhere (Gill 2000; Klein

Table 7.1 United Nations Agencies, Programs, and Funds Involved in Social Justice

United Nations Agencies, Programs, and Funds	Mandates
United Nations High Commissioner for Refugees (UNHCR)	To lead and coordinate international action to protect refugees and resolve refugee problems worldwide. It also has a mandate to help stateless people.
United Nations Population Fund (UNFPA)	To promote the right of every woman, man, and child to enjoy a life of health and equal opportunity. (i.e., poverty reduction, maternal health, HIV prevention, and gender equality).
United Nations Children's Fund (UNICEF)	To advocate for the protection of children's rights; to support in meeting their basic needs; and to expand their opportunities to reach their full potential.
United Nations entity for Gender Equality and the Enpowerment of Women (UN-WOMEN)	To eliminate discrimination against women and girls; to empower women; and to achieve equality between women and men as partners and beneficiaries of development, human rights, humanitarian action, and peace and security.
United Nations Development Programme (UNDP)	To advocate for change and to connect countries to knowledge, experience, and resources to help people build a better life.
United Nations Human Settlements Programme (UN-HABITAT)	To promote socially and environmentally sustainable towns and cities so that adequate shelter is provided for all.
International Labour Organization (ILO)	To promote labour rights and decent employment opportunities; to improve social protections; to strengthen dialogue on labour issues.
World Health Organization (WHO)	To promote equitable access to essential health care and to support the collective defence against transnational (health) threats.
United Nations Educations, Scientific and Cultural Organization (UNESCO)	To contribute to the building of peace, the eradication of poverty, sustainable development, and intercultural dialogue through education, the sciences, culture, communication, and information (with a particular focus on gender equality and Africa).
International Fund for Agricultural Development (IFAD)	To enable poor rural people in developing countries to overcome poverty (i.e., achieve higher incomes and food security).
Food and Agriculture Organization of the United Nations (FAO)	To achieve food security for all men and women; to raise levels of nutrition, improve agricultural productivity, better the lives of rural populations, and contribute to the growth of the world economy.
United Nations World Food Programme (WFP)	To eradicate hunger and poverty. (i.e., use food aid to support economic and social development; to meet refugee and other emergency food needs; and to promote world food security in accordance with the recommendations of the United Nations and FAO).

Source: Prepared by Victoria Simmons on the basis of www.un.org.

2002). They have also been known to support alternative initiatives, such as fair trade, that aim to create a type of trading arrangement that would not only augment the wellbeing of developing world producers by returning to them a larger share of the final sale price of their goods but also create markets that serve the interests of both producers and consumers (see Lyon and Moberg 2010: 7; see also Taylor 2005; Jaffee 2007). Important and critical questions are, however, being raised about the idea of fair trade and fair trade markets (see, for example, Kiely 2005: 2002; Lyon and Moberg 2010).

Oxfam International provides a good example of one transnational organization that engages in and advocates for fair trade. It consists of 15 confederate organizations working in 98 countries and with partners and allies to find "lasting solutions to poverty and injustice" (Oxfam International 2011a). In its aim to find lasting solutions to poverty and injustice, the organization views world trade as a site of necessary change: "World trade rules have been developed by the rich and powerful on the basis of their narrow commercial interests. Rich countries and powerful corporations have captured a disproportionate share of the benefits of trade, leaving developing countries and poor people worse off. Trade rules should be judged on their contribution to poverty reduction, respect for human rights, and environmental sustainability" (Oxfam International 2011a). Oxfam's words are relevant here in that they convey strong social justice goals, such as poverty reduction and environmental sustainability. The organization's focus on bringing about fair trade for those most vulnerable, such as poor people living in the Global South, is, however, premised on neoliberal notions of empowering the poor by making them increasingly more responsible for their routes out of poverty. This neoliberal notion of empowerment is radically different from the feminist notion of empowerment discussed in Chapter 1. Such neoliberal empowerment and responsibility-focused initiatives aimed at the poor are equated with improving human wellbeing with wealth accumulation. However, such initiatives are typically linked to the global market and to an international-trade paradigm that is based on neoliberal policies and agendas (see Bello 2002; Ilcan and Lacey 2011; Shiva 2002). In this way, human dignity and freedom for the poor are often understood as best achieved through liberating individual *entrepreneurial freedoms* and skills and bringing all human action into the domain of the *market* (Keddie 2010: 139).

Consequently, in seeking social justice remedies to problems of poverty and environmental sustainability, fair trade advocates such as Oxfam International are often in the position of pursuing market-based solutions to the problems that emerge from the free market, what Fridell (2007) refers to as "*market-driven social justice*." As Lyon and Moberg astutely claim, "In place of legal and policy remedies by states on behalf of the farmers and workers who reside within their borders, fair trade seeks social justice by embracing the deregulated markets that are themselves often responsible for deepening poverty in rural communities." In this context the authors acknowledge that the social justice undertones of fair trade are constrained by the structure of existing markets and the entities that dominate them, which often leads to "fair trade's cooptation by the very corporations that the [fair trade] movement formerly opposed" (2010: 7). The authors alert us to global corporations such as Starbucks, which is the largest speciality coffee retailer in the United States and one that parades its reputation for social responsibility through fair trade while fighting unionization efforts among its own employees.

Through transnational advocacy work, some organizations present themselves as global institutions that engage in discourses not only of fair trade but also of unrestricted hospitality and humanitarianism. One such organization is the International Organization for Migration (IOM). It consists of 132 members, 97 observers including 17 states and 80 global and regional IGOs and NGOs, has more than 400 field locations, 7300 staff working on more than 2900 projects, and spent more than US$1.4 billion in 2010. Although it is not part of the United Nations, the organization engages in diverse and close working relationships with UN agencies (IOM 2011). It was established in 1951 as an intergovernmental organization and is "committed to the principle that humane and orderly migration benefits migrants and society" (IOM 2011). In broader terms, the IOM "works to help ensure the orderly and humane management of migration, to promote international cooperation on migration issues, to assist in the search for practical solutions to migration problems, and to provide humanitarian assistance to migrants in need, including refugees and internally displaced people" (IOM 2011).

One may often think that it is only nation-states that increasingly restrain the mobility of migrants by stopping potential asylum seekers from reaching sovereign territory to make claims. Much is made public about the detention of asylum seekers, such as those on Guantanamo Bay, Guam, and Tinian, and how their access to asylum is mediated by distance and isolation (see, for example, Nyers 2008; Isin and Nielsen 2008). In the context of the mobile spaces of ports and airports, states engage in activities to position their own immigration control officers in foreign airports in an attempt to identify potential asylum seekers before they reach sovereign territories such as Australia, Canada, New Zealand, the UK, or the US (Ashutosh and Mountz 2011; also see Chapters 3 and 6). The regulation of migrants in many spaces across the globe, however, involves more than state intervention. The IOM serves as a good illustration of the ways in which its own efforts join with other efforts that attempt to shape the movement of migrants through the language of "humane and orderly migration" (Ashutosh and Mountz 2011).

The IOM has been typified as a humanitarian organization that does vital humanitarian work, such as rebuilding housing after the tsunami in Sri Lanka and reintegrating internally displaced people in Colombia. It carries out diverse projects related to human migration that it categorizes as "managing migration," "migrant movement and processing assistance," and "migration research" and it organizes humanitarian projects designed to protect migrants and their human rights, such as anti-trafficking campaigns (Ashutosh and Mountz 2011; Basok and Piper 2012). In 2008, it provided "movement assistance" to 190,647 persons, mostly through resettlement programs and "refugee repatriations" (Ashutosh and Mountz 2011: 28). As with other international organizations that use the language of human rights or humanitarianism in an effort to bring about change and improve the lives of marginal and marginalized peoples, such as the UN Refugee agency (UNHCR), the IOM's employment of humanitarian language can appear to eradicate the coercive practices inherent in detention and the ordering of movement (Ashutosh and Mountz 2011).

However, as Ashutosh and Mountz expose, the IOM engages in neoliberal forms of governance through its role in managing migrant bodies. On a contractual basis, the IOM is employed by federal governments to carry out a range of migration-related services that governments are unable or unwilling to do for legal and political purposes. For example, the IOM was contracted to run the detention of asylum seekers on islands as part of Australia's "pacific solution" to reduce the arrival of asylum seekers by sea, a site that has been known for organizing widespread resistance (hunger strikes and demonstrations by detainees, and citizen movements) both within and outside of Australia's network of asylum seeker detention centres (see Nyers 2008: 160). In its relations with others, the organization serves in a partnership capacity by involving itself in bilateral arrangements for the return asylum seekers, the issuing of travel documents, and providing charter flights for the return of asylum seekers. According to Ashutosh and Mountz (2011: 28–29), it is for these and other similar reasons that No Borders (see Box 7.1) warns us that the IOM is "a Janus-faced organisation, aiming to win trust, cooperate with and [use] NGOs on the one hand but acting as a reliable partner of national governments [on the other]." No Borders has in fact engaged in an international campaign against the IOM by exposing the role and function of the IOM in implementing dominant and repressive migration politics (No Borders 2011).

Similarly, Human Rights Watch has pointed out that the IOM adopts the language of protection but has no mandate to protect and no protocol to investigate human rights violations that transpire under its watch. In this regard, and through the IOM's use of the language of rights and humanitarianism, the organization performs the transnational work of nation-states while managing migrant populations and turning a profit. It is for these reasons that Ashutosh and Mountz (2011: 22) view the IOM as positioned at the intersection of the nation-state, international human rights regimes, and neoliberal governance. Organizations engaging in humanitarian efforts that support neoliberal agendas can sometimes threaten life and livelihoods, produce violent material

BOX 7.1 ❋ NO BORDERS

No Borders emerged from the meeting of campaigns in various European countries at a time when undocumented migrants were organizing and becoming visible through their various actions and demonstrations to bring about fairness for migrant groups, including the freedom of movement and the abolishment of racist policies. No Borders was created in 1999 as a means of connecting various pro-migrant and anti-capitalism protests against restrictive border controls, anti-migrant policies, and deportations. As a loose coalition encircling groups from across Europe, it enables many grassroots groups, including those outside of Europe, to coordinate actions, to exchange information, and to discuss issues relating to migration and border control. The No Borders network aims to "work against all forms of exploitation and division, by working together to create new forms of collaboration and resistance." Network members describe their goals as follows: "We aim to create a platform for exchange of information and experience among groups and individuals involved in different political struggles with an emancipatory anti-capitalist perspective. We also aim to work together with self-organized groups of migrants. We aim to interconnect people working from different political practices and coming with different regional experiences." Anarchists, feminists, civil liberties groups, and migrant and refugee organizations are among the active social and political participants making up this network. (Source: No Borders Network 2011; Walters 2006).

outcomes, and be contested by diverse advocacy groups (see for example Agier 2002: 2011; Ilcan 2009; Nyers 2008).

There are other organizations whose involvement in transnational activism from above embraces the discourses of humanitarianism, rights, and protection. A case in point is The United Nations High Commissioner for Refugees (UNHCR), which was established in 1950 by the United Nations General Assembly. Using the 1951 Geneva Refugee Convention as its major tool, UNHCR's core mandate is to ensure the international protection of 32.9 million uprooted people worldwide through a staff of around 6300 people working in 111 countries. Its directive is to "lead and coordinate international action to protect refugees and resolve refugee problems worldwide. Its primary purpose is to safeguard the rights and well-being of refugees" (UNHCR 2011). Over the years, in addition to its mandate for refugee protection, UNHCR has become the prime coordinator of humanitarian relief operations. More than 500 NGOs work worldwide under contract with the UNHCR to intervene on the ground and organize humanitarian assistance in all its diverse forms (Agier 2002: 321).

Close to 33 million uprooted people around the world are of concern to the UNHCR. This number includes 14.4 million internally displaced people, 10.5 million refugees, 2 million returnees, 6.6 million stateless people, and more than 800,000 asylum seekers. Depending on the year, between 13 and 18 million are refugees in the strict sense, i.e., living outside their country of origin. These refugees are massively concentrated in Africa (over 8 million), in Asia (over 6.3 million), and in Europe (over 2 million). These figures are approximations and do not include large numbers of undeclared refugees, such as Afghan refugees who are not reported as part of the 3 million refugees spread over seventy asylum countries (UNHCR 2009, 30); Somali, Ethiopian, or Rwandan refugees, described as "self-settled" as they prefer to take their chances in illegality and the informal economy rather than being located in refugee camps (see Box 7.2 on Refugee Camps); others wandering for lack of

BOX 7.2 ※ REFUGEE CAMPS

Refugee camps are often created in situations of emergencies, such as famines, conflicts, and wars. The relations within these camps are generally shaped by international refugee and humanitarian organizations in partnership with nation-states. These relations are thought to be protective ones intended to provide for the physical, food, and health requirements of all kinds of survivors of emergency situations. The camps typically house thousands of inhabitants for short and long periods of time, sometimes extending to ten years, and often exceeding the duration of the emergency.

Refugee camps are frequently presented with challenges that undermine or redirect their ability to maintain their integrity—in other words, to ensure the protection and neutrality of the spaces they demarcate. These challenges have sometimes resulted in refugee camps being turned into sites where refugees are forced to return to their home country by national authorities working with international refugee and humanitarian organizations. Refugee camps have also been transformed into training camps for routed armies or the preoccupation of arms traffickers and as a consequence can remain under the control of exiled ethnic or religious groups. Some camps can even provide the guards for or become targets of localized military operations, even when the majority of camp residents play no role in the conflicts.

While some international humanitarian and refugee organizations may engage in practices that aim to protect and control the movement of refugees in the territories of nation-states, other state governments have been known to employ efforts to shield themselves against refugees, which can have other effects. This was the case, for example, with the Zairian government vis-à-vis the Hutu refugees from Rwanda from mid-1994 to November 1996, and with the Turkish government vis-à-vis the Iraqi Kurds between 1988 and 1993. For domestic political reasons or to protect their frontiers, these nation-states endeavoured to concentrate, to abandon, or to organize the forced return of these marginal and marginalized groups who would remain unwanted within their territories. (Sources: Agier 2002: 319; Branch 2009: 489).

official recognition of their refugee status; and exiles from "Black Africa" or the Middle East who are treated as "illegal immigrants" and caught as they cross policed European borders (Agier 2002: 320). It should be noted here that immense migrant fatalities take place in the spaces for controlling mobile populations.

While UNHCR embraces the discourses of human rights and refugee protection, it has come into conflict with various political and security priorities over the years which, in turn, has compelled the organization to engage in certain actions (see Figures 7.1 and 7.2).

FIGURE 7.1 Jean Mbila, a Refugee in Osire Refugee Camp since 1992

Source: www.refugeelives.org/2010/2010/12/16/225/locations/namibia/the-osire-elder. Refugee Lives 2010–11, project of Northwestern University. Photos by Kaitlyn Jakola, contact@refugeelives.org

Figure 7.2 The Osire Refugee Camp, Namibia

Source: www.refugeelives.org/2010/2010/12/16/225/locations/namibia/the-osire-elder. Refugee Lives 2010–11, project of Northwestern University. Photos by Kaitlyn Jakola. contact@refugeelives.org

In 1991, for example, Turkey refused to admit Kurdish refugees fleeing northern Iraq. In response, despite concerns about pushing refugees back at the border, UNHCR decided to participate in the creation of "safe havens" within Iraq and assist the Kurds there. In the former Yugoslavia, UNHCR's role in evacuating people from situations of danger in the country facilitated the process of ethnic cleansing. In central Africa, UNHCR provided support to Rwandan refugee camps, including those people who had participated in genocide at home (Whitaker 2008: 243). In these and other situations, UNHCR engages in actions that may often bring into question its role in and mandate for assisting refugees.

UNHCR engages in practices that control the lives and wellbeing of mobile populations in ways that raise questions about its commitment to "protect refugees and resolve refugee problems" (UNHCR 2011). It is in designated refugee camps that the UNHCR has much influence in controlling the movement of refugees and in categorizing them and making them knowable (i.e., who they are) and countable through census-taking. In the camps of Dadaab in northeast Kenya, for example, the UNHCR has erected fences of thorns and barbed wire several kilometres long to mark the perimeters of the camps. Within the camps, areas or "blocks" are enclosed that consist of two to three hectares containing 100 to 150 shelters housing 300 to 600 refugees on average. Furthermore, according to Agier (2002), camp refugees have been grouped into various blocks according to their place of origin, ethnicity, and sometimes their clan of origin, and are generally referred to in broad ethnic terms (Somalis) or in terms of nationality (Ethiopians, Sudanese) (2002: 325). Additionally, because numbers are essential for appeals for international funding, Harrell-Bond explains that "extraordinary efforts are taken by UNHCR and NGO partners to conduct 'accurate' censuses. Methods involve herding refugees into enclosures and night swoops on camps" (2002: 52). The author brings our attention to the contents of one manual on registration: "Spot checks involve an actual head count and are best carried out at unsocial hours like midnight or dawn when the majority of people will be in their houses. You will need a large number of staff to go round counting every person" (2002: 52). As Liisa Malkki might put it, the refugee camp becomes a "technology of power" which helps "to constitute 'the refugees' as an object of knowledge and control" (1995: 236).

Likewise, in a study of camp refugees in northwest Tanzania, Turner (2006) demonstrates the surveillance and control of refugees in the Lukole refugee camp, which houses approximately 100,000 Burundian refugees. This camp is an example of the increasing use of remote sensing satellite technologies that can, among other things, make refugee populations knowable by generating satellite images that identify the spatial location of refugees and refugee tents; produce a map of a refugee camp (see Giada, De Groeve, Ehrlich, and Soille 2003); and highlight features (e.g., population size, type of available housing) that can be compared to other refugee sites. Refugees in the Lukole camp are under the surveillance of the Tanzanian Ministry of Home Affairs representative and the camp commandant, while UNHCR is in charge of their "care and maintenance." The camp is heavily governed by international relief agencies that justify their surveillance practices by invoking a perceived collapse of the moral order of Burundi inside the camp (Turner 2006: 760). With the support of UNHCR and its partner agencies, camp residents are subject to projects that control the design of the camp, the volume and composition of food rations, the distribution of food, and procedures for defining vulnerable populations. In this context, while UNHCR attempts to protect camp refugees, its practices also point to the ways that this organization, in partnership with other agencies, imagines and directs the conduct of refugees. Other studies reveal the dark side of UNHCR's activities and practices in other refugee camps (see, for example: Agier 2002: 2011; Branch 2009; Harrell-Bond 2002; Ilcan 2012a; Jansen 2008; Nyers 2006).

Refugees housed and detained in various camps around the globe should not, however, be considered passive victims. They have participated and continue to participate in forms of protest, such as enduring solitary confinement; engaging in self-immolation (Nyers 2006: 119); sewing their mouths shut to stress their isolation and lack of rights (Rygiel 2010: 198); engaging in wide-ranging protests and riots to emphasize their demands for social justice

(Ilcan 2012a); and starting hunger strikes (see Figure 7.3) that can trigger the mechanism of law and charitable responses (Aradau and Huysmans 2009: 602). As more and more refugees speak out and engage in contestations of all sorts, and as systematic discrimination and structural disadvantage start to blur, there will be more and more demands for a fundamental redrafting of the 1951 UN Convention and Protocol Relating to the Status of Refugees (see Papastergiadis 2010: 350).

FIGURE 7.3 Participants of a Relay Hunger Strike at Sanischare Camp

Source: www.bhutannewsservice.com/main-news/diaspora_exile_resettlement/relay-hunger-striker-continues-on-third-day

The following section discusses transnational activism "from below." We focus on the advocacy efforts of diverse transnational activist networks and the convergence of some, especially those that are critical of neoliberal policies, practices, and organizations, into one "movement of movements," known as the Global Justice Movement.

Transnational Activism "from Below"

As we discussed earlier, transnational forms of activism from below refers to the advocacy efforts of diverse transnational activist networks that operate on the ground, in local and national circles, and have a global reach. The concept of Transnational Activist Networks, or TANs, was first advanced by Keck and Sikkink (1998). They defined TANs as "those relevant actors working internationally on an issue, who are bound together by shared values, a common discourse, and dense exchanges of information" (1998: 2). TANs' chief actors can include some or all of the following: international and domestic NGOs focused on research and advocacy; local social movements; foundations; the media; churches, trade unions, consumer organizations and intellectuals; parts of regional and international intergovernmental organizations; and parts of executive and parliamentary branches of government (Keck and Sikkink 1998: 9). TANs aim to change the policies and practices of states and international organizations. They do this by contributing new ideas, norms, and discourses. They provide new information and promote norm implementation by pressuring states to adopt new practices and by monitoring state compliance with new commitments. In many cases, they use the language of human rights to call for change in citizenship policies and practices. Keck and Sikkink describe this process as the "boomerang pattern" (1998: 13), represented in Figure 7.4. As seen in Figure 7.4, when State A blocks demands for change advanced by domestic activists, these activists resort to transnational networks for support. The latter then pressure their own states and (if relevant) international organizations to impel State A to respond to domestic advocates. State A subsequently responds to the international pressure of threats (e.g., withdrawal of foreign aid or trade agreements), rewards (e.g., enhanced business opportunities or international loans), or oral persuasion by agreeing to change its practices and policies.

There are numerous examples throughout the globe that underscore the important role TANs have played in influencing national policy and institutions, as well as the understanding of justice and injustice among ordinary people. For example, the International Lesbian and Gay Association, in alliance with Amnesty International and Human Rights Watch, has been instrumental in challenging nation-states to reform their sodomy laws. Advocacy advanced by these TANs has played an important role in the decriminalization of consensual sex between adults of the same sex in a number of countries

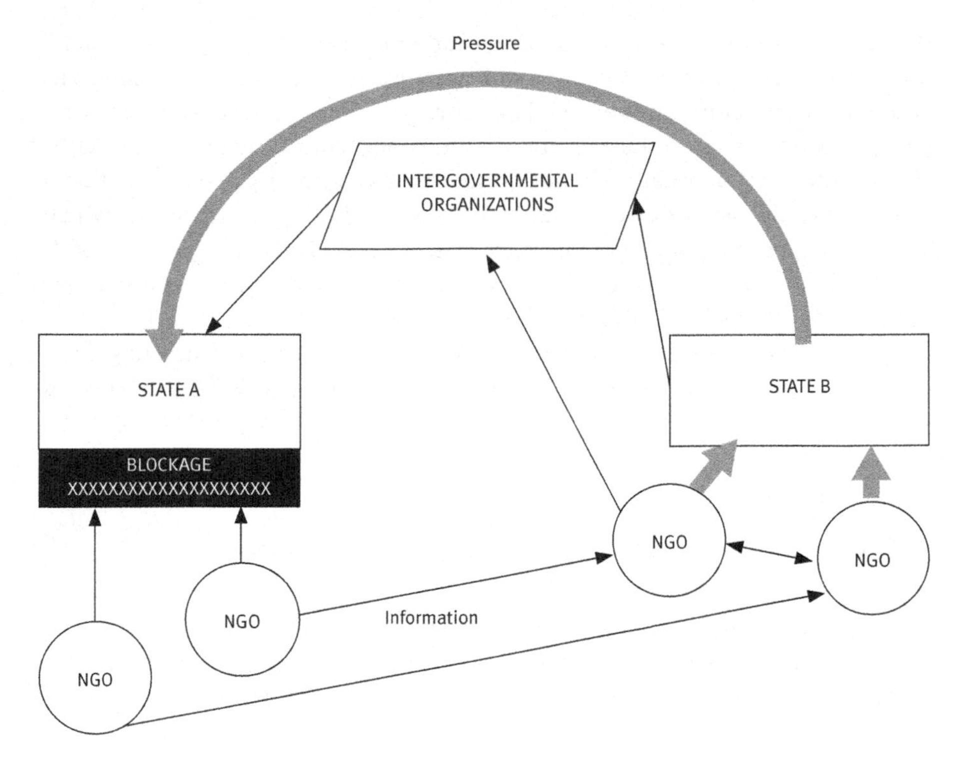

FIGURE 7.4 Transnational Activism
Source: Keck and Sikkink, 1998

(Frank, Boutcher, and Camp 2009). Similarly, TANs' support also improves the likelihood that the North American Agreement on Labour Cooperation's (NAARC) National Administration Offices will accept a petition for a labour rights review in specific workplaces in the NAFTA-ratified countries of Mexico, Canada, and the United States (Nolan Garcia 2011).

It is important to recognize that not all activism against rights violations is likely to gain international support. According to Bob (2001 and 2002), groups that are most likely to succeed in securing backing from transnational advocates are those that can "pitch" their concerns to potential international supporters. In order to be able to do this, they need significant material resources; pre-existing linkages to international actors; skill at international public relations; organizational cohesiveness; and charismatic leadership. Bob illustrates his argument by examining the successful transnationalization of the Ogoni people's movement, an ethnic-based group in Nigeria that mobilized in the 1990s in order to denounce state repression and neglect and to demand political control over Ogoni affairs, economic control over oil-derived revenues, environmental protection, and the preservation of the Ogoni culture, religion and language (see Box 7.3). In addition, Bob (2001) argues that groups are more likely to gain international support if they can "match" their issue focus, preferred tactics, and organizational needs to the concerns and needs of potential supporters. Therefore, in order to attract support, local groups need to adapt to the expectations and concerns of transnational NGOs. Groups that cannot and/or will not do so are unlikely to receive transnational solidarity. This issue, however, raises questions about the degree to which TANs are open to diverse subordinate voices (Bob 2001; Carpenter 2007) and the ways TANs govern local activism. From the social justice perspective put forward in this book, this is a serious concern.

TAN analysts have explored what makes TANs effective in meeting their goals. Keck and Sikkink (1998), for example, have argued that TANs' success

BOX 7.3 THE OGONI PEOPLE ATTRACTING INTERNATIONAL SUPPORT

For many years, the Ogoni people of the Delta region in Nigeria have waged struggles for political, economic, and cultural autonomy and against state repression. When their nation-level protests proved ineffective, the Ogoni leaders solicited international support for their advocacy efforts. While they were unsuccessful in their first year, beginning in 1993, the Ogoni people's cause began to receive increased international media attention and support from transnational NGOs. Foreign governments also began to monitor Nigeria's treatment of the movement's leaders and international organizations shifted the spotlight to the Niger Delta region. This did not happen accidentally. The intense lobbying by the Movement for the Survival of the Ogoni People (MOSOP) played an important role in attracting international attention to the Ogoni cause: the Ogoni people were able to attract the support of the international human rights regime when other groups from the same area have not been as successful. There are four reasons why they were successful. First, MOSOP had a particular ability to "sell" the Ogoni people's cause to international advocacy networks because of the money, professional contacts, and expertise that its local leaders could provide for the purpose of foreign lobbying and publications. For example, Ken Saro-Wiwa and other Ogoni leaders had substantial personal wealth and knowledge to support MOSOP activities, as well as access to professional journalists, writers, and human rights advocates in Great Britain. Second, early in the conflict, the Nigerian government did not restrict local and international activists' travel to and from Oganiland, nor did it place limits on MOSOP's access to communication technologies (i.e., fax and telephone) or to international journalists. Third, early on, MOSOP reframed its goals so as to "match" them to the needs of transnational advocacy networks. For example, MOSOP shifted from minority-rights–focused advocacy for Ogoni political autonomy and cultural-linguistic preservation to an environmental advocacy frame that made claims on multinational oil companies, such as Shell, for ecological damage to Ogoni lands. This shift ultimately attracted important international NGOs, such as Greenpeace International and Friends of the Earth international, to the Ogoni people's cause because the grievances were expressed in terms that were familiar to these organizations. The movement also "matched" INGOs' organizational need to support legitimate movements by organizing a mass mobilization (march) to coincide with the arrival of international representatives, including a Greenpeace photographer, and provide evidence of such legitimacy. And finally, MOSOP was able to present evidence to major NGOs of its legitimacy and representativeness. This evidence was provided in 1993, when Nigerian security forces killed Ogoni protesters, detained MOSOP leaders, and prompted violent attacks on Ogoni villages by other ethnic groups. These events, along with the state's execution of Saro-Wiwa in 1995, served to legitimize the movement's claims and match its needs to those of major international human rights NGOs, such as Human Rights Watch and Amnesty International. (Source: Bob 2001 and 2002).

in affecting changes in the discourse, policies, and programs of states and international organizations depend on both the characteristics of the issues at hand and the characteristics of the actors involved. According to these authors, TANs are more likely to be effective if they focus on the issues that are salient (e.g., bodily harm to vulnerable individuals) and that resonate with the concerns of policy makers and the broader public (e.g., legal equality of opportunities). They have also pointed out that when TANs are dense (that is, comprising many actors) and cohesive, they are also more likely to be effective. At the same time, TANs are more likely to succeed in their campaigns if their targets are vulnerable to either material or moral leverage. States or international organizations that wish to maintain good standing and reputation in the eyes of the international community (for moral or economic reasons) are more susceptible to TANs' leverage tactics (Keck and Sikkink: 25–29).

Much like Keck and Sikkink, Shawki (2011) has illustrated the importance of TANs' organizational strength by comparing the successful International Campaign to Ban Landmines (ICBL) to a considerably less successful campaign led by the International Action Network on Small Arms (IANSA). ICBL emerged from a seed of six NGOs with significant advocacy experience. They had diverse membership involved in a variety of issues and national networks-of-networks around the globe. ICBL developed dense ties among its members through intense information exchange by means of newsletters and mailings; building and maintaining informal and formal relationships with government officials; the use of communication technologies; and the provision of advocacy training for those members who knew about landmines but not about advocacy. Such organization was lacking in the case of IANA. In addition, Shawki (2010) draws attention to the role played by the UN. She illustrates how the UN can offer very valuable opportunities for TANs to influence policy trends, particularly when TAN members are invited to participate and given an opportunity to voice their concerns. The ICBL was successful because its campaigns enjoyed full support from the UN and UN-sponsored conferences. In contrast, IANA did not receive UN endorsement because of the influence of the pro-guns lobby on this organization (Shawki 2010). Shawki views the support provided by the UN as "political opportunities." The "political opportunity structure" is an important concept in the social movement literature. We will discuss this concept in more detail later in this chapter. But the illustration provided by Shawki also points to the importance of viewing the UN in relation to other political and economic actors that often shape its views, policies, and practices.

In addition to the issues discussed above (TANs' organizational strength and the political opportunities available), we have to examine the broader political and economic context that makes certain campaigns successful while blocking change demanded by others. In particular, in the context of the framework put forward in this book, it is important to ask to what extent neoliberal governance creates obstacles (or opportunities) for TANs' advocacy campaigns. Indeed, research has pointed out that TANs that are supportive of neoliberal objectives are, not surprisingly, most likely to gain support from policy makers in the current climate. Consequently, the changes these TANs seek to bring about can be detrimental to many people, particularly poor and marginalized populations. For example, some advocacy networks comprising activists in the US, UK, and India are convinced that neoliberalism, and particularly private schooling, are the solution to India's difficulties in providing high quality universal primary education. They seek to convince the Indian government to expand private schooling in India and accept such neoliberal initiatives as micro-finance advocacy, contracting out of the management of low-performing government-run schools to private foundations, and public–private partnerships between some Indian states and companies able to supply schools with IT and training. These TANs have been creating business infrastructure for private schools while also pressuring the Indian government to open India up to for-profit schools (Nambissan and Ball 2010) which would be beyond the reach of many economically disadvantaged people. Focusing on the detrimental impact of TAN support, Lerche (2008) has illustrated how the support provided by TANs to the Dalit movement in India has tended to de-politicize this movement. Dalit (the "oppressed") is the name given to themselves by people found at the bottom of the Indian caste system (formerly known as "untouchables"). Although, traditionally, the Dalit movement has focused on broad, emancipatory discourses and multi-sectorial initiatives, the current TAN-linked movement focuses on policies which are more compatible with neoliberal discourses. Employment, for example, has received high priority within this new movement. As Lerche puts it, the "empowerment of a social group does not figure in neoliberal individualist policy making, where 'power' is seen in relation to individual capabilities, not to group-level social oppression, and where solutions are based on enabling such individual capabilities" (2008: 257). As a result of such processes, the broader Dalit empowerment agenda has been marginalized.

While TANs that support neoliberal priorities are more likely to gain support from the policy makers, those that oppose exploitative and destructive practices of transnational corporations (and the neoliberal international organizations and states that support them) are least likely to bring about tangible change. Corporate-focused TANs have tried to protect local communities whose lives and environment have been destroyed by production or extraction activities. Activists' appeals to local corporate managers may fail because the latter are protected by local governments. Local authorities are often reluctant to challenge corporate practices for fear of losing financial gains and because they lack the capacity to regulate or to enforce compliance with the imposed regulation. In such situations, local communities may seek support among transnational activists in order to drive change via top-down pressure on senior executives in the corporation's headquarters. The subsidiary's parent corporation then becomes the target of activists' campaigns. Corporate-focused TANs attempt to make change by organizing consumer boycotts, filing lawsuits, and utilizing corporate shareholder structures to convince corporations to cease exploitative and destructive practices (McAtee and Pulver 2009; Dale 2008). Yet, as the examples of oil companies operating in Nigeria clearly illustrate, corporations often introduce cosmetic changes to "whitewash" their image while continuing to inflict damage on the environment, repress opposition, and destroy the lives of local residents (Human Rights Watch 1999; Vidal 2010).

Cross-border labour activism that targets foreign companies responsible for exploitative labour conditions and the denial of workers' right to form independent trade unions has also faced tough opposition. The growing cross-border justice movement has been waging a war against the working conditions and the environmental impact of the maquiladora (assembly plant) industry in Mexico and Central America (Horowitz 2009; Armbruster-Sandoval 2005). Since the early 1990s, Latin American unions, supported by North American labour activists, have struggled to guarantee protection, raise wages, improve working conditions, and create opportunities for collective bargaining. Some cross-border union-organizing campaigns have succeeded (see 7.4 for a discussion of cross-border union activism at a Korean-owned factory named Kukdung, located in Puebla, Mexico). Yet, most struggles have either failed altogether or enjoyed no more than short-lived success. There are two reasons for this. The first is the vulnerability of union organizers and supporters. Numerous maquila workers, no matter how well organized or careful they have been, have been fired for organizing or even joining unions. This situation has created tremendous fear, making organizing nearly impossible. The second reason is that union-organizing drives can be undermined through capital mobility. Companies have closed down and relocated production following workers' success in gaining the right to form a union (Armbruster-Sandoval 2005). What emerges clearly from these examples is the need to fight against neoliberalism (particularly the way it prioritizes market needs

BOX 7.4 ❊ KUKDONG INTERNATIONAL: A VICTORY IN CROSS-BORDER LABOUR ACTIVISM

In early 2001, more than two thirds of the 900 workers at the Korean-owned factory Kukdong International went on strike. The factory, located in Puebla, Mexico, employed mostly young women and teens to produce apparel (mostly sweatshirts) for Nike and Reebok. Prior to the strike, Kukdong had illegally fired a group of workers for protesting poor working conditions (low pay, unsanitary food, physical and verbal abuse, inadequate union representation, and denial of maternity and sick leave) and for trying to organize an independent labour union. In response, the factory workers rallied together to organize a strike in support of their co-workers and the demands they had put forth. The strike provoked violent reactions from riot police, as well as from union officials at the Confederación Revolucionaria de Obreros y Campesinos (CROC) and the company's administrators. Seventeen workers were injured in confrontations with police, workers were fired, and others were forced to sign "oaths" declaring their loyalty to the CROC union.

These events caught the attention of anti-sweatshop and social justice activists in other parts of Mexico, as well as in Canada, Europe, Korea, and the United States. In solidarity, university students and other advocates in these countries pressured Nike and Reebok to impel Kukdong to respect their corporate codes of conduct and to allow the workers to form an independent union. At first, the factory refused to accept these demands, causing Nike—its biggest supplier—to stop sourcing it. Likewise, Mexican state labour officials refused to recognize the workers' independent union. Nevertheless, after months of organized transnational activism, the independent union SITEKIM won recognition in September 2001 and negotiated a collective bargaining agreement with Kukdong (by then renamed "Mexmode"). The CROC union subsequently withdrew from the factory and Nike resumed its business with Kukdong. (Sources: Armbruster-Sandoval 2005: 21–2; Wells 2009: 572–3; Connor 2001: 80–90).

over people's social and economic rights) and those transnational organizations (such as the World Bank, IMF, and the WTO) that propel neoliberal approaches around the globe, as discussed above. This is precisely the objective of the Global Justice Movement, discussed in the next section. Before we move to that section, however, we would like to comment on the Northern bias in the TAN literature.

In much of the literature on transnational activism, there is a tendency to overemphasize the positive impact of Northern-based TANs on activists and policies in the Global South. It appears in this literature as though political change originates in the North and is diffused by TANs to the Global South in a unidirectional manner. Nevertheless, it is important to acknowledge that change often occurs in the opposite direction. For example, visions, organizing strategies, ideologies, and tactics developed by the Zapatista movement in Mexico (discussed in Box 7.5), as well as the riots staged in many cities of the Global South against structural adjustment policies imposed by the IMF, have inspired and influenced activism in the United States, Canada, and other Northern countries (Zugman Dellacioppa 2011; Khasnabish 2008; Smith 2008: 104; Montagna 2010). In fact, as will be discussed below, various forms of activism taking place in the Global South in the 1990s are at the root of the Global Justice Movement.

BOX 7.5 ❋ THE ZAPATISTA MOVEMENT: INSPIRATION FOR THE GLOBAL JUSTICE MOVEMENT

On 1 January 1994, the *Ejército Zapatista de Liberación Nacional* (EZLN) declared war on the Mexican government. *"Hoy Decimos ¡Basta!"* (Today We Say *Enough*!), they stated emphatically in their First Declaration of the Selva Lacandona, denouncing the hunger, poverty, and lack of democratic institutions available to indigenous and many other communities throughout the Mexican Republic. Their rebellion, the Zapatistas proclaimed, was a legitimate exercise of their constitutional right to alter their form of government (without permission) and to demand dignity (without handouts). The armed phase of the Zapatista rebellion lasted just 12 days: the Zapatistas heeded local community members' call for a ceasefire and the Mexican government's repression slackened in response to pressures from national and international civil society. Since this ceasefire and the failure of the 1996 San Andrés Peace Accord, the Mexican government and the Zapatista communities have been engaged in a low-intensity war.

From the beginning, the global dimension of this struggle has been highlighted by the Zapatistas. The date chosen for the uprising—the day the North American

Free Trade Agreement (NAFTA) was to go into effect for Mexico, the US, and Canada—was by no means a coincidence: the EZLN had said that NAFTA meant death to indigenous peoples and the struggles of landless peasants. In their Sixth Declaration of the Selva Lacandona in 2005, the Zapatistas explained this view: "Capitalism," they say, "does as it likes; that is, it destroys and changes what it doesn't like and eliminates whatever gets in its way. For example, those who do not produce, [or] buy, [or] sell modern merchandise, or those who rebel against this order, get in the way of capitalism. And those who are not useful, well, they are despised. That's why the indigenous populations get in the way of neoliberal globalization, and that's why it despises them and wants to eliminate them." The Zapatistas go on to say, however, that "just as there is neoliberal globalization, there is a globalization of rebellion" against it.

The Zapatistas have played a pivotal role in this globalized rebellion. They have engaged both national and international civil society in dialogues about building a more inclusive world, one in which "quepan todos los mundos que resisten" (all worlds in resistance have a place) (Zapatistas, Sexta Declaración). *The First Intercontinental Encuentro (Encounter) for Humanity and Against Neoliberalism*, for example, was organized by the Zapatistas. Drawing thousands of civil society participants from around the world to the jungles of Chiapas, this 1996 *Encuentro* resulted in calls for an "International Order of Hope" to build resistance and alternatives to global neoliberal capitalism. The Second *Encuentro*, held in Spain the following year, provided the opportunity and context to form *Peoples' Global Action* (PGA), a transnational network of global justice movements. Three things have provided a wealth of inspiration to the Global Justice Movement: subsequent international meetings; the Zapatistas' media communications (emitted most notably by the bilingual and eloquent Subcomandante Marcos); and the establishment of autonomous communities that strive to *"mandar obedeciendo"* or "govern by obeying." (Sources: Collier and Lowery 2005; Khasnabish 2008; Stahler-Sholk 2010; EZLN 1993; EZLN 2005; Translation by Victoria Simmons).

In addition, the impact of Northern TANs on improving labour standards in the South has been exaggerated in the literature. It is not Northern-based but rather Southern-based advocates' initiatives and workers' struggles that have produced the greatest improvements in labour standards in Southern countries. While Northern actors can effectively mobilize mass media and consumer consciousness, local workers' struggles in the anti-sweatshop advocacy campaigns have played a much more significant role in bringing about change. Northern supporters are undoubtedly important; however, they play only an auxiliary role in workers' struggles in Southern workplaces (Wells

2009; Armbruster-Sandoval 2005). For example, Wells (2009) discusses the case of Sri Lankan workers in the export processing zones (EPZs) who have struggled to improve their companies' labour standards. Here, the author argues that, while the support provided by the TAN consisting of global unions and NGOs was indeed important, it was the local women's networks, organized around issues of gender inequality and workers' issues, that were key players in bringing about changes (Wells 2009). The militancy and experience of activists in the Global South have been important resources needed to build the Global Justice Movement to which we now turn.

The Global Justice Movement

The Global Justice Movement (GJM) can be defined as "a sustained transnational movement of grassroots activists and organized advocacy groups working for global justice (economic, social, political, and environmental) and against the neoliberal model of international development and the policies of the states and international institutions that advance it, in favour of a model of development aimed at combating the gross inequalities that that model implies" (Hadden and Tarrow 2007: 215). It can be traced back to the international movements of the 1970s and 1980s relating to such issues as peace, human rights, development, ecology, and women's issues. Many of these movements faced few political opportunities during this period, had a small number of internal resources, and were fragmented on many single issues, which made it difficult for them to work transnationally. Despite the persistence of these challenges in the 1990s, these movements were able to begin the construction and consolidation of stable networks (Pianta and Marchetti 2007; Pellow 2007). A number of events, many of which originated in the Global South, served as precursors to the Global Justice Movement. These include: riots taking place in many cities of the Global South against structural adjustment programs imposed by the International Monetary Fund and the World Bank; opposition to Free Trade Agreements (and particularly the North American Free Trade Agreement [NAFTA], and the Multilateral Agreement on Investment [MAI]); the movement in support of Third World Debt forgiveness (particularly the anti-debt campaign called Jubilee 2000); the anti-sweatshop struggles; and the Zapatista movement, an indigenous uprising led by the Zapatista National Liberation Army (known as the EZLN in Spanish; see Box 7.5) (Smith 2008: 100–4; Moghadam 2009: 94–9, Curran 2007; Becker 2007; Gautney 2010: 39–41).

The mobilization of mass protest against the main neoliberal institutions in Seattle in 1999 (known as the "Battle of Seattle") was a watershed event that significantly increased the visibility of the Global Justice Movement. In late November 1999, the WTO's Ministerial Conference was scheduled to address world trade negotiations in Seattle, Washington. There, some thirty thousand militants blocked the delegates' entry to the conference (Smith 2002). This was followed by a cycle of protests against the WTO, World Bank, IMF, and the G8 in various parts of the world (Moghadam 2009: 98; della Porta, Andretta, Mosca and Reiter 2006; Gautney 2010: 41–6).

Why did the Global Justice Movement arise? While the growing awareness of the inequities generated or amplified under neoliberal globalization played a certain role, as social movement theorists argue, these grievances are not sufficient. In addition, transnational political opportunities had to be there for the movement to take shape. For social movement theorists, political opportunities are understood as those elements of the political environment that either encourage or stifle collective action (Tarrow 2005: 23). Two developments have been particularly conducive to the emergence of the Global Justice Movement. First, it has been greatly facilitated by innovations in transportation and communications technologies such as cheaper travel, the affordability of personal computers, and immediate internet communications for the rapid spread of new information (Moghadam 2009: 99; Borras 2008). Second, the United Nations conferences of the 1990s also served as a fertile ground for the formation of what Tarrow (2005) would call "internationalization" or "a dense, triangular structure of relations among states, non-state actors and international institutions, and the opportunities this produces for actors to engage in collective action at different levels of this system (Tarrow 2005: 25). In the 1990s, the UN held a serious of world conferences to which activist groups were invited. NGOs often held parallel fora, which provided the opportunity for activists to network. These growing transnational activist and advocacy networks were able to lobby UN conference delegates and policy makers, voice their concerns, disseminate their literature, and exchange ideas through interpersonal communication (Moghadam 2009: 99–100; Smith 2008: 117). These networks, consisting of both formal (e.g., churches, NGOs, trade unions) and informal (e.g., environmental, women's, and living-wage committees) organizations, serve as what social movement theorists call "mobilizing structures," that is, structures that make it possible for social movements to engage in coordinated action (Smith 2008: 111–17; Moghadam 2009: 104–6).

While the UN conferences played an important role in extending and cementing transnational activist networks, the transnational social movements of the 1980s and 1990s made it possible for these networks to emerge in the first place. Transnational social activism carried out during those decades laid the foundation for new skills, ideas, and structures needed for transnational organizing. In addition to exchanging ideas and learning new ways of engaging in activism through training sessions, internet sites, and ongoing organizing efforts, activists also fostered collective identities to bridge differences between different cultural and special-issue groups (Smith 2008: 104). Box 7.6 illustrates how a transnational agrarian activist network, La Via Campesina,

BOX 7.6 LA VIA CAMPESINA (THE PEASANTS' WAY): A TRANSNATIONAL AGRARIAN MOVEMENT

La Via Campesina—"The Peasants' Way"—is a transnational movement that connects 150 local and national farmers' organizations in 70 countries around the world. The network was founded in 1993 in Mons, Belgium by a group of farmers who saw the need to unite small-scale farmers, foster a common vision and voice, and offer an alternative to the neoliberal global development project. In 1996, the network introduced the principle of "food sovereignty" at an FAO food summit; this concept subsequently became one of its principal platforms for social change and a major theme for discussion among local and international actors around the world. The movement defines food sovereignty as "the right of peoples to healthy and culturally appropriate food produced through sustainable methods and their right to define their own food and agriculture systems. It ensures that the rights to use and manage lands, territories, water, seeds, livestock and biodiversity are in the hands of those who produce food and not of the corporate sector." Today, *La Via Campesina* unites approximately 200 million small- and medium-scale farmers, landless peasants, indigenous people, migrants, and agricultural workers. As an autonomous, pluralist, and multicultural movement, its main goal is to promote small-scale sustainable agriculture as "the way" or "la via" for combating hunger and poverty and protecting the environment. The movement organizes and participates in international meetings, campaigns and public protests, and it publishes policy documents. It focuses primarily on issues such as agrarian reform; biodiversity and genetic resources; food sovereignty and trade; women's rights and gender equality; human rights; migrations and rural workers; sustainable peasant agriculture; and fostering youth involvement in sustainable agriculture. (Sources: http://viacampesina.org; Desmarais 2007; Borras 2008)

formed in the early 1990s, has expanded significantly to become a transnational movement comprising 200 million small- and medium-scale farmers, landless peasants, indigenous people, migrants, and agricultural workers.

The GJM articulates a vision that implies criticism of and alternatives to the neoliberal, military-style globalization that currently dominates. It protests the injustice associated with this model and searches for international democracy, as well as economic and social justice (Pianta and Marchetti 2007). The GJM comprises diverse groups (Gautney 2010; Pianta and Marchetti 2007; Flesher Fominaya 2010) covering a wide spectrum of issues, as illustrated in Table 7.2. della Porta identified two constellations of groups in her analysis of European GJM activists (as she calls them). These constellations differ in terms of their repertoires of action, organizational structure, and discursive frames (see Table 7.3).

Table 7.2 Global Justice Movement: Issues, Networks and Frames

Central Advocacy Issue	Transnational Movements and Networks	Advocacy Frames
Anti-Corporate Governance and Media	ATTAC; 50 Years is Enough!; Public Citizen; Global Trade Watch; CorpWatch; Students Transforming and Resisting Corporations (STARC); Independent Media Center (IndyMedia) Democracy Now!	Democratization of global (corporate) governance; corporate accountability; taxation on financial markets; promotion of diverse, non-corporate, independent media sources
Anti-Poverty	50 Years is Enough!; Oxfam; Jubilee Network; Make Poverty History; Christian Aid; World Council for Churches; Catholic Agency for Overseas Development, United for a Fair Economy	Sustainable development; alternatives to neoliberalism; debt cancellation for countries of the Global South; support for the poor
Environment	Greenpeace; Friends of the Earth International; Earth First!; Sierra Club; Rainforest Action Network	Sustainable development; environmental protection
Food Sovereignty	Via Campesina; Landless Workers Movement	"Biopiracy" relating to plant and seed patents; trade agreements conditioned by gentically modified imports; biodiversity and genetic resources; agrarian reforms; sustainable agriculture
Women and Gender	DAWN; WIDE; Marche Mondiale des Femmes; WLUL; Feminist Articulation Mercosur	Women's rights; gender justice
Human Rights	Amnesty International; Global Exchange; Fédération des droits humains; Global Exchange; No Person (One) is Illegal; ACT UP; Health GAP	Civil, political, and socio-economic rights of persons, regardless of citizenship status
Indigenous Rights	Zapatistas; Congreso Nacional Indígena de México; Confederación de Nacionalidades Indígenas del Ecuador	Cultural and land rights; political autonomy
Labour Rights	International Workers of the World (a.ka. "Wobblies"); International Brotherhood of Teamsters; Service Employees International Union (SEIU); Australian Council of Trade Unions; Canadian Labour Congress; COSATU; Korean Federation of Trade Unions; United Students Against Sweatshops	Labour and collective bargaining rights; betterment of employment wages, stability, and working conditions; worker solidarity

Table 7.2 *continued*

Central Advocacy Issue	Transnational Movements and Networks	Advocacy Frames
Peace	Food not Bombs; Peace Boat; Code Pink; Stop the War Coalition; United for Peace and Justice; WILPF; Raging Grannies International; Seeds for Peace	Against militarization and war; seeks sustainable peace
Universal Access to Basic Needs	Council of Canadians; Water Justice	Against the privatization and corporate control of basic resources such as water; education; health care; the General Agreement of Trade and Services (GTS) and the WTO's Trade-Related Aspects of Intellectual Property (TRIPS) which can privatize basic needs; in support of the right to water
Global South–North Relations	Focus on Global South; Third World Network; Third World Forum	Anti-imperialism: favours local/ regional solutions to Third World development challenges; favours a more just distribution of global resources; fair trade

Sources: Moghadam 2009; Highleyman 2011.

Table 7.3 **Differences within the GJM in European Countries**

	Constellation 1	Constellation 2
Action	Disruptive Protest Dynamics	Lobbying and Media campaigns
Organization	Dense, decentralized networks; informal and formal groups and associations	Srong associations and NGOs
Frames	a. Global Justice linked to fight against neoliberalism at home b. Conception of radical participatory democracy	a. Solidarity with the South b. Conception of associational democracy
Countries where these characteristics dominate	Italy, France, Spain	UK, Germany, Switzerland, US

Source: della Porta 2007.

Yet, despite its diversity, GJM has been successful in uniting different constituencies and in revitalizing working class struggles (della Porta 2007). Many of these groups come together to discuss their particular critiques of neoliberalism, elaborate new visions, and exchange ideas of strategies for change at the World Social Forum (as well as at some regional and national fora), discussed in Chapter 8.

Conclusion

In this chapter, we have discussed a range of issues around transnational activism "from above" and "from below." We have learned about the complexities associated with both forms of activism in such areas as peace, human rights, development, ecology, and women's issues, as well as their strengths and limitations in terms of improving the lives of vulnerable and marginalized peoples.

In light of our discussion of transnational activist practices today, we believe that it is crucial to think about the issue of expanding the political spaces for transnational activism. We are concerned with expanding political spaces that would appeal to more varied social groups in ways that would not advocate for the development of universalistic and centralizing solutions that can work to deny the diversity of marginal and marginalized peoples as well as their different struggles and their diverse demands for social justice.

Key Terms

transnational forms of activism from above advocacy efforts by organizations at the international level that operate on the behalf of others and use the language of rights, protection, or humanitarianism to bring about change for marginalized or vulnerable groups

transnational forms of activism from below advocacy efforts of diverse transnational activist networks

transnational activist networks networks of formal and informal organizations that operate on the ground in local and national circles and that have a global reach

Questions for Critical Thought

1. Identify and discuss the major strengths and challenges facing such transnational organizations as Oxfam International, the IOM, and the UNHCR in terms of their efforts to meet the needs of disadvantaged people. If you were in the position and had the opportunity to improve the lives of disadvantaged people, what would you do differently and why?
2. How and to what extent can TANs effectively attain their goals given the challenges they face as a consequence of neoliberal agendas and policies?
3. What two developments were particularly favourable to the emergence of the Global Justice Movement?
4. Can the Global Justice Movement bring about social justice to all disadvantaged people? If so, how and in what ways would this change be accomplished? If not, explain why.

Annotated Additional Readings

Heather Gautney. 2010. *Protest and Organization in the Alternative Globalization Era: NGOs, Social Movements, and Political Parties*. New York: Palgrave Macmillan. This book details the history of the alter-globalization protests over the last decade and the attempts by various leftist groups to build alternatives to neoliberal development through the mechanism of the World Social Forum.

Valentine M. Moghadam. 2009. *Globalization and Social Movements: Islamism, Feminism, and the Global Justice Movement*. Lanham: Rowman and Littlefield Publishers. This book introduces key issues and debates associated with the fields of globalization and social movements, and provides detailed case studies on transnational social movements, namely Islamic movements, global feminism, and the global justice movement.

Jackie Smith. 2008. *Social Movements for Global Democracy*. Baltimore: The Johns Hopkins University Press. This book addresses the contested processes of globalization and provides valuable insights for understanding and moving towards global democratization.

Sydney Tarrow. 2005. *The New Transnational Activism*, Cambridge: Cambridge University Press. This book demonstrates the broader political meanings associated with new forms of transnational activism, including the manner in which transnational activists draw on the resources, the networks, and the opportunities to make their claims, and the processes that link the local, the national, and the international.

Related Websites

International Organization for Migration
www.iom.int

Oxfam International
www.oxfam.org

United Nations
www.un.org

World Social Forum
www.forumsocialmundial.org.br

8 Conclusion

Learning Objectives

- Explore how processes of globalization create new possibilities for engaging in social justice efforts
- Examine the notions of cosmopolitanism and global citizenship
- Understand the role of Global Justice Networks
- Situate the World Social Forum in the struggle for global social justice
- Examine the potential role of national states and the UN in bringing about global social justice

Introduction

Issues in Social Justice: Citizenship and Transnational Struggles is one book in the social justice studies field that we believe provides a contribution to the growing debates and issues centring on the notion of social justice and its links to citizenship and transnational struggles. Within this thematic focus, our analysis has concentrated on key substantive subjects, ranging from discussions of citizenship and transformations of the welfare state to critical pressures and changes underscoring the voluntary sector, volunteer citizens, and marginal and disadvantaged groups, to debates on human rights and transnational activism. Our analysis raises thematic concerns and questions that move across disciplines and reveal the depth of the dilemmas of social justice as we conceive it and, in the process, provides some constructive, critical ideas for students, researchers, activists, and policy makers. The resulting work is intended to map some of the key debates relating to social justice, citizenship, and transnational struggles, to make connections between related themes and issues, and to assist in developing social change.

In this concluding chapter, our discussion centres on the diverse ways in which social justice has been taken up on a transnational and global scale to bring about change now and in the future. In this discussion we first focus on the ideas of "global social justice" and "global justice networks" and their connections to bringing about a more socially just world. We then turn to the World Social Forum as a site that opens up new spaces for articulating new visions of social justice. Finally, we elaborate on the ways in which various groups may engage in and expand spaces of democratic participation.

Towards Global Social Justice

Many social analysts have observed that processes of globalization and transnationalism can create new possibilities for the quest for social justice (Widows and Smith 2011; Sklair 2011; Cabrera 2011; Routledge and Cumbers 2009). For example, in "The Globalization of Human Rights," Leslie Sklair (2011) suggests that "generic globalization," as he calls it, has created unprecedented opportunities for advances in human rights. He defines generic globalization in terms of four phenomena—moments in the temporal sense and with respect to social forces—of increasing significance since the middle of the twentieth century. These phenomena are the electronic revolution, particularly transformations in the global scope of the electronic mass media (the electronic moment); postcolonialisms (the postcolonial moment); the subsequent development of transnational social spaces (the spatial moment); and new forms of cosmopolitanism (the cosmopolitan moment). He considers that each of these moments offers great potential for the expansion of human rights in terms of the "increasing the numbers of people whose lives can be improved by access to human rights, and qualitatively, in terms of the quality of human rights access" (Sklair 2011: 11–12). In this regard, for example, he considers the electronic revolution as bringing about knowledge of human rights entitlements to millions of people around the world who have been denied these rights and to those who are in positions of authority and who deny human rights to others. Likewise, the postcolonial moment, particularly the postcolonial revolution that began in Latin America in the nineteenth century and continued in the second half of the twentieth century, has encompassed processes (including cross-border migration and multiculturalism) that have met up with the processes of globalization in the field of human rights.

Processes of globalization and transnationalism have positive consequences in terms of the expansion of human rights, although there are underlying conflicts and tensions that can undermine this expansion. Leslie Sklair brings attention to the concept of "capitalist globalization" which has worked to weaken the advances in human rights. This concept, he suggests, upholds the views that globalizing corporations is the most efficient and equitable form of production, distribution, and exchange; that the transnational capitalist class "organizes communities and the global order in the best interests of everyone,"; and that the cultural ideology of consumerism satisfies our needs (2011: 11). He emphasizes that capitalist globalization not only subordinates human rights to the cultural dimensions of consumerism (i.e., identities and values become inextricably linked with what people purchase and consume) but also restricts human rights to the civil and political spheres wherein rights are viewed in terms of freedom from state interference (Sklair 2011: 12–14). Nevertheless, the crucial point that Sklair advances is that there is a way to destabilize capitalist globalization and move towards achieving global social justice, namely taking seriously and advocating for the globalization of human rights. As Widdows and Smith observe, Sklair promotes a two-fold alternative: "First, he emphasizes the need for the nurturing of a culture-ideology of universal human rights in which universally agreed rights and responsibilities—rather than consumerism—become the foundation for the way in which people live their lives." Second, Sklair urges that such rights and responsibilities should no longer be bracketed off from the economic and social sphere but, quite the contrary, should explicitly "incorporate issues such as people's access to adequate shelter, healthcare, education and employment" (2011: 3). In this context, Sklair recognizes that the globalization of human rights can play an important role in transnational transformations that aim towards the gradual elimination of privately owned big businesses, an emerging anti-capitalist globalization movement, and the establishment of more equitable social relations.

Destabilizing the Westphalian Frame: Cosmopolitanism and Global Citizenship

Like Sklair, other researchers are concerned with the necessity of bringing about more equitable social relations as part of the move towards achieving social justice, such as through the abolition of inequalities around the world (Koukouzelis 2011; Cabrera 2011) or through the new globally connected forms of collective action against neoliberalism or what is termed "global justice networks" (Routledge and Cumbers 2009) as we discussed in Chapters 2 and 7. To bring about global social justice, many researchers call for such approaches as "cosmopolitanism," "cosmopolitan citizenship," or "global citizenship" (Linklater 1998; Koukouzelis 2001; Cabrera 2011; Vertovec and Cohen 2002; Dower and Williams 2002). Cosmopolitanism refers both to transnational and international social justice—that is, to principles applicable to relations within states that are the concerns of international legal regulation, and to principles of the rightful distribution among states (or among persons or groups in different states) that defend the continuity of the principle applied (Koukouzelis 2011). In light of theories of global justice, Koukouzelis (2011) recognizes that there has been the need for global solutions to global problems, such as those that aim to resolve the problems of poverty, environmental pollution, and massive inequalities on a global scale.

From a cosmopolitan perspective, Koukouzelis sees the global economy as a site for placing people in legal and economic relations with other people from all over the world (2011: 32). As such, the relationship between the global economy and social justice involves, from his viewpoint, the membership of all people in a global, rather than national, community. It also involves understanding that the kind of rights related to social justice are "rights of membership" (2011: 38). In terms of formulating change towards achieving global social justice in the future, he calls for the eradication of all inequalities regardless of their origins.

Linklater Koukouzelis (1998: 32) argues that cosmopolitan citizenship must imply more than a moral commitment not to exploit the weaknesses of others and to treat all other human beings with care and compassion. He suggests that in order to have real meaning, cosmopolitan citizenship requires political action to build communication communities in which the most vulnerable partners would have the power to refuse and renegotiate offers and contest unjust social structures. Parekh's (2003) associates globally oriented citizenship with: (a) a critical evaluation of the policies of one's country in order to advance the interests of humankind at large; (b) an active interest in, and a sense of responsibility for, the citizens of other countries; and (c) an active commitment to bringing about global justice. Van den Anker suggests that we have an "obligation to build global institutions that are effective in implementing the duties created by global principles of distributive justice" (van den Anker 2002: 159). Concerned particularly about the rights of non-citizens (such as asylum claimants and unauthorized migrants), Cabrera (2011) contends that individuals committed to "global citizenship" have the responsibility to take measures to advance the rights of non-citizens ("contributory duties"); to agree to shoulder the cost of more expansive distributive arrangements ("accommodation duties"); and to engage in advocacy, lobbying, and protesting to promote reforms in national governing institutions as well as in institutions of global governance such as the World Trade Organization, the World Bank, and others (4). These proposals are consistent with Nancy Fraser's call for reframing justice in global (or post-Westphalian) terms (discussed in Chapter 2).

Global Justice Networks

In this book we have placed an important emphasis on how and the extent to which neoliberal policies and agendas undermine efforts towards achieving a more socially just world that can offer inclusive and sustainable social, economic, and cultural relations. We have discussed, for example, the imposition of neoliberal frameworks and their links to the decline of the welfare state and of social support for disadvantaged groups; to the deregulation and flexibilization of employment practices and their effects on vulnerable populations (Chapters 3 and 4); to the marginalization of particular groups, such as women, the poor, and the elderly; and to qualitative changes in social, economic, and environmental conditions on a global scale and the resulting social inequalities these conditions create for particular groups (Chapters 5 to 7). In this context, it is not surprising that an array of struggles and initiatives against neoliberalism has been developing and calling for new visions for social justice. In Chapter 7, for example, we examined the complexities associated with transnational activism and struggles and their potential for fostering and expanding socially just relations around the globe.

As we said in Chapter 7, global justice networks comprise new globally connected forms of collective action against neoliberalism and articulate demands for social, economic, and environmental justice. These forms of action attempt to forge inclusive, democratic forms of globalization and global networks of action, and to retain local autonomy over strategies and tactics. For Routledge and Cumbers (2009), such global justice networks are not examples of "anti-globalization" but rather "represent struggles for inclusive, democratic forms of globalisation, using the communicative tools of the global system. What they are against is the neoliberal form of globalisation" (2009: 16). These forms of action involve the creation of a range of networks including, for example, those of communication, solidarity, information-sharing, and mutual support. It is not merely a matter of forming global justice networks: it is also crucial that these networks be globally active and engage in the production, exchange, and strategic use of information (e.g., email, telephone, circulation of newsletters and bulletins) so that socially or geographically distant actors can potentially be involved in broader global networks of support, action, and debate to bring about social, economic, and environmental justice changes in the future. There are many examples of these kinds of networks, such as global days of action, counter-summits, and campaigns that involve local, national, and international participants from around the world and that aim to resist neoliberal agendas and practices by targeting, for example, international institutions and national governments' adoption of neoliberal policies (see della Porta et al. 2006).

While Routledge and Cumbers recognize the salience of global justice networks in terms of bringing about a more socially just world, they also emphasize the importance of recognizing that such networks, and the movements that comprise them, involve a diversity of struggles that are still territorially based but increasingly advancing their actions to become connected to broader spatial networks (2009: 18–19). While these networks can involve differing conceptions of justice as they vary in different cultural and political circumstances, the authors claim that network participants often share common claims to broadly defined notions of justice that concern issues of redistribution and recognition in attempts to resolve inequitable outcomes and the conditions that give rise to them (see also Chapter 2). Overall, for Routledge and Cumbers, global justice networks represent the ability of different forms of collective action to be able to work together without "attempting to develop universalistic and centralising solutions that deny the diversity of interests and identities that are confronted with neoliberal globalisation processes" (2009: 19).

Our discussion up to this point highlights the ways in which collective forms of action aim to bring about a more socially just world in the future, such as those advocating for "global social justice" or those involved in "global justice networks." From our perspective, it is crucial to recognize the diverse spaces within which individuals and groups can campaign for a world in which social justice is a greater priority. These spaces may operate alongside neoliberal or religious spaces and involve worldwide participants calling for change and articulating new ideas of social justice. From our perspective, we see that there are many spaces that come to inhabit these actions and these visions. The World Social Forum, established to discuss the alternatives to corporate globalization and neoliberalism, provides an important example in this regard.

The World Social Forum

The World Social Forum (WSF) emerged in response to criticisms that the Global Justice Movement (GJM) focused too much on protest against current neoliberal modes of globalization while failing to articulate alternatives. Under the slogan "Another world is possible," annual and (since 2007) biannual WSF meetings provide a space for anti-neoliberal critics to debate and propose alternative visions. WSF also serves as a coordinating assembly of the Global Justice Movement, created by Brazilian activist Oded Grajew. His ideas, along with the efforts of Francisco "Chico" Whitaker Ferreira, a Roman Catholic activist, and Bernard Cassen, president of the French organization ATTAC (Association to Tax Financial Transactions to Aid Citizens) and director of Le Monde Diplomatique, led to the first open invitation to civil society organizations to engage in what would be a counter-forum to the World Economic Forum (an annual meeting of the world's top political and economic powers in Davos, Switzerland). In 2001, the first WSF was held in Porto Alegre, Brazil.

The WSF aims to be "an open meeting place where social movements, networks, NGOs and other civil society organizations opposed to neoliberalism and a world dominated by capital or by any form of imperialism come together to pursue their thinking, to debate ideas democratically, formulate proposals, share their experiences freely and network for effective action" (www.forumsocialmundial.org.br). Each Forum follows an agenda of topics for debate and is organized in accordance with the WSF Charter of Principles, a document elaborated by the original organizing committee in order to ensure that the Forum's founding vision would guide the organization of and participation in the event. Among these principles are respect for diversity, non-violent resistance, the Forum's role as a permanent international space for civil society to network and to build alternatives, horizontal participation and self-organization of activities, and refusal to elaborate a final document or to assign leaders or spokespersons (www.forumsocialmundial.org.br).

The individuals, social movements, and organizations that attend the WSF are diverse in terms of their ideological approaches, organizational structures, political affiliations, geographic origins, and strategic approaches (Conway

2010; Worth and Buckley 2009; Ribeiro 2009; Gautney 2010). Over the course of a few days each year, they address a wide range of global issues, in numerous ways and from a multitude of perspectives. Their self-organized debates, workshops, panels, rallies, and cultural events are carried out in order to rethink and "recreate globalization so that it [will] benefit people, putting human rights, social justice, and ecological sustainability before profits" (Becker 2007). Some of the common themes that are raised at the event include racism, women's equality, food security, land rights, the environment, poverty, debt relief, labour issues, (de)militarization, and war.

Every year, the WSF site is carefully selected to reflect the values and aims of the meetings. It is always located in the Global South based on the reasoning that this is the region of the world which is the most (negatively) affected by neoliberal globalization and that it is an important source of resistance and alternatives to the current system (Curran 2007). Also, through geographical location, the World Social Forum has managed to showcase resistance and the construction of "alternative worlds" situated around the globe. For example, Porto Alegre was chosen as the first site of the Forum in 2001 because of its social movement trajectory and participatory budgeting initiatives (a process that makes it possible for ordinary citizens to participate in debates on municipal budget allocations) (Becker 2007). Likewise, Caracas, Venezuela was one of three sites chosen for the polycentric Forum of 2006 because of its overt resistance to imperial powers such as the United States (Curran 2007).

In the first five years WSF participation rose sharply. It was attended by 20,000 participants from 117 countries in 2001, but by 2005 the number of participants had risen to 155,000 from 135 countries. Since then attendance has fluctuated, depending on the location of the Forum (see Table 8.1). To attract more participants, in 2009 WSF organizers made it possible for people to "attend" the Forum via internet, TV, and radio (Gautney 2010). To foster a stronger link between global and local struggles, and to encourage greater geographic representation, social fora take place throughout the year at local, national, and regional levels in diverse locations of the Global North and South (Smith 2008: 211–13). In Canada, a number of relatively small fora have been organized in the provinces of Quebec, Alberta, and Ontario (Toronto, Ottawa, and London). Quebec also hosted the World Social Forum's International Committee meeting in early 2010 (Conway 2010).

Over the years, critics have identified a number of the Forum's organizational aspects that seemingly betray the very principles of horizontality, egalitarianism, and participatory governance that frame the Forum and represent a major point of collective advocacy. These criticisms include restricted access to WSF International Council membership; relatively closed meetings and top-down organization of the forums; the "star" panels of such intellectuals as Noam Chomsky and Eduardo Galeano; the perceived social distance between activists and intellectuals, as well as the third sector (NGOs) and

Table 8.1 **Overview of World Social Forum (WSF) Locations and Participation**

Year	Place(s)	Attendance
2001	Port Alegre, Brazil	20,000 participants
2002	Porto Alegre, Brazil	50,000 participants
2003	Porto Alegre, Brazil	100,000 participants
2004	Mumbai, India	80,000–100,000 participants
2005	Porto Alegre, Brazil	155,000 participants
2006	3 sites: Caracas, Venezuela; Karachi, Pakistan; and Bamako, Mali	60,000–80,000 participants in Caracas; 30,000–40,000 participants in Karachi; 15,000–17,000 participants in Bamako
2007	Nairobi, Kenya	40,000 participants
2009	Belém, Brazil	133,000 participants
2011	Dakar, Senegal	50,000 participants

Sources: Gautney 2010; Harris 2011.
Note: There was no WSF held in 2008 or 2010. Instead, local-level Social Fora were held throughout the world.

grassroots activists; the gender imbalance among panellists; the lower participation rates of less-professionalized and less resource-abundant civil society organizations;, and the lack of geographic representation (Hammond 2006; Becker 2007; Miles et al. 2009; Eschle and Maiguashca 2010; Worth and Buckley 2009; Ribeiro 2009).

In many ways, WSF organizers have heeded the critical voices and made changes (Becker 2007). The decentralization and democratization of the WSF have been notable changes. Over the years, the Forum has produced less hierarchical relations between organizational collaborators, thus establishing a more open and horizontal space for organizational exchange, networking, and coalition building (Byrd and Jansey 2010). The Organizing Committee has attempted to achieve this through initiatives such as the elimination of "star" panels and the promotion of self-organized themes and activities. Additionally, a Wall of Proposals was introduced in 2005 as a collective bulletin board for idea-sharing among all Forum participants. Finally, the multi-city (polycentric) forum sites in 2006 and the Nairobi, Kenya site in 2007 were attempts at further globalizing the discussion space and opening up the event to all civil society organizations from around the globe, regardless of their resource levels. The Organizing Committee, which consisted of just eight civil society organizations in 2001, now comprises 129 (WSF 2004). The WSF agendas are no longer determined by the WSF International Council; instead, the Council now provides a very general theme for the annual meeting and encourages WSF participants to propose their own topics for specific debates and panels (Hammond 2006). Additionally, in response to feminist criticisms of the under-representation of women and feminist issues, as well as incidents of violence against women in WSF Youth Camps, feminist groups at the fourth and fifth WSF were put in charge of some key sessions. With approximately half of the participants being women, women are also among the WSF's most prominent speakers (Moghadam 2009: 109–10). Some criticisms have subsided in recent years as the critics themselves have either stopped attending or have felt satisfied with the changes made to the WSF in response to their feedback (Hammond 2006). Some critics, however, still question whether the WSF truly represents those who have been most affected by neoliberal globalization (Worth and Buckley 2009).

Despite these limitations, however, for many analysts and activists the WSF "remains without a doubt the most open and diverse space where global policy issues are considered" (Smith 2008: 213). The WSF has strengthened the GJM in a number of ways. It has made it possible for activists to exchange information about the impact of neoliberal agendas on their specific communities and to share strategies to resist it. WSF participants have solidified transnational networks and improved the channels of communication among themselves. Activists are able to produce visions for an alternative society at the WSF. Additionally, the WSF has cemented common identities. This is expressed through a Zapatista slogan frequently cited at these meetings—"against neoliberalism and for humanity"—which emphasizes the unity of the human community. The WSF has also put in place models of global participatory democracy that might serve as a model for the democratic global order. As such, it actively promotes economic democracy by enhancing scrutiny of TNCs' activities and by supporting local economic activities. And, finally, the WSF inspires and coordinates new movement initiatives, campaigns, and appeals for action. The WSF's power, in this sense, has been demonstrated through its successful campaign launches and massive mobilizations, such as the Global Calls to Action. The protest against the US-led Iraq War in February 2003, which united millions of people around the world in public demonstrations, is one of the most salient examples of this accomplishment (Smith 2008: 213–24; Vivas 2010; Hammond 2006).

The World Social Forum, the Occupy Movement, and other popular resistance struggles discussed throughout this book do not only call for redistribution, recognition, and ordinary political representation. For Fraser (2005), they are also claiming a say in a post-Westphalian process of frame-setting. "Rejecting the standard view, which deems frame-setting the prerogative of states and transnational elites, they are effectively aiming to democratize the process by which the frameworks of justice are drawn and revised. Asserting their right to participate in constituting the 'who' of justice, they are simultaneously transforming the "how"—by which I mean the accepted procedures for determining the 'who'" (Fraser 2005: 84).

Expanding Spaces of Democratic Participation

While WSF is an important political space for the articulation of global justice visions, Smith (2008) contends that it is essential to expand the spaces of democratic participation beyond this forum. Jackie Smith calls for public involvement in some global policy processes (e.g., global parliament). For her, these initiatives should not replace but rather complement the WSF (237). Furthermore, she suggests that activists need to connect the politics of the WSF with "routines of people's everyday political lives" and recommends engaging with political parties, trade unions, and states (240). The role of the states in advancing social justice, however, is somewhat controversial.

As we have seen throughout this book (particularly in Chapters 3 and 4), states, especially neoliberal states, have been largely responsible for (re)creating practices of social exclusion. It is no wonder that some social activists, such as anarchists and members of other anti-authoritarian movements, are especially critical of the coercive, undemocratic, and inequitable nature of the state (Gautney 2010: 126–7). Nevertheless, we recognize that states can provide social benefits and protections against the detrimental effects of unregulated markets. Furthermore, some states (e.g., left-wing governments in countries such as Venezuela, Bolivia, Brazil, and Argentina) have asserted strong positions against neoliberal institutions, such as the IMF and World Bank, and promoted social policies aimed to redress the instabilities of these countries under neoliberal rule (Klein 2007). Peter Evans (2008) recognizes the progressive role that states can play: "More progressive state actors provide transnational movements with potential national allies at the global level, strengthening these transnational movements and enhancing their ability to act as allies for domestic movements" (295). It is in this regard that Smith argues that global activists should work to strengthen and support states instead of opposing them. She asserts, "Reclaiming the state as an institution for the promotion and protection of human rights—rather than an instrument for advancing economic growth—is essential to any strategy for resisting global neoliberalism" (2008: 232).

In addition to "reclaiming the state," Smith calls for "reclaiming the United Nations". In reclaiming the UN, she refers to "efforts to seriously transform this institution in democratic ways." As discussed in this book (particularly in Chapters 4, 6, and 7), the UN has been complicit in supporting neoliberal agendas and directing voluntary organizations and individuals towards market-based alternatives. While remaining critical of the way the UN currently operates, Smith nevertheless remains optimistic about the potential for this institution to support a global human rights culture. She believes that a reformed UN can provide essential institutional support for global social justice networks.

In conclusion, we view social justice as a process of change that links local and global struggles for redistribution, recognition, and representation (as well as other struggles not captured by these notions), and that calls into question the Westphalian social justice frame. We also envisage social justice as a potential space for fostering the practices of democratic participation that involve deciding not only on the "what" of social justice but also on the "how." This complex process involves multiple players and, as such, can be full of contradictions, tensions, and conflicts. Nevertheless, the ever-increasing assertiveness of global social justice activists makes it imperative for other global actors to heed to their voices and open up institutional spaces for more democratic popular participation.

Questions for Critical Thought

1. What are the key features associated with the concept "global social justice"? Think of one or two global social justice initiatives that you are familiar with and discuss their characteristic features. Describe how and the extent to which this initiative(s) can bring about change.
2. Keeping in mind the ideas discussed in both Chapter 7 and this chapter, how might researchers and activists explain or account for the growth in transnational struggles over the past few decades?
3. What linkages can be made between neoliberalism and "global justice networks," and what do these linkages reveal about competing claims for change? How and to what extent do global justice networks have the potential to bring about social change? Which types of social change do you think can emerge and why?
4. What potential do you think transnational advocacy initiatives, networks, or struggles have to challenge social, economic, and political inequalities?

Annotated Additional Readings

T. Olesen. 2011. *Power and Transnational Activism*. London: Routledge. This book focuses on the strengths and limitations of global activism in the era of globalization.

H. Widdows and N. Smith, Eds. 2011. *Global Social Justice*. London: Routledge. From a multi-disciplinary perspective, this book examines the debates on global justice and global ethics and explores a diversity of themes relating to global social justice.

Related Websites

Amnesty International, World Social Forum
www.amnesty.org/en/activism-center/event/world-social-forum-%E2%80%93-community-activists-share-their-experiences-fighting-forc

Centre for Citizenship, Identities, and Governance
www8.open.ac.uk/ccig

Centre for the Study of Social and Global Justice
www.nottingham.ac.uk/cssgj/about/index.aspx

Global Social Justice
www.globalsocialjustice.eu

The Global Justice Network
www.theglobaljusticenetwork.org

United Nations
www.un.org/en

References

Abramovitz, Mimi. 2006. Welfare Reform in the United States: gender, race and class matter. *Critical Social Policy* 26, 2: 336–64.

Abu-Laban, Yasmeen. 2009. The Welfare State Under Siege? Neo-liberalism, Immigration, and Multiculturalism. In *Women and Public Policy in Canada: Neoliberalism and After?*, edited by A. Dobrowolsky, 146–65. Oxford: Oxford University Press.

———, and Gabriel, Christina. 2002. *Selling Diversity: Immigration, Multiculturalism, Employment Equity and Globalization*. Peterborough: Broadview Press.

Adamson, Nancy, Linda Briskin and Margaret McPhail. 1988. *Feminists Organizing for Change: The Contemporary Women's Movement in Canada*. Toronto: Oxford University Press.

Agier, Michel. 2011. *Managing the Undesirables: Refugee Camps and Humanitarian Government*. Cambridge: Polity Press.

———. 2002. Between War and City: Towards an Urban Anthropology of Refugee Camps. *Ethnography* 2002: 3; 317–41.

Agustín, Laura. 2005. Migrants in the Mistress's House: Other Voices in the 'Trafficking' Debate. *Social Politics: International Studies in Gender, State and Society* 12, 1: 96–117.

Alfredson, Lisa, S. 2009. *Creating Human Rights: How Noncitizens Made Sex Persecution Matter to the World.* Pennsylvania Studies in Human Rights. Philadelphia: University of Pennsylvania Press.

Amin, A. 2005. Local community on trial. *Economy and Society* 34, 4: 612–33.

Anderson, Elizabeth S. 2004. Against luck egalitarianism: What is the point of equality? In *Social Justice*, edited by M. Clayton and A. Williams,154–85. Malden: Blackwell Publishing.

Andrijasevic, Rutvica. 2003. The Difference Borders Make: (Il)legality, Migration and Trafficking in Italy among Eastern European Women in Prostitution. In *Uprootings/Regroundings: Questions of Home and Migration*, edited by Sara Ahmed, Claudia Castañeda, Anne-Marie Fortier, and Mimi Sheller, 251–72. Oxford, UK: Berg.

Ansley, Fran. 2010. Constructing Citizenship without a Licence: The Struggle of Undocumented Immigrants in the USA for Livelihoods and Recognition. *Studies in Social Justice* 4, 2: 165–78.

Aradau, Claudia and Jef Huysmans. 2009. Mobilising (global) democracy: A political reading of mobility between universal rights and the mob. *Millennium: Journal of International Studies* 37, 3: 583–604.

Arce, Moisés. 2006. The Societal Consequences of Market Reform in Peru. *Latin American Politics and Society* 48, 1: 27–54.

Arendt, H. 1979 [1951]. *The Origins of Totalitarianism*. New York: Harcourt Brace Jovanovich.

Armbruster-Sandoval, Ralph. 2005. Workers of the World Unite? The Contemporary Anti-Sweatshop Movement and the Struggle for Social Justice in the Americas. *Work and Occupations* 32, 4: 464–85.

Armstrong, Pat and Hugh Armstrong. 2002. Women, privatization, and health care reform: the Ontario case. In Pat Armstrong et al. (eds). *Exposing Privatization: Women and Health Care Reform in Canada*. Aurora: Garamond Press: 163–215.

Ashutosh, Ishan and Alison Mountz. 2011. Migration management for the benefit of whom? Interrogating the Work of the International Organization for Migration. *Citizenship Studies* 15, 01: 21–38.

Backstrand, Karin. 2008. Accountability of Networked Climate Governance: The Rise of Transnational Climate Partnerships. *Global Environmental Politics* 83: 74–102.

Baer, Madeline and Alison Brysk. 2009. New Rights for Private Wrongs: Female Genital Mutilation and Global Framing Dialogues. In *The International Struggle for New Human Rights*, edited by Clifford Bob, 93–107. Philadelphia: University of Pennsylvania Press.

Baines, Donna. 2010. Neoliberal Restructuring, Activism/Participation and Social Unionism in Nonprofit Social Services. *Nonprofit and Voluntary Sector Quarterly* 39, 1: 10–28.

Balibar, Etienne. 2007. (De)constructing the Human as Human Institution: A Reflection on the Coherence of Hannah Arendt's Practical Philosophy. *Social Research* 74, 3: 727–38.

Banerjee, Subhabrata Bobby. 2008. Corporate Social Responsibility. The Good, the Bad and the Ugly. *Critical Sociology* 34, 1: 51–79.

Basok, Tanya. 2009. Counter-Hegemonic Human Rights Discourses and Migrant Rights Activism in the U.S. and Canada. *International Journal of Comparative Sociology*, 50 (2): 179–201.

———. 2004. Post-national Citizenship, Social Exclusion, and Migrants Rights: Mexican Seasonal Workers in Canada. *Citizenship Studies* 81: 47–64.

———. 2002. *Tortillas and Tomatoes. Mexican Transmigrant Harvesters in Canada.* Montreal: McGill-Queen's University Press.

———. 1996. Canadian Refugee Policy: Globalization, Radical Challenge or State Control? in *Political Economy* 50: 133–66.

———, and Emily Carasco. 2010. Advancing the Rights of Non-Citizens in Canada: A Human Rights Approach to Migrant Rights. *Human Rights Quarterly* 32, 2: 342–66.

———, Suzan Ilcan, and Jeff Noonan, Eds. 2006. Special Journal Issue: "Citizenship, Human Rights, and Social Justice." *Citizenship Studies*. 10(3): 267–372.

———, and Nicola Piper. 2012. Regulation versus Rights: Migration of Women and Global Governance Organizations in Latin America and the Caribbean, *Feminist Economics* 18, 2.

Beck, Ulrich and Natan Sznaider. 2006. Unpacking Cosmopolitanism for the Social Sciences: A Research Agenda. *British Journal of Sociology 57*, 1: 1–23.

Becker, Mark. 2007. World Social Forum. *Peace & Change* 32, 2: 203–20.

Bello, W. 2002. The Oxfam Debate: From Controversy to Common Strategy. *South Bulletin* 36: 13–16.

Benhabib, Seyla. 2007. Twilight of Sovereignty or the Emergence of Cosmopolitan Norms? Rethinking Citizenship in Volatile Times. *Citizenship Studies* 111: 19–36.

———. 2002. Political Geographies in a Global World: Arendtian Reflections. *Social Research* 69, 2: 539–66.

Berman, Jaqueline. 2010. Biopolitical Management, Economic Calculation and 'Trafficked Women.' *International Migration* 48, 4: 84–113.

Bezanson, Kate. 2006. *Gender, the State and Social Reproduction: Household Insecurity in Neo-liberal Times*. Toronto: University of Toronto Press.

Bob, Clifford, ed. 2009. *The International Struggle for New Human Rights*. Philadelphia: University of Pennsylvania Press.

———. 2002. Globalization and the Social Construction of Human Rights Campaigns. In *Globalization and Human Rights*, edited by Alyson Brysk, 133–47. Berkeley, California: University of California Press.

———. 2001. Marketing Rebellion: Insurgent Groups, International Media, and NGO Support. *International Politics* 38: 311–34.

Borras Jr., Saturnino M. 2008. La Via Campesina and its Global Campaign for Agrarian Reform in *Transnational Agrarian Movements Confronting Globalization*, edited by Saturnino M. Borras Jr, Marc Edelman and Cristóbal Kay. Malden, MA: Wiley-Blackwell.

Bosniak, Linda. 2006. *The Citizen and the Alien: Dilemmas of Contemporary Membership.* Princeton: Princeton University Press.

Braidotti, Rosi. 2003. Becoming woman: Or sexual difference revisited. *Theory, Culture & Society*. 20, 3: 43–64.

Branch, Adam. 2009. Humanitarianism, Violence, and the Camp in Northern Uganda. *Civil Wars* 11, 4: 477–501.

Brock, Kathy and Keith Banting 2001. The nonprofit sector and government in a new century: an introduction. In Kathy Brock and Keith Banting (eds). *The Nonprofit Sector and Government in a New Century.* Montreal and Kingston: McGill-Queen's University Press:1–20.

Brodie, Janine. 2008a. We are all equal now: Contemporary gender politics in Canada. *Feminist Theory*. 9, 2: 145–64.

———. 2008b. The Social in Social Citizenship. In *Recasting the Social in Citizenship*, edited by E. F. Isin, 20–43. Toronto: University of Toronto Press.

Brubaker, William Rogers. 1989. The French Revolution and the Invention of Citizenship. *French Politics and Society* 7, 3: 30–49.

Buechler, Steven M. 2000. *Social Movements in Advanced Capitalism*, New York and Oxford: Oxford University Press.

Buğra, Ayse, and Çağlar Keyder. 2006. The Turkish Welfare Regime in Transformation. *Journal of Social Policy* 16, 3: 211–28.

Burchardt, Tania. 2008. Monitoring inequality: Putting the capability approach to work. In *Social Justice and Public Policy: Seeking Fairness in Diverse Societies*, edited by G. Craig, T. Burchardt, and D. Gordon, 205–29. Bristol: Policy Press.

Butler, Judith. 2004. *Undoing Gender*. London and New York: Routledge.

———. 1999. *Gender Trouble: Feminism and the Subversion of Identity*. New York: Routledge.

Byrd, Scott C. and Lorien Jansy. 2010. Transnational Movement Innovation and Collaboration: Analysis of World Social Form Networks. *Social Movement Studies* 9, 4: 355–72.

Cabrera, Luis. 2010. *The Practice of Global Citizen-ship.* Cambridge: Cambridge University Press.

Canadian Encyclopedia. 'Potlatch'. Accessed 10 October 2011. www.thecanadianencyclopedia.com/index.cfm?PgNm=TCE&Params=A1ARTA0006431

Carpenter, R. Charli. 2009. "Orphaned Again? Children Born of Wartime Rape as a Non-Issue for the Human Rights Movement." In *The International Struggle for New Human Rights*, edited by Clifford Bob, 14–29. Philadelphia, Pennsylvania: University of Pennsylvania Press.

———. 2007. "Studying Issue (Non)-Adoption in Transnational Advocacy Networks." *International Organization* 61: 643–67.

Carroll, William. 2007. Hegemony and Counter-hegemony in a Global Field. *Studies in Social Justice* 1, 1: 36–66.

Castles, Francis G. 1985. *The Working Class and Welfare: Reflections on the Political Development of the Welfare State in Australia and New Zealand, 1890–1980*. Allen and Unwin.

CBC News. 2011. Occupy Canada protests persist as work week begins. Published and accessed online on 17 October. www.cbc.ca/news/canada/edmonton/story/2011/10/17/occupy-canada-wrap.html

Centre for Constitutional Studies. 2011. Health Services and Support—Facilities Subsector Bargaining Assn. Accessed 16 June. www.law.ualberta.ca/centres/ccs/rulings/facilitiessubsectorbargainingassn.php

Chakrabortty, Aditya. 2011. Athens protests: Syntagma Square on frontline of European austerity protests. Guardian (UK), 19 June. Accessed online 23 November 2011. www.guardian.co.uk/world/2011/jun/19/athens-protests-syntagma-austerity-protests

Chapkis, Wendy. 2003 Trafficking, Migration and the Law—Protecting Innocents, Punishing Immigrants. *Gender & Society* 17, 6: 923–37.

Chivers, Sally. 2008. Barrier by Barrier: The Canadian Disability Movement and the Fight for Equal Rights. In *Group Politics and Social Movements in Canada*, edited by Miriam Smith, 307–28. Toronto: Broadview Press.

Chong, Daniel. 2009. Economic Rights and Extreme Poverty: Moving toward Subsistence. In *The International Struggle for New Human Rights*, edited by Clifford Bob, 108–29. Philadelphia: University of Pennsylvania Press.

Chouinard, Vera. 2008. Negotiating Neo-liberal Environments in British Columbia and Ontario, Canada: Restructuring of State—Voluntary Sector Relations and Disability Organizations' Struggles to Survive. *Environment and Planning C: Government and Policy* 26: 173–90.

Citizenship and Immigration Canada. Final Text of the Safe Third Country Agreement. Accessed 5 July 2011. www.cic.gc.ca/english/department/laws-policy/safe-third.asp.

Cloke, Paul, Sarah Johnsen and Jon May. 2007. Ethical citizenship? Volunteers and the ethics of providing services for homeless people. *Geoforum* 386: 1089–1101.

Cohen, Jean. 1999. Changing Paradigms of Citizenship and the Exclusiveness of the Demos. *International Sociology* 14, 3: 245–68.

Cohen, Marjorie Griffen and Marcy Cohen. 2006. Privatization: A Strategy for Eliminating Pay Equity in Health Care in Bezanson, Kate and Meg Luxton (eds) Social Reproduction. *Feminist Political Economy Challenges Neo-liberalism*. Montreal and Kingston McGill-Queen's University Press, pp.117–44.

Collier George with Elizabeth Lowery Quaratiello. 2005. *Basta! Land and the Zapatista Rebellion in Chiapas*, Third Edition. Oakland, CA: Food First Press.

Collins, Patricia Hill. 1991. *Black Feminist Thought*. London, UK: Routledge.

Connor, Tim. 2001. *Still Waiting for Nike to Do It. Nike's Labor Practices in Three Years since CEO Phil Knight's Speech to the National Press Club*. Global Exchange. May 2001, 80–90. Accessed 17 August 2011. www.globalexchange.org/campaigns/sweatshops/nike/NikeReport.pdf

Conway, Janet. 2010. World Social Forum: Canadian Contexts and Questions. *Canadian Social Economy Hub*. 26 January. Accessed online 1 February 2010. www.socialeconomyhub.ca/?q=content/january-26-2010-world-social-forum-canadian-contexts-and-questions.

Cordero-Guzmán, Hector, Nina Martin, Victoria Quiroz-Becerra and Nik Theodore. 2008. Voting With Their Feet: Nonprofit Organizations and Immigrant Mobilization. *American Behavioral Scientist* 524: 598–617.

Coulter, Kendra. 2009. Women, Poverty Policy, and the Production of Neoliberal Politics in Ontario, Canada. *Journal of Women, Politics, & Policy* 301: 23–45.

Council of Canadians 2010. Canada Abstains on Historic Water Rights Resolution at UN: UN General Assembly Passes Historic Human Right to Water and Sanitation Resolution over Harper's Objections, PublicValues.ca, www.publicvalues.ca/ViewArticle.cfm?Ref=00748

Council of Canadians with Disabilities. 2008. *A Disability Rights Analysis of Canada's Record Regarding the Human Rights of Persons with Disabilities: A Submission by CCD to the Human Rights Council in Relation to the 2009 Periodic Review of Canada*. Accessed 8 February 2011: www.ccdonline.ca/en/humanrights/promoting/periodic-review-2009.

———. 2007. *From Vision to Action: Building an Inclusive and Accessible Canada: A National Action Plan*. Accessed 8 February 2011: www.ccdonline.ca/en/socialpolicy/actionplan/inclusive-accessible-canada

Cowan, Jane K., Marie-Benedict Dembour, and Richard Wilson, eds. 2001. *Culture and Rights*. Cambridge: Cambridge University Press.

Cronin, Ciaran and Pablo De Greiff, eds. 2002. *Global Justice and Transnational Politics*. Cambridge, MA: MIT Press.

Curran, Giorel. 2007. Making Another World Possible? The Politics of the World Social Forum. *Social Alternatives* 26, 1: 7–12.

Dagnino, Evelina. 2005. 'We all have rights, but . . .': Contesting Concepts of Citizenship in Brazil. In *Inclusive Citizenship: Meanings & Expressions,* edited by Naila Kabeer, 149–63. New York: Zed Books.

Dale, John G. 2008. Burma's Boomerang: Human Rights, Social Movements and Transnational Legal Mechanisms 'from Below.' *International Journal of Contemporary Sociology* 45, 1: 151–84.

Daly, Tamara. 2007. Out of Place: Mediating Health and Social Care in Ontario's Long-Term Care Sector. *Canadian Journal on Aging* 261: 63–76.

Dauer, Sheila. 2001. Indivisible or Invisible. Women's Human Rights in the Public and Private Sphere. In *Women, Gender, and Human Rights,* edited by Marjorie Agosín, 65–82. New Brunswick, New Jersey and London: Rutgers University Press.

Dauvergne, Catherine. 2008. *Making People Illegal: What Globalization Means for Migration and Law*. Cambridge: Cambridge University Press.

Davey, Monica and Steven Greenhouse. 2011. Angry Demonstrations in Wisconsin as Cuts Loom. New York Times. 16 February. Accessed online 23 November 2011. www.nytimes.com/2011/02/17/us/17wisconsin.html?_r=1

Dean, Mitchell. 2010. *Governmentality: Power and Rule in Modern Society*. London: Sage (2nd Edition).

———. 2007. *Governing Societies*. Berkshire, England: Open University Press.

Declaration of the Rights of Man and Citizen from the Constitution of Year I. Accessed 15 February 2011. www.columbia.edu/~iw6/docs/dec1793.html

de Gaay Fortman, Bas. 2011. *Political Economy of Human Rights*. London and New York: Routledge.

De Genova, Nicholas. 2010. The Queer Politics of Migration: Reflections on 'Illegality' and Incorrigibility. *Studies in Social Justice* 4, 2: 101–26.

———. 2007. The Production of Culprits: From Deportability to Detainability in the Aftermath of Homeland Security. *Citizenship Studies* 115: 421–48.

———. 2004. The Legal Production of Mexican/Migrant 'Illegality.' *Latino Studies* 2: 160–85.

della Porta, Donatella. 2007. The global justice movement in context. In *The Global Justice Movement. Cross-National and Transnational Perspectives*, edited by Donatella della Porta. 232–251. Boulder, CO: Paradigm Publications.

della Porta, Donatella, Massimiliano Andretta, Lorenzo Mosca, and Herbert Reiter. 2006. *Globalization from Below: Transnational Activists and Protest Networks*. Minneapolis: University of Minnesota Press.

Desmarais, Annette. 2007. *Globalization and the Power of Peasants*. London: Pluto.

Devlin, Richard and Dianne Pothier. 2006. Introduction: Toward a Critical Theory of Dis-Citizenship. In *Critical Disability Theory: Essays in Philosophy, Politics, Policy and Law*, edited by Dianne Pothier and Richard Devlin, 1–24. Vancouver: UBC Press.

Dhanda, Amita. 2008. Constructing a New Human Rights Lexicon: Convention on the Rights of Persons with Disabilities. *International Journal on Human Rights* 8: 43–59.

Dilger, Hansjorg. 2009. Doing Better? Religion, the Virtue-Ethics of Development, and the Fragmentation of Health Politics in Tanzania. *Africa Today* 561: 89–110.

Dillabough, Jo-Ann and Madeleine Arnot (2000). Feminist Political Frameworks: New Approaches to the Study of Gender, Citizenship and Education. In *Challenging Democracy: International Perspectives on Gender, Education and Citizenship*, edited by Madeleine Arnot and Jo-Ann Dillabough, 21–40. London and New York: Routledge.

Dillenburger, Karola, Montserrat Fargas and Rym Akhonzada. 2008. Evidence-Based Practice: An Exploration of the Effectiveness of Voluntary Sector Services for Victims of Community Violence. *British Journal of Social Work* 388: 1630–1647.

Dobrowolsky, Alexandra. 2008. Interrogating 'Invisibilization' and 'Instrumentalization': Women and Current Citizenship Trends in Canada. *Citizenship Studies* 12, 5: 465–79.

——— and Ruth Lister. 2006. Social Exclusion and Changes to Citizenship: Women and Children, Minorities and Migrants in Britain. In *Women, Migration, and Citizenship: Making Local, National and Transnational Connections,* edited by Evangelia Tastsoglou and Alexandra Dobrowolsky, 149–82. Hampshire, England: Ashgate Publishing Ltd.

Dobrowolsky, Alexandra and Jane Jenson. 2004. Shifting Representations of Citizenship: Canadian Politics of 'Women' and 'Children.' *Social Politics* 11, 2: 154–80.

Donzelot, Jacques. 1988. The promotion of the social. *Economy and Society* 17, 3: 395–427.

Dower, Nigel and John Williams, eds. 2002. *Global Citizenship: A Critical Introduction.* New York: Routledge.

Elias, J. 2008. Struggles over the Rights of Foreign Domestic Workers in Malaysia: The Possibilities and Limitations of 'Rights Talk.' *Economy and Society 372*: 282–303.

Elson, Diana. 2002. Gender Justice, Human Rights, and Neo-liberal Economic Policies. In *Gender Justice, Development, and Rights,* edited by Maxine Molyneux and Shahra Razavi, 78–114. New York: Oxford University Press Inc.

Engle, Karen. 2011. On Fragile Architecture: The UN Declaration of the Rights of Indigenous People in the Context of Human Rights. *The European Journal of International Law* 221: 141–63.

Eschle Catherine and Bice Maiguashca. 2010. *Making Feminist Sense of the Global Justice Movement.* New York: Rowman & Littlefield Publishers.

Esping-Andersen, Gosta. 1999. *Social Foundations of Post-Industrial Societies,* Oxford: Oxford University Press.

———.1996. After the Golden Age: The Future of the Welfare State in the New World Order. *Desarrollo Económico* 36, 142: 523–54.

———. 1990. *The Three Worlds of Welfare Capitalism.* N.J.: Princeton University Press.

Evans, Peter. 2008. Is an Alternative Globalization Possible? *Politics & Society* 36, 2: 271–305.

Evans, Tony. 2011. *Human Rights in the Global Political Economy: Critical Processes,* London: Lynne Rienner Publishers.

Ewig, Christina. 2006. Global Processes, Local Consequences: Gender Equity and Health Sector. *Social Politics: International Studies in Gender, State & Society* 133: 427–55.

EZLN. 1993. La Primera Declaración. Accessed on 26 Aug 2011 at http://palabra.ezln.org.mx/comunicados/1994/1993.htm.

———. 2005. La Sexta Declaración. Accessed on 22 August 2011 at http://palabra.ezln.org.mx/comunicados/2005/2005_06_SEXTA.htm

Fairweather, C. 2000. Review of "Is Multiculturalism Bad for Women? Susan Moller Okin with Respondents." *Canadian Women's Studies* 20, 2: 150+.

Falk, Richard. 2002. Interpreting the Interaction of Global Markets and Human Rights. In *Globalization and Human Rights,* edited by Alyson Brysk, 61–76. Berkeley, California: University of California Press.

Farrior, Stephanie. 2009. Human Rights Advocacy on Gender Issues: Challenges and Opportunities. *Journal of Human Rights Practice* 1, 1: 83–100.

Febbraro, Angela R., Michael H. Hall, and Marcus Parmegiani. 1999. *Developing a Typology of the Voluntary Health Sector in Canada: Definition and Classification Issues.* Ottawa: Health Agency of Canada.

Federal Task Force on Disability Issues. 1996. *Equal Citizenship for Canadians with Disabilities: The Will to Act.* 21 October 1996. Accessed 11 February 2011. www.teamworkcooperative.ns.ca/Documents/EQUAL%20CITIZENSHIP%20FOR%20CANADIANS%20WITH%20DISABILITIES.PDF

Ferguson, Barry, Simon Langlois and Lance W. Roberts. 2009. Social Cohesion in Canada. *The Tocqueville Review* 302: 69–101.

Fisher, Tracy. 2006. Race, Neoliberalism, and 'Welfare Reform' in Britain. *Social Justice* 33, 3: 54–65.

Flesher Fominaya, Cristina. 2010. Creating Cohesion from Diversity: The Challenge of Collective Identity Formation in the Global Justice Movement. *Sociological Inquiry* 80, 3: 377–404.

Frank, David John, Steven A. Boutcher, and Bayliss Camp. 2009. The Reform of Sodomy Law from a World Society Perspective. In *Queer Mobilizations:* LGBT *Activists Confront the Law,* edited by Scott Barclay, May Bernstein, and Anna-Maria Marshall, 123–41.

Franzway, Suzanne and Fonow, Mary Margaret. 2011. *Making Feminist Politics. Transnational Alliances between Women and*

Labour. Illinois: The Board of Trustees of the University of Illinois.

Fraser, Arvonne S. 2001. Becoming Human: The Origins and Development of Women's Human Rights. In *Women, Gender, and Human Rights,* edited by Marjorie Agosín, 15–64. New Brunswick, New Jersey and London: Rutgers University Press.

Fraser, Nancy. 2005 Reframing Justice in a Globalizing World, *New Left Review* 36, 69–88.

———. 1997. *Justice Interruptus: Critical Reflections on the "Postsocialist" Condition.* New York: Routledge.

———. 2003. Social Justice in the Age of Identity Politics: Redistribution, Recognition, and Participation. In *Redistribution or Recognition: A Political-Philosophical Exchange*, edited by Nancy Fraser and Axel Honneth, 7–109. London: Verso.

Freitas, Anthony J. 1998. Belongings: Citizenship, Sexuality, & the Market. In *Everyday Inequalities: Critical Inquiries*, edited by J. O'Brien and J.A. Howard, 361–84. Malden: Blackwell.

Frericks, Patricia, Robert Maier and Willibrord de Graaf. 2007. European Pension Reforms: Individualization, Privatization and Gender Pension Gaps. *Social Politics: International Studies in Gender, State and Society* 14, 2: 212–37.

Fridell, Gavin. 2007. *Fair Trade Coffee: The Prospects and Pitfalls of Market-Driven Social Justice.* Toronto: University of Toronto Press.

Fudge, Judy and Vosko, Leah. 2001. Gender, segmentation and the standard employment relationship in Canadian labour law, legislation and policy. *Economic and Industrial Democracy* 22: 271–310.

Garton, Stephen and Margaret E. McCallum. 1996. Workers' Welfare: Labour and the Welfare State in 20th-century Australia and Canada, *Labour/Travail*, 38, 116–41.

Gaer, Felice D. 2001. Mainstreaming a Concern for the Human Rights of Women. In *Women, Gender, and Human Rights,* edited by Marjorie Agosín, 98–122. New Brunswick, New Jersey and London: Rutgers University Press.

Gasser, Rachel. 2007. *UN and Business: Where do we stand?* Programme on Global Issues & Civil Society Centre for Applied Studies in International Negotiations, Geneva: Switzerland.

Gautney, Heather. 2010. *Protest and Organization in the Alternative Globalization Era: NGOs, Social Movements, and Political Parties.* New York: Palgrave Macmillan.

Gazso, Amber and Harvey Krahn. 2008. Out of Step or Leading the Parade? Public Opinion about Income Support Policy in Alberta, 1995 and 2004. *Journal of Canadian Studies* 421: 154–78.

Giada, Silvia, Tom De Groeve, Daniele Ehrlich, and Pierre Soille. 2003. Information Extraction from very High Resolution Satellite Imagery over Lukole Refugee Camp, Tanzania. *International Journal of Remote Sensing* 24, 22: 4251–66.

Giddens, Anthony. 1971. *Capitalism and modern social theory. An analysis of the writings of Marx, Durkheim and Max Weber.* Cambridge: Cambridge University Press.

Gill, Stephen. 2000. Towards a Postmodern Prince? The Battle of Seattle as a Moment in the New Politics of Globalisation. *Millennium* 29, 1: 131–40.

Glass, Christy M. and Nancy Kubasek. 2008. The Evolution of Same-Sex Marriage in Canada: Lessons the U.S. can learn from its Northern Neighbour regarding Same-Sex Rights. *Michigan Journal of Gender and Law 2008-2009* 15: 143–204.

Global Commission on International Migration (GCIM). 2005. *Migration in an Interconnected World: New Directions for Action.* A report of the Global Commission on International Migration, Switzerland.

Goldston, James. 2006. Holes in the rights framework: Racial discrimination, citizenship, and the rights of noncitizens. *Ethics and International Affairs* 203: 321–47.

Goodale, Mark. 2009. *Surrendering to Utopia: An Anthropology of Human Rights.* Stanford, CA: Stanford University Press.

Goodwin-Gill, Guy S. and Jane McAdam. 2007. *The Refugee in International Law*, 3rd edition, Oxford: Oxford University Press.

Gordon, Neve and Nitza Berkovitch, 2007. Human Rights Discourse in Domestic Settings: How Does it Emerge? *Political Studies* 55, 1: 243–66.

Greenaway, Norma and Douglas Quan. 2010. "Tories Take Aim at 'Refugee Fraudsters' and Smugglers." Accessed 21 October. http://www.globalnws.ca/tories+take+aim+at+refuee+fraudsters+and+smugglers/86438/story.html.

Griffin, Penny. 2011. Sexuality, power and global social justice. In Global Social Justice, edited by Heather Widdows and Nicola J. Smith, 138–52. London and New York: Routledge.

Grosz, Elizabeth. 2005. Bergson, Deleuze and the becoming of unbecoming. *Parallax* 2, 4: 4–13.

Grugel, Jean and Nicola Piper. 2007. *Critical Perspectives on Global Governance*. London and New York: Routledge.

Guardian UK. 2011. Egypt's military rulers 'continuing Mubarak-era abuses'. November 22. Accessed 22 November. www.guardian.co.uk/world/2011/nov/22/egypt-military-rulers-abuses

Hadden, Jennifer and Sidney Tarrow. 2007. The Global Justice Movement in the United States since Seattle. In *The Global Justice Movement. Cross-National and Transnational Perspectives*, edited by Donatella Della Porta, 210–31. Boulder, CO: Paradigm Publications.

Hammond, John L. 2006. Whither the Social Forum? *New Labor Forum* 15, 3: 41–51.

Hanes, Roy. 2010. *None is Still Too Many: An Historical Exploration of Canadian Immigration Legislation as It Pertains to People with Disabilities*. Report prepared for the Council of Canadians with Disabilities. Accessed 15 November. www.ccdonline.ca/en/socialpolicy/access-inclusion/none-still-too-many

Hanlon, Neil, Mark Rosenburg and Rachael Clasby. 2007. Offloading social care responsibilities: recent experiences of local voluntary organisations in a remote urban centre in British Columbia, Canada. *Health & Social Care in the Community* 154: 343–51.

Hardt, Michael and Antonio Negri. 2011. The Fight for 'Real Democracy' at the Heart of Occupy Wall Street. *Foreign Affairs*. 11 October. Accessed online 23 November 2011. www.foreignaffairs.com/articles/136399/michael-hardt-and-antonio-negri/the-fight-for-real-democracy-at-the-heart-of-occupy-wall-street

———. 2004. *Multitude: War and Democracy in the Age of Empire*. New York: Penguin.

Harrell-Bond, Barbara. 2002. Can Humanitarian Work with Refugees be Humane? *Human Rights Quarterly* 24: 51–85.

Harris, David Evan. 2011. World Social Forum is So Much More than Evo Morales. February 27. *The Guardian* (UK). Accessed 10 September. www.guardian.co.uk/commentisfree/2011/feb/27/world-social-forum-evo-morales.

Harvey, David. 2005. *A Brief History of Neoliberalism*. New York: Oxford University Press. New York.

———. 2003. *The New Imperialism*. Oxford, UK: Oxford University Press.

———. 1999. *Limits to Capital*. London and New York: Verso.

Hiemstra, Nancy. 2010. Immigrant 'Illegality' as Neoliberal Governmentality in Leadville, Colorado *Antipode*. 42, 1: 72–102.

Higgins, Vaughan, Jacqui Dibden and Chris Cocklin. 2008. Neoliberalism and natural resource management: Agri-environmental standards and the governing of farming practices. *Geoforum* 39: 1776–85.

Highleyman, Liz. The Global Justice Movement. In *Encyclopedia of American Social Movements*, edited by Immanuel Ness, Verso, forthcoming. Accessed 7 Sept 2011. www.black-rose.com/articles-liz/globjustice.html

Holzner, Claudio A. 2007. The Poverty of Democracy: Neoliberal Reforms and Political Participation of the Poor in Mexico. *Latin American Politics and Society* 492: 87–122.

Horowitz, Mark. 2009. Maquiladora Production, Rising Expectations, and Alterglobalization Strategy. *Critical Sociology* 35, 5: 677–88.

Hörschelmann, Kathrin. 2008. Transitions to work and the making of neo-liberal selves growing up in (former) East Germany. In *Social Justice and Neoliberalism: Global Perspectives*, edited by Adrian Smith, Alison Stenning, and Katie Willis. London: Zed Books.

Human Rights Watch. 1999. *The Price of Oil: Corporate Responsibility and Human Rights Violations in Nigeria's Oil Producing Communities*. New York: Human Rights Watch. Accessed 2 September 2011. www.hrw.org/legacy/reports/1999/nigeria/nigeria0199.pdf.

Hurley, Mary C. 2010. Sexual Orientation and Legal Rights. *Library of Parliament Background Paper. Publication No. 08-49-E*. Social Affairs Division. Parliamentary Information and Research Service. Accessed online 24 October 2011. www.parl.gc.ca/Content/LOP/ResearchPublications/prb0849-e.htm

Ilcan, Suzan. 2012a. Paradoxes of Humanitarian Aid: Mobile Populations, Biopolitical Knowledge, and Acts of Social Justice in Osire Refugee Camp. In *Mobilities, Knowledge, and Social Justice*, edited by Suzan Ilcan. Montreal and London: McGill-Queen's University Press. Forthcoming.

———. Ed. 2012b. *Mobilities, Knowledge, and Social Justice*. Montreal and London: McGill-Queen's University Press. Forthcoming.

———. 2009. Privatizing Responsibility: Public Sector Reform under Neoliberal Government. *Canadian Review of Sociology*. 46(3): 207–34.

———. 2006. Global Governing Organizations: Order-Building and Waste Management. *Current Sociology*. 54(6): 851–72.

———. 2002. *Longing in Belonging: The Cultural Politics of Settlement*. Westport and London: Praeger Publishers.

———, and Tanya Basok. 2004. Community Government: Voluntary Agencies, Social Justice, and the Responsibilization of Citizens. *Citizenship Studies* 82: 129–44.

———, and Anita Lacey. 2011. *Governing the Poor: Exercises of Poverty Reduction, Practices of Global Aid*. Montreal and London: McGill-Queen's University Press.

———, and Anita Lacey. 2006. Governing through Empowerment: Oxfam's Global Reform and Trade Campaigns. *Globalizations*. 3(2): 207–25.

———, Marcia Oliver, and Daniel O'Connor 2007. Spaces of Governance: Gender and Public Sector Restructuring in Canada. *Gender, Place and Culture*. 14(10): 75–92.

Inda, Jonathan. 2006. *Targeting Immigrants: Government, Technology, and Ethics*. Malden, MA: Blackwell Publishing.

Inder, Claire. 2011. International Refugee Law, 'Hyperlegalism' and Migration Management: The Pacific Solution. In *The New Politics of Migration Management: Actors, Discourses and Practices,* edited by Martin Geiger and Antoine Pécoud, 220–51. London and New York: Palgrave Macmillan.

International Labour Office (ILO). 2012. www.ilo.org/ipec

International Labour Organization. 2011. International Labour Standards by Subject. Accessed 17 June. www.ilo.org/ilolex/english/subjectE.htm.

———. 2011. ILOLEX Database of International Labour Standards. Accessed 17 June. www.ilo.org/ilolex/english/index.htm.

International Organization for Migration (IOM). 2011. Homepage. Accessed 10 October. www.iom.int/jahia/Jahia/about-iom/lang/en).

Isin, Engin and Greg Nielsen, eds. 2008. *Acts of Citizenship*. London and New York: Zed Books.

———, Janine Brodie, Danielle Juteau, and Daiva Stasiulis 2008. Recasting the Social in Citizenship. In *Recasting the Social in Citizenship,* edited by Engin Isin, 3–19. Toronto: University of Toronto Press.

———, and Patricia K. Wood. 1999. *Citizenship and Identity*. London: Sage Publications.

Jaeger, Hans-Martin. 2007. 'Global Civil Society' and the Political Depoliticization of Global Governance. *International Political Sociology* 1: 257–77.

Jaffee, Daniel. 2007. *Brewing Justice: Fair Trade Coffee, Sustainability, and Survival*. Berkeley: University of California Press.

Jansen, Bram. 2008. Between Vulnerability and Assertiveness: Negotiating Resettlement in Kakuma Refugee Camp, Kenya. *African Affairs* 107: 569–87.

Jenkins, Katy. 2009. 'We have a lot of goodwill, but we still need to eat': Valuing Women's Long Term Voluntarism in Community Development in Lima. *Voluntas: International Journal of Voluntary and Nonprofit Organizations* 201: 1–14.

Jenkins, Rob. 2007. India's Unlikely Democracy: Civil Society Versus Corruption. *Journal of Democracy* 182: 55–69.

Jenson, Jane. 2009. Lost in Translation: the Social Investment Perspective and Gender Equality. *Social Politics: International Studies in Gender, State and Society* 164: 446–83.

Jenson, Jane and Susan D. Phillips. 2001. Redesigning the Canadian Citizenship Regime: Remaking the Institutions of Representation. In *Citizenship, Markets, and the State,* edited by C. Crouch, K. Eder, and D. Tambini, 69–89. Oxford: Oxford University Press.

Johnston, Christina. 2006. The PACS and Post-Queer Citizenship in Contemporary Republican France. *Sexualities* 116: 688–705.

Joya, Angela, Patrick Bond, Rami El-Amine, Adam Hanieh and Mostafa Henaway. 2011. *The Arab Revolts against Neoliberalism*. Socialist Project. Socialist Interventions Pamphlet Series.

Juteau, Danielle. 2008. Multicultural Citizenship beyond Recognition. In *Recasting the Social in Citizenship,* edited by Engin Isin, 69–99. Toronto: University of Toronto Press.

Kabeer, Naila. 2002. *Citizenship and the Boundaries of the Acknowledged Community: Identity, Affiliation and Exclusion. IDS Working Paper 171*. Brighton: Institute of Development Studies.

———. 1999. *The Conditions and Consequences of Choice: Reflections on the Measurement of Women's Empowerment*. UNRISD Discussion Paper No. 108.

Kallen, Evelyn. 2004. *Social Inequality and Social Injustice: A Human Rights Perspective,* New York: Palgrave Macmillan.

Kaufman, Natalie and Stefanie Lindquist. 1995. Critiquing gender-neutral treaty language: The convention on the elimination of all forms of discrimination against women. In J. Peters and A. Wolper (Eds), *Women's rights, human rights: International Feminist Perspectives* (pp. 114–25). New York: Routledge.

Keck, Margaret and Kathryn Sikkink. 1998. *Activists Beyond Borders: Advocacy Networks in International Politics*. Ithaca and London: Cornell University Press.

Keddie, Amanda. 2010. Neo-liberalism and New Configurations of Global Space: Possibilities, Tensions and Problematics for Gender Justice. *Journal of Gender Studies* 19, 2: 139–52.

Khasnabish, Alex. 2008. *Zapatismo Beyond Borders. New Imaginations of Political Possibility*. Toronto: University of Toronto Press.

Kiely, Ray. 2005. *The Clash of Globalisations: Neoliberalism, the Third Way and Anti-Globalisation*. Leiden, Boston and the Netherlands: Brill.

———. 2002. Actually Existing Globalization, Deglobalisation, and the Political Economy of Anti-Capitalist Protest. *Historical Materialism* 10, 1: 93–121.

Kinney, Nancy Thomas and Mary L. Carver. 2007. Urban Congregations as Incubators of Service Organizations. *Nonprofit Management & Leadership* 182: 193–214.

Kivisto, Peter and T. Faist. 2007. *Citizenship: Discourse, Theory, and Transnational Prospects*. Malden, MA: Blackwell Publishing.

Klein, Naomi. 2007. Latin America's Shock Resistance. *The Nation*. Accessed 23 November 2011. www.thenation.com/article/latin-americas-shock-resistance.

———. 2002. *Fences and Windows. Dispatches from the Front Lines of the Globalization Debate*. London: Flamingo.

Klooster, Dan. 2010. Standardizing sustainable development? The Forest Stewardship Council's plantation policy review process as neoliberal environmental governance. *Geoforum* 41: 117–29.

Koukouzelis, Kostas. 2011. Liberal Internationalism and Global Social Justice. In *Global Social Justice*, edited by Heather Widdows and Nicola J. Smith, 29–41. London: Routledge

Krause, Monika. 2008. Undocumented Migrants: An Arendtian Perspective. *European Journal of Political Theory* 7, 3: 331–48.

Kymlicka, Will. 2008. Multiculturalism, social justice and the welfare state. In *Social Justice and Public Policy: Seeking fairness in diverse societies*, edited by G. Craig, T. Burchardt, and D. Gordon, 53–75. Bristol: The Policy Press.

Ladner, Kiera L. (2008) *Aysaka'paykinit:* Contesting the Rope Around the Nations' Neck. In *Group Politics and Social Movements in Canada*, edited by Miriam Smith, 227–50. Toronto: Broadview Press.

Laforest, Rachel and Michael Orsini, 2005. Evidence-based Engagement in the Voluntary Sector:Lessons from Canada. *Social Policy and Administration*. 39, 5: 481–97.

Lakoff, Andrew. 2005. The private life of numbers: pharmaceutical marketing in post-welfare Argentina. In Aihwa Ong and Stephen J. Collier (eds). *Global Assemblages: Technology, Politics, and Ethics as Anthropological Problems* Malden, MA: Blackwell: 194–213.

Larner, Wendy and Richard Le Haron. 2004. Global Benchmarking: Participating 'At a Distance' in the Globalizing Economy. In *Global Governmentality*, 212–32. New York: Routledge.

La Via Campesina. 2011. What is La Via Campesina? Last Modified 9 February. Accessed 30 August. http://viacampesina.org/en/index.php?option=com_content&view=category&layout=blog&id=27&Itemid=44

Lemke, Thomas. 2002. Foucault, governmentality, and critique." *Rethinking Marxism* 14: 49–64.

Lerche, Jens. 2008. Transnational Advocacy Networks and Affirmative Action for Dalits in India. *Development and Change* 39, 2: 239–61.

Lightman, Ernie, Andrew Mitchell and Dean Herd. 2008. Globalization, Precarious Work and the Food Bank. *Journal of Sociology and Social Work*. 35, 2: 9–28.

Linklater, Andrew. 1998. Cosmopolitan Citizenship. *Citizenship Studies* 2, 1: 23–41.

Lister, Ruth. 2008. Recognition and voice: The challenge for social justice. In *Social Justice and Public Policy: Seeking fairness in diverse societies*, edited by G. Craig, T. Burchardt, and D. Gordon, 105–22. Bristol: Policy Press.

———. 2003. *Citizenship: Feminist Perspectives*, Basingstoke: Macmillan.

Logan, Shannon and Gerda R. Wekerle. 2008. Neoliberalizing environmental governance? Land trusts, private conservation and nature on the Oak Ridges Moraine. *Geoforum* 39: 2097–2108.

Lord, Janet. 2009. Disability Rights and the Human Rights Mainstream: Reluctant Gatecrashers? In *The International Struggle for New Human Rights*, edited by Clifford

Bob, 83–92. Philadelphia, Pennsylvania: University of Pennsylvania Press.

Lovenduski, Joni. 2005. *Feminizing Politics*. Cambridge, UK: Polity Press.

Lyon, Sarah and Mark Moberg, eds. 2010. *Fair Trade and Social Justice: Global Ethnographies*. New York and London: New York University Press.

McDaniel, Susan. 2003. Social cohesion and gender: reflections on tendencies and tensions. *Canadian Journal of Sociology* 28, 1: 43–50.

MacDonald Roderick A. and Robert Wolfe. 2009. Canada's Third National Policy: The Epiphenomenal or the Real Constitution? *University of Toronto Law Journal* 59, 4: 469–523.

Macklin, Audrey. 2009. Particularized Citizenship: Encultured Women and the Public Sphere. In *Migrations and Mobilities: Citizenship, Borders, and Gender,* edited by S. Benhabib, 276–303. New York and London: New York University Press.

———. 2003. Dancing Across Borders: 'Exotic Dancers,' Trafficking, and Canadian Immigration Policy. *International Migration Review* 37, 2: 464–500.

Malkki, Liisa. 1995. *Purity and Exile: Violence, Memory, and National Cosmology among Hutu Refugees in Tanzania*. Chicago, IL: University of Chicago Press.

Marchevsky, Alejandra and Jeanne Theoharis. 2008. Dropped From the Rolls: Mexican Immigrants, Race and Rights in the Era of Welfare Reform. *Journal of Sociology and Social Welfare* 35, 3: 71–96.

Marshall, T.H. 1965 [1950]. Citizenship and Social Class. In *Class, Citizenship, and Social Development.* USA: Anchor Books.

Matthews, J. Scott. 2005. The Political Foundations of support for Same-Sex Marriage in Canada. *Canadian Journal of Political Science* 38, 4: 841–66.

May, Jon, Kavita Datta, Yara Evans, Joanna Herbert, Cathy MCIlwaine, and Jane Wills. 2008. Travelling Neoliberalism: Polish and Ghanaian migrant workers in London in Adrian Smith, Alison Stenning, and Katie Willis, eds, *Social Justice and Neoliberalism: Global Perspectives*. London: Zed Books, pp. 61–89.

Mayer, Victoria. 2008. Crafting a New Conservative Consensus on Welfare Reform: Redefining Citizenship, Social Provision, and the Public/Private Divide. *Social Politics: International Studies in Gender, State and Society* 15, 2: 154–81.

Mayer, Margit. 2007. Contesting the neoliberalization of urban governance. In *Contesting Neoliberalism: The Urban Frontier*, edited by H. Leitner, J. Peck and E. Shepherd, 99–125. New York: Guilford.

Mayo, Marjorie. 2005. *Global Citizens: Social Movements & The Challenge of Globalization*. Toronto: Canadian Scholars' Press Inc.

Mayor, Federico and Jerome Binde. 2001. *The World Ahead: Our Future in the Making*. Paris: Unesco Publishing, Zed Books.

McAdam Doug, Sydney Tarrow, and Charles Tilly. 2001. *Dynamics of Contention*. Cambridge: Cambridge University Press.

McAteer, Emily and Simone Pulver. 2009. The Cooperate Boomerang: Shareholder Transnational Advocacy Networks Targeting Oil Companies in the Ecuadorian Amazon. *Global Environmental Politics* 9, 1: 1–30.

McLaughlin, Janet and Jenna Hennebry. 2010. Pathways to Precarity: Structural Vulnerabilities and Lived Consequences in the Everyday Lives of Migrant Farmworkers in Canada. Paper presented at the *Research Alliance on Precarious Status Workshop, entitled "Producing and Negotiating Precarious Migratory Status in Canada,"* York University, Toronto, 16 September.

Mégret, Frédéric. 2008. The Disabilities Convention: Human Rights of Persons with Disabilities or Disability Rights? *Human Rights Quarterly* 30, 2: 494–516.

Melucci, Alberto. 1989. *Nomads of the Present: Social Movements and Individual Needs in Contemporary Society*, Philadelphia: Temple University Press.

———. 1996. *Challenging Codes: Collective Action in the Information Age*, edited by John Keane and Paul Mier. Cambridge: Cambridge University Press.

Merry, Sally Engle. 2006. *Human Rights and Gender Violence: Translating International Law into Local Justice*. Chicago: Chicago University Press.

———. 2001. Women, Violence, and the Human Rights System. In *Women, Gender, and Human Rights,* edited by Marjorie Agosín, 83–97. New Brunswick, New Jersey and London: Rutgers University Press.

Mihr, Anja and Hans Peter Schmitz. 2007. Human Rights Education (HRE) and Transnational Activism. *Human Rights Quarterly* 29, 4: 973–93.

Miller, David. 2004. The concept of desert. In *Social Justice*, edited by M. Clayton and A. Williams, 186–200. Malden: Blackwell Publishing.

Miles, Larmer, Peter Dwyer, and Leo Zeilig.

2009. Southern African social movements at the 2007 Nairobi World Social Forum. *Global Networks* 9, 1: 41–62.

Mirza, Heidi Safia and Diane Reay (2000). Redefining Citizenship: Black Women Educators and 'The Third Space." In *Challenging Democracy: International Perspectives on Gender, Education and Citizenship*, edited by Madeleine Arnot and Jo-Ann Dillabough, 58–72. London and New York: Routledge.

Moghadam, Valentine M. 2009. *Globalization and Social Movements: Islamism, Feminism, and the Global Justice Movement.* Lanham: Rowman and Littlefield Publishers.

Mohanty, Chandra Talpade. 2003. 'Under Western Eyes' Revisited: Feminist Solidarity through Anticapitalist Struggles. *Signs* 28, 2: 499–535.

Mold, Alex and Virginia Berridge. 2007. "Crisis and Opportunity in Drug Policy: Changing the Direction of British Drug Services in the 1980s." *Journal of Policy History*, Volume 19, Number 1: 29–48.

Molyneux, Maxine. and Shahra Razavi. 2002. Introduction. In M. Molyneux and S. Razavi (Eds), *Gender, Justice Development and Rights*. Oxford: Oxford University Press.

Montagna, Nicola. 2010. The Making of a Global Movement: Cycles of Protest and Scales of Action. *The Sociological Review* 58, 4: 638–55.

Moxham, Claire, and Ruth Boaden. 2007. The impact of performance measurement in the voluntary sector: Identification of contextual and processual factors. *International Journal of Operations & Production Management* 278: 826–45.

Muhumuza, William. 2010. State-Civil Society Partnership in Poverty Reduction in Uganda. *Eastern Africa Social Science Research Review* 261: 1–21.

Mullally, Siobhán. 2006. Introduction. In *Gender, Culture and Human Rights. Reclaiming Universalism,* xxix–xlv. Oxford and Portland, Oregon: Hart Publishing.

Nambissan, Geetha B. and Stephen J. Ball. 2010. Advocacy networks, choice and private schooling of the poor in India." *Global Networks* 10, 3: 324–43.

Nash, Kate. 2002. Human rights for women: An argument for 'deconstructive equality'. *Economy and Society* 31, 3: 414–433.

———. 2000. *Contemporary Political Sociology: Globalization, Politics, and Power*. Malden, MA: Blackwell Publishing.

Nickson, Robert A. 2009. Governance and the Revitalization of the Guarani Language in Paraguay. *Latin American Research Review* 443: 3–26.

Nicol, Nancy and Miriam Smith. 2008. Legal Struggles and Political Resistance: Same-Sex Marriage in Canada and the USA. *Sexualities* 11, 6: 667–87.

No Borders. 2011. Homepage. Accessed 9 October www.noborder.org/iom/

Nolan García, Kimberly A. 2011. Transnational Advocates and Labor Rights Enforcement in the North American Free Trade Agreement. *Latin American Politics and Society* 53, 2: 29–60.

Noorbaksh, Mehdi. 2008. Politics, Economy, and the Threats of AIDS in Africa: The Case of Botwana. *Comparative Studies of South Asia, Africa and the Middle East* 282: 351–66.

Novik, Marta, Miguel Lengyl, and Marianela Sarabia. 2009. De la protección laboral a la vulnerabilidad social. Reformas neoliberales en la Argentina. *Revista Internacional del Trabajo* 128, 3: 257–75.

Noxolo, Pat, Parvati Raghuram, and Clare Madge. 2011. Unsettling responsibility: postcolonial interventions. *Transactions of the Institute of British Geographers*, 1–12.

Nussbaum, Martha C. 1992. Human functioning and social justice: In defense of Aristotelian essentialism. *Political Theory* 20, 2: 202–46.

Nyers, Peter. 2008. No One is Illegal between City and Nation. In *Acts of Citizenship*, edited by Engin Isin, 160–81. London and New York: Zed Books.

———. 2006. *Rethinking Refugees: Beyond States of Emergency*. New York: Routledge.

O'Connor, Daniel and Willem de Lint. 2009. Frontier Government: The Folding of the Canada–US Border. *Studies in Social Justice*. 3,1: 39–66.

O'Connor, Daniel and Suzan Ilcan. 2005. The folding of liberal government: Contract governance and the transformation of the public service in Canada. *Alternatives: Global, Local, Political* 30, 1: 1–23.

Occupy Wall Street Home Page. 2011. Occupy Wall Street Marks One Month. Last modified and accessed on 17 October 2011. http://occupywallst.org/

Offe, Claus. 1982. Some Contradictions of the Modern Welfare State. *Critical Social Policy* 2, 2: 7–16.

Office of the United Nations High Commissioner for Human Rights. 2011. International Law. Accessed 17 June. www2.ohchr.org/english/law/index.htm.

Okereke, Chukwumerije, Harriet Bulkeley and Heike Schroeder. 2009. "Conceptualizing

Climate Governance beyond the International Regime." *Global Environmental Politics* 91: 58–78.

Okin, Susan M. 1999. Is Multiculturalism Bad for Women? In *Is Multiculturalism Bad for Women?*, edited by Joshua Cohen, Matthew Howard, and Martha Nussbaum, 9–24. Princeton, N.J.: Princeton University Press.

Olesen, Thomas. 2011. Introduction. *Power and Transnational Activism*. London and New York: Routledge.

O'Malley, Pat. 2004. *Risk, Uncertainty and Government*. London and Portland: The GlassHouse Press.

Ong, Aihwa. 2006. *Neoliberalism as Exception: Mutations in Citizenship and Sovereignty*. Durham, NC: Duke University Press.

Oppenheimer, Melanie. 2005. Voluntary Action and Welfare in Post-1945 Australia: Preliminary Perspectives. *History Australia* 23: 82.1–82.16.

Oorschot, Wim. 2006. Making the difference in social Europe: deservingness perceptions among citizens of European welfare states. *Journal of European Social Policy* 16, 1: 23–42.

Osborne, Stephen P., Gyorgy Jenei, and Gergely Fabian. 2008. Whispering at the Back Door"? Local Government— Voluntary and Community Sector Relationships in Post-Accession Hungary. *Public Policy and Administration* 234: 331–50.

Ouziel, Pablo. 2011. Spain's 'Indignados': Vanguard of a Global Nonviolent Revolt against Neoliberalism. *Global Research*. August 6. Accessed 23 November 2011. www.globalresearch.ca/index.php?context=viewArticle&code=20110806&articleId=25911

Oxfam International. 2011a. About Us. Accessed 14 October 2011. www.oxfam.org/en/about

Oxfam International. 2011b. Home page. Accessed 14 October 2011. www.oxfam.org/en/campaigns/trade/about

Papastergiadis, Nikos. 2010. Wars of Mobility. *European Journal of Social Theory* 13, 3: 343–61.

Parekh, Bhikhu. 2003. Cosmopolitanism and global citizenship. *Review of International Studies* 29: 3–17.

Parpart, Jane L., Shirin M. Rai, and Kathleen Staudt. 2002. Rethinking em(power)ment, gender and development: an introduction. In *Rethinking Empowerment: Gender and development in a global/local world*, edited by Jane L. Parpart, Shirin M. Rai and Kathleen Staudt, 3–21. London and New York: Routledge.

Parry, Emma, and Clare Kelliher. 2009. Voluntary sector responses to increased resourcing challenges. *Employee Relations* 311: 9–24.

Peck, James and Adam Tickell. 2002. Neoliberalizing Space. *Antipode* 343: 380–404.

———, Nik Theodore, and Neil Brenner. 2009. Neoliberal Urbanism: Models, Moments, Mutations. *SAIS Review* 291: 49–66.

Pécoud, Antoine and Paul de Guchteneire, eds. 2007. *Migration without Borders: Essays on the Free Movement of People*. New York: UNESCO and Berghahn Books.

Pellow, David N. 2007. *Resisting Global Toxins: Transnational Movements for Environmental Justice*. Cambridge, MA: MIT Press.

Perkins, Harold A. 2009. Out from the Green shadow? Neoliberal hegemony through the market logic of shared urban environmental governance. *Political Geography* 287: 395–405.

Phillips, Anne. 1998. Democracy and Representation: Or, Why Should it Matter Who Our Representatives Are? In *Feminism and Politics*, edited by Anne Phillips, 224–41. Oxford, UK: Oxford University Press.

Phillips, Lynne and Suzan Ilcan. 2004. Capacity-Building: The Neoliberal Governance of Development. *Canadian Journal of Development Studies* 25, 3: 393–409.

Phoenix, Jo. 2007. Governing Prostitution: New Formations, Old Agenda. *Canadian Journal of Law and Society* 222: 73–94.

Piachaud, David. 2008. Social justice and public policy: A social policy perspective. In *Social Justice and Public Policy: Seeking Fairness in Diverse Societies*, edited by G. Craig, T. Burchardt, and D. Gordon, 33–51. Bristol: Policy Press.

Pianta, Mario and Raffaele Marchetti. 2007. Global Justice Movements. The Transnational Dimension. In *The Global Justice Movement. Cross-national and Transnational Perspectives*, edited by Donatella Della Porta, 29–51. Boulder, CO: Paradigm Publications.

Pogge, Thomas. 2008. *World Poverty and Human Rights: Cosmopolitan Responsibilities and Reforms. 2nd edition*. Cambridge: Polity Press.

Preibisch, Kerry. 2007. Local Produce, Foreign Labour: Labour Mobility Programs, and Global Trade Competitiveness in Canada. *Rural Sociology* 723: 418–49.

Pringle, Peter. 2007. So Shall We Reap. In *World Hunger*, edited by C. Stanford, 117–32. New York: H.W. Wilson.

Pullenayegem, Chris. 2007. Dismantling the Safe Third Country Agreement. *Citizens for Public Justice*, 13 December. Accessed 5 July 2011. www.cpj.ca/en/content/dismantling-safe-third-country-agreement.

Raco, Mike. 2009. "From Expectations to Aspirations: State Modernisation, Urban Policy, and the Existential Politics of Welfare in the UK. *Political Geography* 28: 436–454.

Rauch, Angela and Johanna Dornette. 2006. Equal Rights and Equal Duties? Activating Labour Market Policy and the Participation of Long-Term Unemployed People with Disabilities after the Reform of the German Welfare State. *Journal of Social Policy* 39, 1: 53–70.

Rawls, John. 2003. Distributive Justice. In *Equality & Justice: Social Contract and the Currency of Justice, Ethical Investigations*, edited by P. Vallentyne, 52–76. New York: Routledge.

———. 2003. Justice as Fairness. In *Equality & Justice: Social Contract and the Currency of Justice, Ethical Investigations*, edited by P. Vallentyne, 20–50. New York: Routledge.

Razin, Assaf and Efraim Sadka. 2005. *The Decline of the Welfare State*. Boston: Massachusetts Institute of Technology.

Ribeiro, Gustavo Lins. 2009. Non-hegemonic Globalizations. Alter-native Transnational Processes and Agents. *Anthropological Theory* 9, 3: 297–329.

Risse, Thomas, Stephen C. Ropp, and Kathryn Sikink, eds. 1999. *The Power of Human Rights: International Norms and Domestic Change*. Cambridge: Cambridge University Press.

Ritzer, George. 2008. Karl Marx: A Biographical Sketch. In *Modern Sociological Theory*, 24–25. New York: McGraw-Hill Higher Education.

Routledge, Paul and Andrew Cumbers. 2009. *Global Justice Networks: Geographies of Transnational Solidarity*. Manchester and New York: Manchester University Press.

Royal Commission of Aboriginal Peoples (RCAP). *Report of the Royal Commission of Aboriginal Peoples 1996. Looking Forward Looking Back*. Vol.1. Accessed 24 September 2011. www.collectionscanada.gc.ca/webarchives/20071124130216/http://www.ainc-inac.gc.ca/ch/rcap/sg/sgm10_e.html

Rubin, Michael. 2003. Are Kurds a pariah minority? *Social Research* 70, 1: 295–330.

Rutowski, Kara D., Jeffery K. Guiler and Kurt E. Schimmel. 2009. Benchmarking Organizational Commitment Across Nonprofit Human Services Organizations in Pennsylvania. *Benchmarking: An International Journal* 161: 135–50.

Rygiel, Kim. 2010. *Globalizing Citizenship*. Vancouver and Toronto: University of British Columbia Press.

Sainsbury, Diane. 2006. Immigrants' Social Rights in Comparative Perspective: Welfare Regimes, Forms of Immigration and Immigration Policy Regimes. *Journal of European Social Policy* 16, 3: 229–44.

Sanders, Edmund. 2011. Israel Rent Protests Underscore Middle Class Frustration. *Los Angeles Times*. July 29. Accessed 23 November 2011. http://articles.latimes.com/2011/jul/29/world/la-fg-israel-protests-20110730-27

"Sandra Lovelace v. Canada, Communication No. R.6/24 (29 December 1977), UN Doc. Supp. No. 40 (A/36/40) at 116 (1981)." *Lawsite, Carleton University*. Accessed 18 May 2011 www.lawsite.ca/WLSC/Lovelace_w.htm.

Sangameswaran, Priya. 2009. Neoliberalism and Water Reforms in Western India: Commercialization, Self-sufficiency, and Regulatory Bodies. *Geoforum* 40: 228–38.

Satzewich, Vic and Nikolaos Liodakis. 2007. *"Race" and Ethnicity in Canada: A Critical Introduction*. Don Mills, Ontario: Oxford University Press.

Scott, Alan. 1990. *Ideology and the new social movements*. London, England and Boston: Unwin Hyman.

Sen, Amartya. 2003. Equality of What? In *Equality & Justice: Social Contract and the Currency of Justice, Ethical Investigations*, edited by P. Vallentyne, 324–48. New York: Routledge.

———. 2003. Justice: Means versus Freedoms. in *Equality & Justice: Social Contract and the Currency of Justice, Ethical Investigations*, edited by P. Vallentyne, 348–59. New York: Routledge.

Shawki, Noha. 2011. Organizational Structure and Strength and Transnational Campaign Outcomes: A Comparison of Two Transnational Advocacy Networks."*Global Networks* 11, 1: 97–117.

———. 2010. Political Opportunity Structures and the Outcomes of Transnational Campaigns: A Comparison of Two Transnational Advocacy Networks. *Peace and Change* 35, 2: 381–411.

Shiva, Vandana. 2002. Oxfam's Free Trade Recipe: Export at Any Cost. *South Bulletin* 36: 10–13.

Shore, Cris. 2008. Audit Culture and Illiberal Governance: Universities and the Politics of

Accountability. *Anthropological Theory* 83: 278–98.

Simmons, Alan B. 2010. *Immigration and Canada: Global and Transnational Perspectives*. Toronto: Canadian Scholars Press.

Skinner, Mark W. and Alun E. Joseph. 2007. The Evolving Role of Voluntarism in Ageing Rural Communities. *New Zealand Geographer* 632: 119–29.

Sklair, Leslie. 2011. The Globalization of Human Rights. In *Global Social Justice*, edited by Heather Widdows and Nicola J. Smith, 11–28. London and New York: Routledge.

Smith, Jackie. 2008. *Social Movements for Global Democracy*. Baltimore: The Johns Hopkins University Press.

———. 2002. Globalizing Resistance: The Battle of Seattle and the Future of Social Movements. In *Globalization and Resistance: Transnational Dimensions of Social Movements*, edited by J. Smith and H. Johnston, 183–99. Lanham, MD: Rowman and Littlefield.

Smith, Miriam. 2008. Identity and Opportunity: The Lesbian and Gay Rights Movement. In *Group Politics and Social Movements in Canada,* edited by Miriam Smith, 181–202. Toronto: Broadview Press.

Smyth, L. 2008. Gendered spaces and intimate citizenship. *European Journal of Women's Studies*. 15, 2: 83–99.

Solway, Jacqueline. 2009. Human Rights and NGO 'Wrongs': Conflict Diamonds, Culture Wars and the 'Bushman Question.' *Africa: the Journal of the International African Institute* 793: 321–46.

Somers, Margaret R. and Christopher N.J. Roberts. 2008. Toward a new sociology of rights: A genealogy of 'buried bodies' of citizenship and human rights. *Annual Review of Law and Social Science* 4: 385–425.

South, Jane, Tracy J. Higgins, James Woodall and Simon M. White. 2008. Can Social Prescribing Provide the Missing Link? *Primary Health Care Research & Development* 94: 310–18.

Souza, Karen A. and Mandeep K. Dhami. 2008. A Study of Volunteers in Community-Based Restorative Justice Programs."*Canadian Journal of Criminology and Criminal Justice* 501: 31–58.

Soysal, Yasemin. 1994. *Limits of Citizenship: Migrants and Postnational Membership in Europe*. Chicago: University of Chicago Press.

Squires, Judith. 2007. Negotiating Equality and Diversity in Britain: Towards a Differentiated Citizenship. *Critical Review of International Social and Political Philosophy* 10, 4: 531–59.

Stahler-Sholk, Richard. 2010. The Zapatista Social Movement: Innovation and Sustainability. Alternatives 35, 3: 269–90.

Stammers, Neil. 2009. *Human Rights and Social Movements*. London: Pluto Press.

Stanford Encyclopedia of Philosophy. 2011. Hannah Arendt. Accessed 15 May. http://plato.stanford.edu/entries/arendt/

———. 2010. Karl Marx. Accessed on 31 October 2011. http://plato.stanford.edu/entries/marx/

Stasiulis, Daiva and Darryl Ross. 2006. Security, Flexible Sovereignty, and the Perils of Multiple Citizenship. *Citizenship Studies* 103: 329–48.

Staeheli, Lynn A. 2008. Citizenship and the problem of community. *Political Geography* 27: 5–21.

Statistics Canada. 2010. Accessed 11 July. www.statcan.gc.ca/daily-quotidien/100526/dq100526b-eng.htm

Stromquist, Nelly P. 2002. Education as a means for empowering women. In *Rethinking Empowerment: Gender and Development in a Global/Local World* , edited by Jane L. Parpart, Shirin M. Rai and Kathleen Staudt, 22–38. London and New York: Routledge.

Tarrow, Sydney. 2005. Introduction. The New Transnational Activism, 15–34. Cambridge: Cambridge University Press.

———. 1994. *Power in Movement: Social Movements, Collective Action and Politics*. New York: Cambridge University Press.

Taylor, P.L. 2005. In the Market but Not of It: Fair Trade Coffee and Forest Stewardship Council Certification as Market-based Social Change. *World Development* 33: 129–47.

Teeple, Gary. 2007. Honoured in the Breach: Human Rights as Principles of a Past Age. *Studies in Social Justice* 1, 2: 136–45.

———. 2005. *The Riddle of Human Rights*. Merlin Press UK and Garamond Press Ltd. Canada.

Teplova, Tatyana. 2007. Welfare State Transformation, Childcare, and Women's Work in Russia. *Social Politics* 143: 284–322.

Thane, Pat, ed. 2010. *Unequal Britain. Inequalities in Britain since 1945*. London: Continuum.

Tilly, Charles. 2004. *Social Movements, 1768–2004*. Boulder, Colorado: Paradigm.

Tombs, Steve and David White. 2010. A Deadly Consensus: Worker Safety and Regulatory

Degradation under New Labour. *British Journal of Criminology* 50: 46–65.

Tong, Rosemarie. 2009a. Long-Term Care for the Elderly Worldwide: Whose Responsibility is it? *International Journal of Feminist Approaches to Bioethics* 22: 5–30.

———. 2009b. Enacting state restructuring: NGOs as 'translation mechanisms'. *Environment and Planning D: Society and Space* 27: 1117–34.

Trudeau, Dan. 2008a. Towards a Relational View of the Shadow State. *Political Geography* 276: 669–90.

Trudeau, Dan. 2008b. Junior Partner or Empowered Community? The Role of Non-Profit Social Service Providers amidst State Restructuring in the US. *Urban Studies*. 45, 13: 2805–27.

Turner, Bryan S. 1993. Contemporary Problems in the Theory of Citizenship. In *Citizenship and Social Theory*, edited by Bryan S. Turner, 1–18. London: Sage Publications.

Turner, Simon. 2006. Negotiating Authority between UNHCR and 'The People.' *Development and Change* 37, 4: 759–78.

UNHCR. The United Nations Refugee Agency Official Website. 2011. Accessed 5 July. www.unhcr.org.

United Nations. 2011. International Covenant on Civil and Political Rights. *The Official Website of the Office of the United Nations High Commissioner for Human Rights*. Accessed 18 May. www2.ohchr.org/english/law/ccpr.htm#art27.

———. 2011. The Universal Declaration of Human Rights. *The Official Website of United Nations*. Accessed 5 July. www.un.org/en/documents/udhr.

———. 2001. The convention on the rights of the child. *Health and Human Rights* 5, 2: 175–200.

United Nations Treaty Collection. 2011. Accessed 31 March. http://treaties.un.org/pages/ParticipationStatus.aspx.

UN News Centre (2010). General Assembly Declares Access to Clean Water and Sanitation is a Human Right. UN News Service. www.un.org/apps/news/story.asp?NewsID=35456&Cr=SANITATION

University of Minnesota Human Rights Library. 2011. International Human Rights Instruments. Accessed 5 July. www1.umn.edu/humanrts/instree/ainstlsa2.html

Urry, John. 2007. *Mobilities*. Oxford: Polity Press.

———. 2000. Mobile sociology. *British Journal of Sociology* 51, 1: 185–203.

Van den Anker, Christien. 2011. Cosmopolitanism, Trafficking and Migrant Labour Exploitation. In *Global Social Justice*, edited by Heather Widdows and Nicola J. Smith, 117–27. London and New York: Routledge.

———. 2002. Global Justice, Global Institutions and Global Citizenship. In *Global Citizenship: A Critical Introduction*, edited by Nigel Dower and John Williams, 158–68. New York: Routledge.

Varsanyi, Monica. 2006. Interrogating 'Urban Citizenship' vis-a vis Undocumented Migration. *Citizenship Studies* 102: 229–49.

Veronis, Luisa. 2010. Immigrant Participation in the Transnational Era: Latin Americans' Experiences with Collective Organising in Toronto. *International Migration and Integration*.

Vertovec, Steven and Robin Cohen, eds. 2002. *Conceiving of Cosmopolitanism: Theory, Context, and Practice*. Oxford: Oxford University Press.

Vidal, John. 2010. NIGERIA: Nigeria's agony dwarfs the Gulf oil spill. The US and Europe ignore it. *The Guardian* (UK), 30 May. Accessed 9 September 2011. www.corpwatch.org/article.php?id=15592

Vivas, Esther. 2009. Foro Social Mundial, diez años. Accessed 2 February 2010. www.adital.com.br/site/noticia.asp?idioma=ES&cod=44646.

Wacquant, Löic. 2010. Crafting the Neoliberal State: Workfare, Prisonfare, and Social Insecurity. *Sociological Forum* 25, 2: 197–219.

———. 2009. Welfare 'Reform' as Poor Discipline and Statecraft in *Punishing the Poor: The Neoliberal Government of Insecurity*. Duke University Press: Durham and London. pp. 76–109.

Walby, Sylvia. 1997. *Gender Transformations*. London, UK: Routledge.

———. 1994. Is Citizenship Gendered? *Sociology* 28: 379–95.

Waldinger, Renée, Phillip Dawson and Isser Woloch, eds. 1993. *The French Revolution and the Meaning of Citizenship*. Westport, CT: Greenwood Press.

Walks, R. Alan. 2009. The Urban in Fragile, Uncertain, Neoliberal Times: Towards New Geographies of Social Justice? *The Canadian Geographer* 533: 345–56.

Walters, William. 2006. No Border: Games With(out) Frontiers. *Social Justice* 33, 1: 21–39.

———. 2000. *Unemployment and Government: Genealogies of the Social*. Cambridge: Cambridge University Press

Walzer, Michael. 1996. Membership. In *Social Justice in a Diverse Society*, edited by R.C. Manning and R. Trujillo, 242–60. Mountain View: Mayfield Publishing Company.

Wells, Don. 2009. Local Worker Struggles in the Global South: reconsidering Northern impacts on international labour standards. *Third World Quarterly* 30, 3: 567–79.

Whitaker, Beth. 2008. Funding the International Refugee Regime: Implications for Protection. *Global Governance* 14: 241–58.

Widdows, Heather and Nicola Smith. 2011. Global Social Justice: An Introduction. In *Global Social Justice*, edited by H. Widdows and N. Smith, 1–10. London: Routledge.

Winchester, N.B. 2009. Emerging Global Environmental Governance. *Indiana Journal of Global Legal Studies* 161: 7–23.

World Social Forum (WSF). 2004. Who Organizes It? Accessed 13 Sept. 2011. www.forumsocialmundial.org.br/main.php?id_menu=3&cd_language=2

———.2002. What the World Social Forum Is. 22 August. Last modified and accessed 10 Sept. 2011. www.forumsocialmundial.org.br/main.php?id_menu=19&cd_language=2

Worth, Owen and Karen Buckley. 2009. The World Social Forum: postmodern prince or court jester? *Third World Quarterly* 30, 4: 649–61.

Wright, Erik Olin. 2010. *Envisioning Real Utopias*. London and New York: Verso.

Young, Iris Marion. 2008. Structural Injustice and the Politics of Difference. In *Social Justice and Public Policy: Seeking Fairness in Diverse Societies*, edited by G. Craig, T. Burchardt and D. Gordon, 77–104. Bristol: Policy Press.

——— 1996. Social Movements and the Politics of Difference." In *Social Justice in a Diverse Society*, edited by R.C. Manning and R. Trujillo, 445–68. Mountain View: Mayfield Publishing Company.

Yuval-Davis, Nira. 2007. Intersectionality, Citizenship, and Contemporary Politics of Belonging. *Critical Review of International Social and Political Philosophy* 10, 4: 561–74.

Xu, Ying and Ngan-Pun Ngai. 2011. Moral Resources and Political Capital: Theorizing the Relationship between Voluntary Service Organizations and the Development of Civil Society in China. *Nonprofit and Voluntary Sector Quarterly* 402: 247–69.

Youde, Jeremy. 2009. From Resistance to Receptivity: Transforming the HIV/AIDS Crisis into a Human Rights Issue. In *The International Struggle for New Human Rights*, edited by Clifford Bob, 68–82. Philadelphia: University of Pennsylvania Press.

Zaman, Habiba. 2006. *Breaking the Iron Wall: Decommodification and Immigrant Women's Labour in Canada*. Oxford: Lexington Books.

Zugman Dellacioppa, Kara. 2011. The Bridge Called Zapatismo. Transcultural and Transnational Activist Networks in Los Angeles and Beyond. *Latin American Perspectives* 176, 1: 120–37.

Index

CPSIA information can be obtained
at www.ICGtesting.com
Printed in the USA
LVOW03s0550200118
563251LV00002B/4/P